Mark -

Some light reading for the holidays.

Thanks to you and Peg for all your support through the years.

Brother John

EVERY ARMY MAN IS WITH YOU

Also by Nicolaus Mills

American and English Fiction in the Nineteenth Century (1973)
The Crowd in American Literature (1986)
Like a Holy Crusade: Mississippi 1964—The Turning of the Civil Rights Movement in America (1992)
The Triumph of Meanness: America's War Against Its Better Self (1997)
Their Last Battle: The Fight for the National World War II Memorial (2004)
Winning the Peace: The Marshall Plan and America's Coming of Age as a Superpower (2008)

As Editor and Coeditor

Comparisons: A Short Story Anthology (1972)
The Great School Bus Controversy (1973)
The New Journalism (1974)
Busing USA (1979)
Culture in an Age of Money (1990)
Debating Affirmative Action (1994)
Arguing Immigration (1994)
Legacy of Dissent: Forty Years of Dissent Magazine (1994)
The New Killing Fields: Massacre and the Politics of Humanitarian Intervention, with Kira Brunner (2002)
50 Years of Dissent, with Michael Walzer (2004)
Getting Out: Historical Perspectives on Leaving Iraq, with Michael Walzer (2009)

EVERY ARMY MAN IS WITH YOU

The Cadets Who Won the 1964 Army–Navy Game, Fought in Vietnam, and Came Home Forever Changed

Nicolaus Mills

ROWMAN & LITTLEFIELD
Lanham • Boulder • New York • London

Published by Rowman & Littlefield
A wholly owned subsidiary of The Rowman & Littlefield Publishing Group, Inc.
4501 Forbes Boulevard, Suite 200, Lanham, Maryland 20706
www.rowman.com

Unit A, Whitacre Mews, 26-34 Stannary Street, London SE11 4AB

British Library Cataloguing in Publication Information Available

Library of Congress Cataloging-in-Publication Data

Mills, Nicolaus.
Every army man is with you : the cadets who won the 1964 Army–Navy game, fought in Vietnam, and came home forever changed / Nicolaus Mills.
pages cm
Includes bibliographical references and index.
ISBN 978-1-4422-3985-2 (cloth : alk. paper) — ISBN 978-1-4422-3986-9 (electronic)
1. Army–Navy Football Game. 2. United States Military Academy—Football—History 3. United States Naval Academy—Football—History 4. Football players—United States—Biography. 5. Soldiers—United States—Biography. 6. Vietnam War, 1961–1975—Influence. 7. Football—United States—History. I. Title.
GV957.A7.M55 2015
796.332'630973—dc23
2014027177

™ The paper used in this publication meets the minimum requirements of American National Standard for Information Sciences Permanence of Paper for Printed Library Materials, ANSI/NISO Z39.48-1992.

Printed in the United States of America

For Susan Cheever

CONTENTS

PREFACE

The epitaph on Dennis Lewis's headstone in the West Point Cemetery consists of just one line: "A West Point Football Player." The epitaph, which appears above the Ranger tab and airborne wings that have been carved into the headstone, is taken from a quote attributed to General

The plaque, with the quote attributed to World War II Army chief of staff George Marshall, that West Point football players touch before every home game. (Courtesy Athletic Communications Office, USMA)

George Marshall when he was Army chief of staff during World War II: "I want an officer for a secret and dangerous mission. I want a West Point football player." The quote is apocryphal, but that has not changed its significance for Army football players. The quote appears on the bronze plaque the players touch before they take the field for home games. For the players, who over the years have made a ritual of touching the plaque, the quote expresses the inner resolve they seek to live by.[1]

Dennis Lewis was one of the West Point players who did his best to embody that resolve, but he was far from being a typical West Point football player. Lewis did not get on the field for a single varsity game during his four years at West Point. After his plebe year, he was assigned to the B squad, Army's practice squad, and there he stayed. In his senior year Lewis was not included in the group photo of the 1964 team.

Army B-squad players who fail to make it onto the varsity team after a year or two usually quit football. They don't see the training and the long practices as paying off for them. For Lewis, the opposite was true, and the varsity players he practiced against all week long admired him for staying with the football program throughout his four years at West Point. At Lewis's funeral service at Army's Old Cadet Chapel, Rollie Stichweh, the quarterback and captain of Army's 1964 varsity team, delivered a eulogy and the chapel pews were filled with players from the team.

I did not expect to be writing about Dennis Lewis when I began *Every Army Man Is with You*. My subject was the Army players who, in the 1964 season, made headlines across the country by beating a Navy team led by All-American quarterback Roger Staubach and then shipped off to Vietnam soon after their required military service began. What interested me when I started my research was how the players balanced the highs they achieved as West Point football players with their experiences in a war the country turned against long before it was over.

I learned of Lewis because the players kept bringing up his name in the interviews I did with them. Lewis died in 2009 while awaiting a heart transplant at the University of Pittsburgh Medical Center, but for the players I spoke with, he was still very present. From the players I learned that when their classmate Bob Jones returned to the United States after spending more than five years as a North Vietnamese prisoner of war, it was Lewis who organized a reception at his home in Warren, Ohio, for Jones. The players also told me how, when another classmate and Vietnam vet, Tim Vogel, was suffering from progressive supranuclear palsy, a rare brain disorder that has Parkinson's-like symptoms, it was Lewis who stepped in and took over custodianship of Vogel when his family could no longer do so.

When they thought about Lewis, what struck the players most was that he never acted like a do-gooder. He was too busy just being himself. "He was one of those guys who was the backbone of my experience at West Point," Bill Zadel, the giant starting tackle who played the same position as Lewis, remembered. John Johnson, who played both wingback and cornerback for Army in 1964, felt the same way. For Johnson, Lewis was "the heart and soul of our team."[2] When Paul Dietzel, Army's coach during Lewis's West Point years, learned of Lewis's death two months after it occurred, he was stricken by the thought that Lewis's wife, Marie, might think that as a B-squad player, Lewis never caught his attention. "My deepest apologies for not writing sooner," he began his letter to her by saying. "It is my distinct honor to have been Dennis's coach." Dennis was, Dietzel wrote, "not a star," but something better, "one of those people loved by everyone who was lucky enough to call him friend."[3]

In 2000 the newly formed Army Football Club, using its power to award letters for service to West Point football, gave Lewis the "A" he had never gotten while a cadet. The award surprised Lewis, but it also struck the right note. The ceremony turned out to be a joyful, as well as a tearful, occasion, more moving, many of Lewis's teammates believed, than the time when they got their Army "A" at the awards banquet held at the end of the season. For the remaining years of his life, Lewis kept the letter in an 8" x 10" gold picture frame on the dresser in his bedroom.[4]

Marie, who had been watching Lewis play football since he was captain of his Youngstown East, Ohio, high school team, knew how proud he was of the letter, but when she spoke of her husband, she talked most of all about the kind of father Lewis was to their son and daughter. When Lewis was shipped off to Vietnam, his son was just three months old, and the timing of the assignment worried Lewis. Fearing he might be killed, Lewis wanted his son to have his name, and when he returned, he embraced fatherhood with a passion and gentleness that let his children find their own way. Lewis's granddaughter is now a West Point cadet, but his son (like Lewis, an Ohio high school football star) went to Harvard, where, instead of playing football, he rowed on the crew team.

In Vietnam, Lewis was advisor to a Vietnamese infantry unit, whose nickname for Lewis was "Captain of Many Kilos." Lewis was the recipient of a Bronze Star, but his family remembers him making a point of not talking about the war or what he did to be awarded a Bronze Star. The Army story that Marie tells that is most revealing of her husband occurred while he was undergoing Ranger training in the United States. Lewis and the men he was with were given a goat and chicken that they were expected to kill and eat while on patrol. The exercise was supposed to toughen up the men and give them the survival skills they might need if they had to go without food for very long.

For Lewis, who had faced the varsity running plays against him his entire time on the West Point practice squad, the challenge seemed more brutal than practical. He did not need to prove how tough he was by killing a couple of helpless animals, and he was not someone who could be intimidated by pressure. By the time Lewis finished his Ranger training, he had lost more than twenty pounds, Marie remembers, but he had never laid a finger on the goat and the chicken he was expected to kill.[5]

The Ranger story provided me with a window into Lewis's life, but it also brought me back to the players I was writing about. The story made it even clearer why the players cherished Lewis as much as they did. At Ranger School Lewis was a tough guy in a world of tough guys, but for him, real toughness meant caring for those who depended on you. If any belief summed up the players I was writing about, here it was. In making the transition from the football field, where there was plenty of glory to go around, to the Vietnam battlefield, where glory was hard to come by, the players found that when they thought about it, the bedrock in their lives was one another and what they stood for together.[6]

In contrast to so many of those who were drafted, the players did not enter the Vietnam War reluctantly. Their education had been about fighting wars. Their transition from West Point to Airborne and Ranger schools was as natural for them as the transition from college to business school or law school for an Ivy League grad. Vietnam was the problem. The players took pride in serving with honor, but it was not possible to come away believing that they were part of a successful war effort. Combat experience allowed the players to see the failings of America's military strategy, with its focus on body counts, and beginning in 1971, with the publication of *The Pentagon Papers*, the players were forced to deal with the revelation that the war they had been asked to risk their lives for was one that the president and secretary of defense, who sent them into battle, came to doubt could be won.

Had the players shared the politics of so many college students their age, it would have been easy for them to turn against the war and grow cynical about the country, treating America as *Amerika*. Any number of the best and brightest of their generation did both, but the players belonged to a different group of 1960s young. They don't fit neatly into anyone's category—liberal or conservative—of what a Vietnam vet is supposed to be like. For them, going to Vietnam was inseparable from living up to their obligations as West Pointers and citizen soldiers. Although they regularly pay homage to teammates and classmates who died in Vietnam, the players have never written off their lives as tragic, let alone lost. Their perspective on Vietnam and their postwar lives goes far beyond the disillusionment that characterizes the soldiers in a book such as Tim O'Brien's *The Things They Carried* or in a film such as Oliver Stone's *Platoon*.[7]

When I started *Every Army Man Is with You*, I often found myself wishing I had known the players when they were cadets at West Point or junior officers in Vietnam, but the more I interviewed the players, the more I stopped worrying about personally missing out on that earlier time in their lives. Circumstances have, I think, worked in my favor when it comes to the players' biographies. I have been lucky, I believe, to know them as mature men who could measure, without handwringing or defensiveness, the extremes they experienced while still in their twenties.

Front Row, L-R: Rollie Stichweh, John Johnson, Tom Schwartz, Bill Zadel, Pete Braun, Ron Butterfield, Sonny Stowers, John Carber, Sam Champi, John Seymour, Don Parcells, Coach Paul Dietzel. 2nd Row: Fred Barofsky, Ray Hawkins, Ed Unruh, Mike Neuman, Billy Sims, Mike O'Grady, Tom Dusel, John Montanaro, Barry Nickerson, Mark Hamilton, Curt Lindler. 3rd Row: Frank Cosentino, Tony Pyrz, Sam Bartholomew, Vince Casillo, Jim Hennen, Townsend Clarke, Mike Berdy, Dave LaRochelle, Dave Rivers, Don Dietz, Ed Noble. 4th Row: Coach George Terry, Tom Abraham, Stan Brodka, Curt Cook, Pete Krause, Jack Wood, Warren Albrecht, Greg Steele, Jim Siket. Absent when picture was taken: Bill Sherrell, Dave Ray, Bill McKinney, Claude Herman, Dick Black, Dave Baggett.

1964 Army football team photo. (Courtesy Athletic Communications Office, USMA)

CAST OF CHARACTERS

GENERALS

Dwight Eisenhower, United States Military Academy (USMA) Class of 1915 (1890–1969)

Thirty-fourth president of the United States, supreme commander of Allied Forces in Europe during World War II, and Army chief of staff. Eisenhower was a star running back on the 1912 West Point football team until a knee injury ended his football career. On the eve of the 1964 game with Navy, he wired the Army football team a telegram of support.

Douglas MacArthur, USMA Class of 1903 (1880–1964)

Supreme commander of Allied Forces in the Southwest Pacific during World War II and Army chief of staff. MacArthur was awarded varsity "A" in 1902 as manager of the football team. Superintendent of West Point, 1919–1922. Delivered his West Point farewell address in 1962, which the football team listened to before going to the final scrimmage of spring practice.

Eric Shinseki, USMA Class of 1965

Secretary of Veterans Affairs for the Obama administration. Twice wounded in Vietnam, Shinseki was asked by the Army to retire because of the severity of his injuries, but he remained in the service, becoming Army chief of staff in 1999. In 2003 he challenged as too low the George W. Bush administration's estimate of the number of troops needed for the pending war in Iraq. He was a hero to his classmates, who saw him as standing up for the ordinary soldier rather than buckling under pressure.

William Westmoreland, USMA Class of 1936 (1914–2005)

World War II hero and commander of American forces in Vietnam from 1964 to 1968, Army chief of staff, and West Point superintendent from 1960 to 1963. In Vietnam Westmoreland commanded many of the same West Pointers he first knew as cadets. He was responsible for hiring Paul Dietzel as West Point's football coach after Army lost three years in a row to Navy.

PLAYERS AND COACHES

Earl "Red" Blaik, USMA Class of 1920 (1897–1989)

As head football coach from 1941 through 1958, Blaik led Army to six undefeated seasons and two national championships. He was a lifelong friend of Douglas MacArthur, who was superintendent at West Point when Blaik was a cadet. Provided the standard by which all West Point coaches after him were judged. His overall West Point coaching record was 121-33-10.

Peter Braun, USMA Class of 1966

Mainstay on Army's football team for three years, Braun played guard on offense and linebacker on defense in the 1964 game with Navy. Military advisor to the First Vietnamese Division from the summer of 1968 to the summer of 1969. When his required military service was over, Braun returned to civilian life for a career in finance.

Sam Champi, USMA Class of 1966

As an offensive end, Champi was a big target for Army quarterbacks and an excellent blocker on a team that ran more than it passed. In Army's 1964 game with Navy, he scored the team's only touchdown. Champi served in Vietnam from the summer of 1968 to the summer of 1969 with the 577th Engineer Battalion. He left the Army in 1973 and later founded his own construction company.

Paul Dietzel, Miami University of Ohio Class of 1948 (1924–2013)

Head Army football coach from 1962 to 1966. A B-29 pilot in World War II, Dietzel twice served as an assistant coach for Red Blaik. Named coach of the year in 1958 for leading Louisiana State University to an undefeated season and number-one national ranking. Brought to West Point to stop Army's losing streak to Navy. His Army coaching record was 21-18-1. The only year his team beat Navy was 1964.

John Johnson, USMA Class of 1965

One of the most versatile players of West Point's football team, Johnson played wingback and defensive back in the 1964 game with Navy. Johnson served two tours in Vietnam. The first tour, which began in 1967, was cut short by hepatitis. His second tour in 1970 was as a staff officer with the 173rd Airborne Brigade. Johnson became a career officer in the Army, retiring in 1989 as a colonel.

John Seymour, USMA Class of 1965

Seymour missed most of the 1964 season with a shoulder injury. At full strength for his final game against Navy, he led Army in rushing. In Vietnam, Seymour served with the First Air Cavalry from August 1967 to August 1968. He left the Army when his period of required service ended to work in private industry.

Roger Staubach, United States Naval Academy (USNA) Class of 1965

As the quarterback for Navy, Staubach was West Point's most feared competitor from 1962 through 1964. In 1963 he won the Heisman Trophy and led Navy to a number-two ranking in the nation. Following graduation in 1965, he served four years in the Navy, including a tour of duty in Vietnam. Staubach then joined the Dallas Cowboys, playing for them from 1969 through 1979. He was named to the Pro Bowl six times and took Dallas to four Super Bowls. He later founded his own real estate company.

Rollie Stichweh, USMA Class of 1965

Quarterback and captain of West Point's 1964 football team, Stichweh played defense and offense in the team's 1964 game with Navy. He served in Vietnam from spring 1967 to spring 1968 with the 173rd Airborne Brigade. He left the Army in 1970 and spent most of his career in private industry. He retired as senior executive and managing director of the Towers Perrin (now Towers Watson) management consulting firm.

Sonny Stowers, USMA Class of 1966

In Army's 1964 game with Navy, Stowers played guard on offense and linebacker on defense, but, as one of his teammates noted, he was capable of playing any position. In 1965 he was captain of the team and, as a tailback, led Army in rushing. From the fall of 1967 to the fall of 1968, he served in Vietnam with the 71st Artillery. Stowers left the Army to work in private industry.

Bill Zadel, USMA Class of 1965 (1943–2011)

A starter on the West Point football team for three years, Zadel was a blocking mainstay for Rollie Stichweh. He played offense and defense in Army's 1964 game with Navy. On graduating, he took advantage of a little-used West Point option and joined the Marine Corps, serving in Vietnam from the spring of 1967 through the spring of 1968. After leaving the Marines, he embarked on a long and successful business career.

INTRODUCTION

Preparation for Battle

On September 28, 2012, I drove from New York City to West Point to watch Rollie Stichweh, the captain of the 1964 Army football team that defeated Navy and its All-American quarterback, Roger Staubach, be inducted into the Army Sports Hall of Fame. Forty-eight years earlier, Stichweh, playing quarterback on offense and safety on defense, had led Army to an 11–8 victory over Navy in the final game of his college career. After five straight losses to Navy, the victory was a must-win for Army, but for me what made Stichweh and his teammates special was the way in which their football lives gave way to their military lives. Before the 1960s were over, they would all be in Vietnam. In the coming years, they could not look back on the greatest triumph of their football careers without thinking of the war that changed them and took the lives of so many of their classmates.

Army's 1964 defeat of Navy meant that neither Stichweh nor his West Point class would, like the seniors before them, have to graduate without a victory over Navy. In a school with a culture that linked winning in football to winning in war, the triumph was no small accomplishment. "Football, beyond any game invented by man, is closest to war," Earl "Red" Blaik, West Point's legendary head coach of the 1940s and 1950s, always insisted, and for Blaik the "preparation for battle" that football provided had a natural corollary: "The primary objective of Army football must be victory over Navy."[1]

As I watched Stichweh's teammates and classmates gather around him at his Army Sports Hall of Fame ceremony, it was clear that they had not forgotten how much the 1964 victory over Navy meant to them. Even Stichweh's former coach, eighty-eight-year-old Paul Dietzel, had made the trip from his home in Baton Rouge, Louisiana, to be at West Point. The evening ceremonies were not the kind of backslapping occasions so many sports gatherings are. Held in the massive banquet room of West Point's Eisenhower Hall, the ceremonies started with the singing of "God Bless America" followed by the National Anthem, and for the rest of the evening the patriotism and formality never went away. Most of the players came in tuxedos, but a number of the older West Point grads wore their Army blue mess jackets, complete with medals and campaign ribbons.

Admittance to Army's Sports Hall of Fame was important to Stichweh. He prized the letters on his behalf that came from, among others, Army football great Pete Dawkins, as well as his own classmate Lieutenant General Dan Christman, a former superintendant of West Point. But at the evening awards ceremony, it was not just West Pointers who spoke on Stichweh's behalf. Roger Staubach, Stichweh's Navy rival, who in the 1970s became an All-Pro quarterback for the Dallas Cowboys despite four years of military service, presented Stichweh with a plaque from Navy's players praising him as "a fierce competitor and feared opponent." Then, in an emotional tribute, Staubach spoke of Stichweh as a brother in arms, who in Vietnam and afterward had experienced the same "crazy world" that he had.[2]

Staubach's appearance at Stichweh's Army Sports Hall of Fame ceremony was not a surprise to those who knew both men. The closeness between Stichweh and Staubach had started when the two visited one another's academies as part of the exchange visits Army cadets and Navy midshipmen regularly make. A visit that might have begun and ended as a pro forma meeting turned into a friendship that over the years has expanded to include family and friends as well as sitting together at the annual Army–Navy football game.[3]

Staubach's presence at Stichweh's Army Sports Hall of Fame induction spoke to much more, however, than their personal friendship. By coming to West Point, Staubach was also demonstrating his understanding of the special importance the 1964 game had for Army's players. As John Seymour, Army's leading runner in the game, later observed, win-

Navy quarterback Roger Staubach (right) joins Rollie Stichweh at Stichweh's induction into the Army Sports Hall of Fame. (Courtesy Lucille Braun)

ning "validated" how the players saw each other as individuals and as a team.[4]

For most Americans, 1964 was a year of tremendous social and political change. The Beatles arrived in February. The Civil Rights Act became law in July, the Berkeley Free Speech Movement began in October, and in November Lyndon Johnson won a landslide presidential victory over conservative Barry Goldwater. At West Point, by contrast, the currents of social upheaval never found a home in a student body that had grown up in the 1950s and admired President Kennedy for declaring America would "pay any price, bear any burden, meet any hardship" in defense of freedom. Army's 1964 football team, which ran far more than it passed and had an all-white roster, was all about tradition. Army's 1964 victory over Navy was part of a West Point sports era that harkened back to 1958, when, at the end of an undefeated season, Red Blaik retired after eighteen years of coaching.

For the next five years, Army, without the coach whose name had become synonymous with winning football, failed to beat Navy in the most important game on the schedules of both teams. Blaik's successor, Dale Hall, who had played for Blaik in the 1940s and later served on his coaching staff, was fired with a year to go on his contract after three straight losses to Navy, and Paul Dietzel, the 1958 coach of the year at Louisiana State University, was hired in his stead in 1962. "The best professional advice I can give my successor is to beat Navy," the departing Hall told the *New York Times*. But the hiring of Dietzel did not produce an Army victory over Navy in the first two years of his coaching tenure, and as the 1964 game approached, Dietzel and Army's players were feeling the pressure to win. For the Army–Navy rivalry to remain meaningful, it had, they knew, to be competitive on the field.[5]

Today, there are sentimental reasons for watching the Army–Navy game, but it is no longer the pivotal moment in American popular culture that it once was. The appeal of the game lies in the character of its players, who, bound for military service rather than the pros, play as gifted amateurs set on a higher calling. Showtime rightly titled its 2011 documentary on the Army–Navy rivalry "A Game of Honor." In 1964 the amateur appeal was part of the Army–Navy game, but the caliber of Army–Navy football was never in question. Army consistently held its own against the nation's football powers. In 1964 Texas, Penn State, Syracuse, and Pittsburgh were all on Army's schedule. In the 1960s the annual Army–Navy game, like the World Series, was an event the entire nation followed. In 1963 Navy was the number-two team in the nation, earning an invitation to the Cotton Bowl that would have gone to Army if it had won their annual game. CBS, anticipating the large audience it would have for its 1963 Army–Navy telecast, even chose the game to debut its newest television achievement—instant replay.[6]

The excitement surrounding the 1964 Army–Navy game was set up by the two teams' 1963 encounter. As a result of the assassination of President John Kennedy, the 1963 game was almost cancelled by the Defense Department, but at the request of the Kennedy family, the game was instead postponed a week until December 7 and dedicated to the president's memory. The death of Kennedy caused both teams to downplay their pregame rallies, and prior to the kickoff, Philadelphia's huge Municipal Stadium, where the two teams had played for many years, reflected the nation's state of mourning. The stadium, as *New York Times* sports columnist Arthur Daley noted, looked like an outdoor cathedral. The president's box was draped with black rosettes, and the bands of both schools joined together for a playing of "America the Beautiful" and "The Star-Spangled Banner."[7]

Nothing, though, was restrained about the play in the 1963 game. Army's strategy was to keep in check Navy's marquee quarterback, Roger Staubach, who days earlier had been awarded the Heisman Trophy as the outstanding player in college football. At the beginning of the game, Army's strategy worked. Army got on the scoreboard first with Rollie Stichweh going in for a touchdown on a ten-yard run. But after Stichweh's run, Navy came roaring back. Its fullback Pat Donnelly shredded Army's defenses, rushing for three touchdowns on drives that Staubach engineered.[8]

With ten minutes and fifty-two seconds left on the clock in the fourth quarter, Navy had a comfortable 21–7 lead after Donnelly's third touchdown. It was at this point that Stichweh took control of the game. Following Navy's kickoff, he led Army to a touchdown on a nine-play series in which he took the ball the final yard on a run over right end. Then, on a fake handoff, he kept the ball himself and ran over left end for a two-point conversion to bring the score to 21–15.

Stichweh had scored fourteen of Army's fifteen points, and he would come close to scoring more. Rather than risk giving Navy another chance to score, Army tried an onside kick. The gamble worked: Navy was caught by surprise. Stichweh recovered the kick on Navy's forty-nine-yard line, and with over six minutes remaining, Army was poised to go ahead for good. Seven running plays followed by an eleven-yard pass brought Army to Navy's seven-yard line with a minute and thirty-eight seconds left to play. There was still plenty of time to score. Three more runs then moved the ball to the two-yard line, and with seconds remaining on the clock, Army was on the verge of breaking its losing streak to Navy.

The biggest problem for Army at this point was not Navy. It was crowd noise, made more intense by excited fans pouring onto the field. Stichweh turned to the referee to ask for a timeout, expecting him to halt play until there was enough quiet for Army's players to hear the signals he was calling. The referee had already granted one such timeout during the drive, and Stichweh assumed the referee would do as he had done before and start the clock once again with the snap of the ball. This time, however, as Stichweh stepped back from the line of scrimmage to indicate that the crowd noise was making it impossible for him to be heard, the referee did not stop the clock. Instead, he signaled that time had run out and the game was over.[9]

"The 1963 Army–Navy game will surely be remembered for the play that never was," Dan Jenkins wrote in *Sports Illustrated*. Army's players agreed. They were sure that they were about to score, but equally important, they were sure that they had figured out how to beat Navy. "We felt we got screwed," Peter Braun, Army's offensive guard, remembers himself and his teammates thinking. One year later, the defeat still rankled, and as Army took the field for its 1964 game against Navy in Philadelphia's Municipal Stadium, now renamed John F. Kennedy Stadium, Army's players felt more than ever that their backs were against the wall. There would be no more chances to defeat Roger Staubach before he graduated.[10]

To counter Navy's team depth, Army's coach Paul Dietzel decided to throw caution to the wind. In a decision that would be unthinkable today, he opted to play five of his best players on offense and defense. In the middle of a season, such a strategy would have been too risky, but with no more games left, Dietzel reasoned that did not have to worry if his players could not recover in a week from the pounding they were sure to take. The big danger for Army, as far as Dietzel was concerned, was that one of his two-way players might get worn out in the course of the game.[11]

Dietzel's gamble was a desperate move, but it proved effective. Army's defense especially benefited from having the team's best athletes on the field. Before a minute was gone in the game, Army scored on an all-out blitz, trapping Roger Staubach in his own end zone for a safety. The safety immediately changed the complexion of the game, bolstering Army's confidence in its two-way plan and making it clear how much pressure Navy and Staubach were going to be under. Then, in the second quarter, with its running attack in high gear, Army added to its lead, scoring on a fifty-four-yard drive. Army's touchdown came on a quarterback option play on which Rollie Stichweh took advantage of Navy's expectation that he would run and lobbed a short pass to Sam Champi, his wide-open end.[12]

Kicker Barry Nickerson's extra-point attempt was no good, but Army still had an eight-point lead. There was, however, no shutting out a team with as many offensive weapons as Navy for an entire game. As the second quarter drew to a close, Navy, aided by a fifteen-yard holding penalty on Army, scored a touchdown and then tied the game on a two-

Barry Nickerson (82) kicking the winning field goal against Navy. (Courtesy Athletic Communications Office, USMA)

point conversion when Staubach, despite being in the grasp of Army tacklers, completed a pass to his end Phil Norton. Staubach's completion was a reminder of how dangerous he was, even under pressure. Despite outplaying Navy for most of the first half, Army now found itself deadlocked 8–8 as it went into the locker room.[13]

The tie was dismaying for Army's players, given how well they had played, but as the second half began, they picked up their defensive intensity once more. Navy never scored again, and in the fourth quarter Army engineered a final scoring drive of its own. The key to the drive was a thirty-three-yard pass from Stichweh to Sam Champi that set up a short field goal attempt by Barry Nickerson. This time Nickerson, who would break his leg the following season and never play in another Army–Navy game, was perfect with his kick. Army took a lead it would never relinquish.

There was nothing glamorous about an 11–8 win, but it was proof of who they were as a team as far as Army's players were concerned. The normally elusive Staubach was held to a minus twenty-two yards rushing

Sam Champi making his touchdown catch against Navy. (Courtesy Athletic Communications Office, USMA)

as a result of Army's constant blitzing, and on offense Army tailback John Seymour, healthy for the first time since sustaining a shoulder separation in training camp, ran for more yards than the entire Navy backfield.[14]

West Point's superintendent, Major General James Lampert, was so happy about the victory that he did not even wait for the team to get back to the Academy before announcing that he was adding three-and-a-half days to the cadets' Christmas vacation. It did not matter to Lampert or to anyone else at West Point that as a result of injuries Army had actually finished the 1964 season with a losing record. The following week, at the luncheon of the Football Writers of New York, Paul Dietzel, relieved to have at last justified his hiring, told the press that his feet were still not on the ground.[15]

The victory put Army's players at the center of the sports world. The *New York Times*, *New York Herald Tribune*, *Washington Post*, and *Philadelphia Inquirer* all featured Army's win on their sports pages, and all struck the theme that the *New York Times* headline captured best: "Long Grey Wait Ends for Corps." For Stichweh, who was named the game's outstanding player, the ultimate accolade came in a *Sports Illustrated* article that declared, "The Army quarterback outplayed Staubach as no player had before."[16]

At virtually any other college in the country, the players' stories would end at this point. Most of them would go on to graduate, and then get more schooling or begin jobs. A few would even end up having pro-football careers. But the engagement of Army's players with the history of their times was just beginning. The headline on the front page of the Sunday *Washington Post* that carried the story of their victory over Navy read, "LBJ Decries Talk of Wider Viet War." The president was being misleading. By 1965, the year the seniors on the team graduated, America would have 184,300 troops in Vietnam. Within a few years, all the players would be in Vietnam. Two members of the team would die in Vietnam, as would more than fifty cadets from the West Point classes to which the juniors and seniors on the team belonged. At a very early age, the players would thus be set apart by having their lives marked by two extremes—a football victory that made headlines across the country and a controversial war that became unpopular with the American public.[17]

Every Army Man Is with You—the phrase comes from a telegram that former president Dwight Eisenhower wired the team on the eve of its 1964 game with Navy—is the story, told through the lives of seven players who survived the Vietnam War, of how the 1964 West Point football team made the transition from the football field to the Vietnam battlefield and then back to the States before their twenties were over. The emotional core of this book lies in this journey, which began at West Point as a collective undertaking but quickly changed course in Vietnam, where as junior officers the players were dispersed throughout the country. The players' encounters with three of the most famous generals America has ever produced, Dwight Eisenhower, Douglas MacArthur, and William Westmoreland (their West Point superintendent, and later their Vietnam commander), were turning points for them, but it is the players' interpretation of their own lives and the history they were part of as athletes and soldiers that lies at the center of the linked biographies that dominate *Every Army Man Is with You.*

The seven players were chosen because of the key roles they played in the 1964 Army–Navy game. Five of them—quarterback Rollie Stichweh, wingback John Johnson, tackle Bill Zadel, and guards Peter Braun and Sonny Stowers—were offensive-team starters whom coach Dietzel asked to play the entire game on defense as well. The two other players—end Sam Champi and tailback John Seymour, who also did West Point's punting—were crucial to Army's scoring. Champi caught the pass that accounted for Army's only touchdown, and Seymour kept drive after drive alive with his running.[18]

The players at the center of *Every Army Man Is with You* were the cream of the football crop at West Point, and if their Vietnam War experience had been anything like the World War II experience of their fathers' greatest generation, victory on the football field would have been followed by victory on the battlefield. But the opposite was the case. Vietnam shook to its foundations the sense of America that reigned when the 1964 Army–Navy game was played and that the game itself helped to define. Six of the seven players whose lives are the subject of *Every Army Man Is with You* left the service rather than make a career in the military.

West Point football was also changed by the Vietnam War. As the war grew in unpopularity and pro-football teams offered college stars increasingly lucrative contracts, more and more high school athletes decided against going to West Point, with its compulsory military service requirement. In 1973, the year America withdrew all its combat troops from Vietnam and switched to an all-volunteer Army, West Point lost all ten of its football games and was beaten by Navy 51–0, the most lopsided defeat in the history of their rivalry. Army no longer had the ability to recruit the types of players who would allow it to play a schedule filled with nationally ranked teams.[19]

The players' post-Vietnam lives were no less a struggle to balance past and present. The players had not opposed the war before they were sent to Vietnam, and they would not join the antiwar movement after they came home. They believed antiwar protests by returning vets such as themselves harmed the morale of troops still in combat. The players did not, though, minimize the toll that General Westmoreland's attrition strategy, with its emphasis on body counts, took on everyone who fought in Vietnam. Nor did the players hide the bitterness they later felt on learning that President Lyndon Johnson and Secretary of Defense Robert McNamara had come to doubt the war in Vietnam could be won, even as they sent more troops into battle.[20]

It did not surprise the players that so many of them and so many of their classmates decided against making a career of the Army, opting instead to return to civilian life once their period of required military service ended. The players had experienced nothing in Vietnam different from other vets, but they did come back from the war with a level of disappointment that was special to them. As Army tackle Bill Zadel put it, "We were idealistic." The players' West Point experience both on the football field and in the classroom had primed them to believe the Vietnam War would result in the kind of victory that the generals whom they admired believed in. They took seriously General MacArthur's dictum that "in war there is no substitute for victory." But they found themselves forced to realize—long before America's wars in Iraq and Afghanistan became the norm—that such unambiguous military victories belonged in the past.

Although the players had grown up as the loyal sons of World War II's greatest generation, they were not, it was clear to them, going to be able to transmit World War II's victory culture intact to their own generation, nor was anyone else their age going to accomplish that feat. What they should do instead was the legacy question that these players faced.

It was not easy being the first generation of West Pointers to fight a war widely viewed by Americans as a failure. Nothing in their West Point educations and nothing in the hypercompetitive West Point football culture had prepared the players for such a turn of events or for having antiwar dissent, traditionally directed against the government, directed against troops like them.[21]

In 1975, the year North Vietnam took control of Vietnam and America evacuated its embassy in Saigon, the future National Book Award winner James Fallows published a personal account of his Vietnam experience in a *Washington Monthly* essay, "What Did You Do in the Class War, Daddy?" Fallows was the players' opposite with respect to Vietnam. In his essay, he recounted how, in the fall of 1969, he, along with many of his Harvard classmates, gamed the draft system to avoid both the Army and service in Vietnam. They took what Fallows ironically labeled "the thinking-man's routes to escape." It was not an episode in his life that Fallows was proud of. Much of his essay is an apology for personally risking so little during the Vietnam era. What made the essay especially telling in 1975 was that the draft avoidance Fallows described was widespread. Of the twenty-seven million men who became draft eligible between 1965 and 1973, only eleven million ever served in the military, and of these only 1.6 million went to Vietnam. Pro athletes were particularly adept at avoiding the war at this time. The Pro Football Hall of Fame lists just twenty-eight National Football League players, three of them Hall of Famers, who served in the military during the Vietnam War.[22]

The figures reflect why Army's football players so often felt divided from their own generation. Their thinking on Vietnam never came down to a single viewpoint, despite their closeness with one another and their recognition that the war had not gone as planned. They returned home with multiple perspectives on the politics of the Vietnam War, its conduct, its justification, but behind these multiple perspectives there remained the players' awareness that they had reached their conclusions on Vietnam through direct experience. When America went to war, they had paid their dues, rather than ask others to pay their dues for them.

In the players' minds, there was honor in such an act. It meant, they believed, that no apologies from them were in order when it came to explaining their time in Vietnam or the decisions so many of them finally made to lead private lives rather than continue in the military (a choice the players also respected). In post-Vietnam America, rejecting a career in the Army did not, from the perspective of Army's 1964 football team, involve settling for a diminished life or retreating into a shell. It meant coming to terms with what was feasible, putting aside the expansive habits of mind and unearned confidence behind so much of the over-reaching in Vietnam. As they began their postwar lives, the players knew they could never have the faith they once did in their government and its leaders, but they also did not have a sense of restarting their lives from zero. When it came to shared undertakings, they were very clear about what they had achieved together in the game by which they measured themselves.

Part I

The Generals

1

IKE'S TELEGRAM

On the night before the Army–Navy game of 1964, Coach Paul Dietzel read his team a telegram that had just been forwarded to him from the adjutant general's office at West Point. "Fifty years ago this date, Army met Navy as you will today. We, too, had to win because it was our last game and it was Navy," the telegram began. "The final score, Army 20–Navy 0 has been the source of undiminished pride to our Class, despite the varied paths down which this half-Century has led us. You will always have what you give today. The more you give the more you will keep. Every Army man is with you all the way. BEAT NAVY!"[1]

There was no mistaking the sentiments behind the telegram, but what made this telegram different from the many others that Coach Dietzel received that night was who had sent it—former president Dwight Eisenhower, who, since finishing his second term in office, had been quietly living in retirement in Gettysburg, Pennsylvania.

Today, Eisenhower's name does not resonate with most Americans the way it once did, but in 1964 he was a rare combination of icon and folk hero. Only George Washington, who became a two-term president after leading the country to victory in the Revolutionary War, and Ulysses Grant, who became a two-term president after leading the North to victory in the Civil War, occupy a place similar to Eisenhower's in American history. Neither Washington nor Grant was, however, someone whom Americans thought to refer to by a nickname. Eisenhower was different. He had acquired the nickname "Ike" in high school, and it stayed with him for the rest of his life. His troops called him Ike with affection, and when he ran for president, the "I like Ike" slogan he campaigned on was a natural fit. Eisenhower was too long a name for someone who seemed as down to earth as Ike.

At West Point the affection for Ike among the players, who had grown up when he was president, was even greater than that of the nation. Ike was one of them. Getting a telegram from him meant hearing from a West Pointer who had walked in their shoes. This was not the first time that Ike had sent his encouragement to a West Point football coach and his team on the eve of an Army–Navy game. In 1945, shortly after being made Army chief of staff, Ike addressed a rally at West Point over a long-distance telephone hookup to the West Point public-address system. On that call, Ike, who at the time was in the hospital recovering from pneumonia, did not hesitate to talk about his own football days at West Point. "I understand we're talking on sort of a family line, with all the cadets and everyone else at the football rally listening in. How I'd like to be there!" Ike began. "Due to injury I never had the priceless privilege of playing against the Navy. So will you throw every block just a little harder—will you make every tackle a bit sharper. . . . That will help make up, for me, the tackles and blocks that I had always hoped to try against those crabtown pirates!"[2]

Years later, while president of Columbia University, Ike went out of his way to send Army football coach Red Blaik another message about West Point football. "In these times of tension and conflict, it is especially important that West Point's Corps of Cadets continue to give all of us a flawless example of perfection in teamwork, skill, and loyalty," Ike wrote. "Good luck, and may blocking be sharp, tackling clean, and ball handling perfect." Even while president, Ike never lost his enthusiasm for West Point football. "If I didn't get so darn excited at a football game when 'my team' is playing, I would never miss an Army game," he confessed to Red Blaik in 1957.[3]

Ike's 1964 telegram grew out of a meeting with Ross Wollen, a West Point senior at the time and the features editor of the cadet-run *Pointer* magazine. On the day before the Army–Navy game, Wollen was in Gettysburg interviewing Ike, who up to this point had been the hardest-to-reach figure for the interviews Wollen was doing with the West Point class of 1915, best known as "the class the stars fell on" because 59 of its 164 graduates rose to the rank of brigadier general or higher. When Ike scheduled a meeting with Wollen on the day before the 1964 game,

Dwight Eisenhower as a West Point football player in 1912. (Courtesy Athletic Communications Office, USMA)

Wollen sought to do more than just conduct the interview he had planned. "The opportunity to see him in Gettysburg in conjunction with the Army–Navy game in Philadelphia on November 28, 1964, seemed perfect," Wollen later wrote. "It gave me the idea to propose that Ike send a telegram to the Army team and, especially, to my '65 classmates."

An earlier interview by Wollen with General Omar Bradley, the best-known member of the class of 1915 after Ike, ended up as a national news story when Bradley made a point of criticizing British Field Marshal Bernard Montgomery for failing to close the Falaise Gap during the allied breakout from Normandy in the summer of 1944. Wollen's interview with Ike produced no such bombshell. Ike made sure that critical remarks he made to Wollen about President Truman, which certainly would have generated headlines, were stricken from the official transcript of their conversation. "Thinking that we were conversing informally and on a fairly confidential basis, I made some remarks about my predecessor that, while a truthful expression of my opinion, would be nothing but troublesome if ever found in the records," Ike wrote. "Consequently, I request that you carefully eliminate from the record all portions of the tape having to do with anything I said that could be construed as critical in any way."[4]

As a result of his yielding to Ike's request, Wollen's interview, as he later acknowledged, "became pretty much worthless Pablum." But the interview did capture how closely Ike continued to follow West Point football. During the morning they spent together, Ike made a point of telling Wollen, "I was hoping we'd be talking a lot more about Army football." Ike was serious. Seven months later, when he returned to West Point for his fiftieth reunion, Ike remembered enough about Army's 1964 victory over Navy to give a "good game" greeting to Rollie Stichweh.[5]

When it came time to send the telegram that Wollen had proposed, Ike made sure the final version he sent out reflected his personal feelings about the Army–Navy game. His handwritten changes are very visible on the copy of the telegram that exists at the Eisenhower Presidential Library. Ike redid the telegram's beginning so that it was now addressed to Coach Paul Dietzel as well as the Army team and the class of 1965, and he rewrote the ending so that before its concluding "BEAT NAVY," the telegram contained his much more personal observation: "The more you give the more you will keep. Every Army man is with you all the way."[6]

Ike's feelings about the Army–Navy game reflected his own complicated West Point football experience. He went to the Academy desperately wanting to be a football star. Succeeding at football, Ike believed, was the

President Eisenhower and West Point superintendent Major General James Lampert, June 1965, on Ike's fiftieth class reunion. (Courtesy Signal Corps Collection, USMA Archives)

fastest way to distinguish himself from other cadets and shed the anonymity of his Kansas roots. "It would be difficult to overemphasize the importance I attached to participation in sports," Ike later wrote. "I so

President Eisenhower, West Point Class of 1915, returns for his fiftieth reunion, June Week 1965. (Courtesy Signal Corps Collection, USMA Archives)

loved the fierce bodily contact of football that I suppose my enthusiasm made up somewhat for my lack of size." Ike arrived at West Point in 1911 standing 5'11" and weighing 152 pounds, which made him undersized even by the standards of the period. "I was muscular and strong, but very

From the desk of the Honorary President of the Class of 1915.

To the Army Team and the Class of 1965.

Fifty years ago this date Army met Navy as you will today. We, too, had lost to them 5 out of 6 times and we, too, had to win because it was our last game and it was Navy. The final score, Army 20-Navy 0 has been the source of undiminished pride to our Class despite the varied paths down which this half-Century has led us. You will always have what you give today - ~~that which you keep you will lose forever.~~ BEAT NAVY!

Telegram sent by President Eisenhower to the 1964 Army team on the eve of the Navy game. (Courtesy Dwight D. Eisenhower Presidential Library)

spare," Ike recalled. "It was dismaying, then, to find that I was too light in comparison to men who were then on the team to be taken seriously."[7]

Ike swallowed his early disappointment and spent his first year playing on the Cullum Hall squad, then the equivalent of West Point's junior varsity. Ike knew that he had to do something about his weight if he ever wanted to be a starter on the varsity, and in the summer of 1912 he set about transforming himself. "I indulged my appetite at the table to the limit," Ike wrote of his effort to put on weight. But getting heavier was only the first step he took in transforming himself into a varsity football player. To improve his speed, Ike worked out on West Point's track, practicing fast starts, and to increase his strength, he adopted "a severe regimen of gymnastics." The result was that in the fall of 1912, Ike showed up for varsity practice much faster than he had been the year before and weighing a respectable 174 pounds.[8]

The hard work paid off. In 1912, his sophomore year, Ike became a featured running back on offense and a linebacker on defense, playing outstanding early games against Yale and Colgate. He was in the starting lineup when Army lost by a lopsided score of 27–6 its historic 1912 game against the legendary Jim Thorpe and the Carlisle Indian School team. "Army has a rattling good back in Eisenhower, who was the best man to carry the ball in the Indian game," the *New York Sun* told its readers. "Good linebacker," Thorpe remarked years later during Eisenhower's presidency when he was asked to rate Eisenhower as a football player. The *New York Times* hailed Ike as "one of the best backs Army had," and in the 1915 *Howitzer*, West Point's yearbook, he was remembered by his classmates as once being "the most promising back in Eastern football." The pictures of Ike in his football letter sweater and on the practice field show how much the game meant to him. In contrast to the solemn Ike we find in the photos taken of him during World War II and his presidency, Ike the football player takes enormous pleasure in appearing before the camera. He knows he is being watched, and he goes out of his way to make eye contact with the viewer. Marty Maher, the longtime trainer for the West Point football team, once complained, "Ike was the first cadet on the field for football practice and the very last to leave. I used to curse him because he would practice so late that I would be collecting footballs he had kicked away in the darkness."[9]

Ike was on the verge of fulfilling his football dreams when, near the end of the 1912 season in a game against Tufts, he twisted his knee so badly that he had to be sidelined. After the game, he was hospitalized for several days, but the swelling in his knee soon went away, and when he was discharged from the hospital, it was, as Ike recalled years later, "with no warning from the medical men that the joint was permanently weakened and with no instructions to be cautious in using it." Ike's only fear was that the coaches might bench him for the upcoming Navy game, but once he started feeling better, he stopped worrying. Later in the week, Ike was confident enough of his recovery to go to the riding hall and participate in what was then called the "monkey drill"—a riding maneuver in which a cadet was supposed to swing off his horse while it was cantering, run alongside it, and then leap over the horse's back, landing on his feet on the opposite side from which he had begun the monkey drill.[10]

Ike and his doctors had underestimated the severity of his injury. The monkey drill was a maneuver that his weakened knee could not take, and Ike's determination to meet the demands of West Point's riding instructor was the mistake of a lifetime. The minute he landed, Ike crumpled to the ground in pain. The shock of hitting the floor of the riding ring instantly turned a painful injury into a permanent one. Ike was sent back to the hospital, but now with severely damaged tendons, ligaments, and cartilage. At a time before arthroscopic surgery, the treatment for Ike's knee was crude. "In the hospital, the doctors spent four days straightening my leg, a process so painful that I scarcely slept during the ordeal," he remembered. Ike's season was over, and when doctors removed the cast on his leg, so was his football career.[11]

"The end of my career as an active football player had a profound effect on me," Ike later acknowledged. In the aftermath of the Tufts game, he had worried about losing his first "chance for glory against Navy." Now all his dreams of football glory were permanently over. In an interview with one of his early biographers, John Gunther, Ike spoke of the shame he felt as a result of his knee injury. "I was like a man with his nose cut off going out into society," he told Gunther.

Ike's shame reflected the depression that overtook him once he realized the consequences of his injury. "I had every reason to think that I had another two seasons ahead of me with the hope, as weight was added and experience gained, I might make a reputation that would endure for a few years," he wrote in his memoir *At Ease*. For a while, Ike thought about leaving West Point and giving up a career in the Army: "I was almost despondent and several times had to be prevented from resigning by the persuasive efforts of classmates. Life seemed to have little meaning; a need to excel was almost gone."[12]

Ike tried a football comeback the following year—to no avail—but then, as his depression lifted, his interest in football revived. In 1913 he helped coach the Cullum Hall junior varsity squad, establishing a winning record while sending a number of players up to the varsity, and in his senior year, Ike served as head cheerleader, a role in which speaking to the entire West Point corps of cadets before games became one of his duties.[13]

The football bug was now permanently part of Ike's life, as was the pain his knee would cause him over the years. The historian Stephen

Ambrose has noted how, as a commander in World War II, Ike continually used football expressions, urging his men "to pull an end run" or "get that ball across the goal line." But the most far-reaching consequence of Ike's West Point football experience was the belief he carried with him for the rest of his life regarding the value of football. Ike the general and president would never forget Ike the cadet, who saw football as a way to make his mark. "I noted with real satisfaction how well ex-footballers seemed to have leadership qualities," he observed to a group of generals he had led and promoted during World War II. "I believe that football, perhaps more than any other sport, tends to instill in men the feeling that victory comes through hard—almost slavish—work, team play, self-confidence, and an enthusiasm that amounts to dedication."[14]

As president, Ike continued to keep track of how the West Point football team did. When the newly appointed superintendent of West Point, General William Westmoreland, visited Ike at the White House in 1960, Ike made a point of letting him know how closely he was following the team.[15]

During his White House years, Ike was so aware of his partisanship when it came to the Army–Navy game that he never attended one for his two terms in office. He felt he could not follow the presidential custom of switching from one team's side to the other at halftime without being a hypocrite. In 1957 Ike had, despite his good intentions, let his guard down after telegramming Navy coach Eddie Erdelatz, "Please accept my personal best wishes to each member of your squad as it goes into the big game today. I know that regardless of the outcome every American will be proud of them." In his telegram to Army coach Earl Blaik, Ike quoted the wire that he had just sent Erdelatz, and then observed, "The requirements of neutrality are thus scrupulously observed. But over a span of almost half a century on the day of The Game, I had only one thought and one song: On Brave Old Army Team."[16]

As he read Ike's telegram to his players on the night before their 1964 game with Navy, Paul Dietzel was glad to have a message that might give them added confidence. Ike embodied the West Point ideal of a cadet who went from success on the football field to success on the battlefield. "On the terrace of the Manufacturers Country Club, the night before the Army–Navy game, I read your wire to the assembled football team," Dietzel later told Ike. "It was certainly very wonderful to me as their coach, and thrilling to them as a team!" In their postgame letters, Dietzel and Ike were still celebrating Army's victory weeks later. "West Point is my first love," Dietzel, a World War II vet, assured Ike. "These are the men who make our country great." Ike, in turn, wished Dietzel a "long and successful" career at West Point, telling him, "I am pleased by your obvious dedication to West Point and what it stands for."[17]

"It was like talking to a fellow coach," Dietzel later recalled of his first meeting with Ike, but as he got his players ready for a game that was less than twenty-four hours away, it did not matter to Dietzel whether Ike knew a little or a lot about football. It was enough that the man who had planned the Normandy invasion and served two terms as president telegraphed to say how much the game West Point was about to play meant to him.[18]

2

WESTMORELAND AND HIS COACH

When in the spring of 1960 he went to the White House to meet with President Eisenhower after being appointed superintendent of West Point, General William Westmoreland did not know what to expect. Their difference in rank was so great that the two had never really gotten to know each other when they were in the Army. During World War II, Westmoreland met Ike in 1944 just before the Battle of the Bulge when Ike visited the 9th Infantry Division, in which Westmoreland was then serving. Their White House meeting was the first time Westmoreland had seen Ike since 1946, when, as Army chief of staff, Ike visited the 82nd Airborne Division, into which Westmoreland had transferred after the war.

Their conversation in the Oval Office of the White House, Westmoreland recalled in his memoir, *A Soldier Reports*, was an informal one. Ike, who had graduated from West Point more than twenty years before Westmoreland, spent most of their visit reminiscing about his days as a cadet. Only as Westmoreland was about to leave did Ike offer him advice. "The only thing I specifically charge you to do, Westmoreland," the president said, "is to buck up that football team."

The advice was in keeping with Ike's football background as a West Point halfback and with his lifelong, rooting interest in the team, but nobody would have blamed Westmoreland if he had politely listened to Ike's advice and then ignored it in order to focus on the larger educational problems that came with running West Point. Westmoreland did not, though, see the failings of West Point's football team as a small problem.

He believed, as he wrote years later, that "football success at West Point means beating the Naval Academy." During his tenure as Academy superintendent, Westmoreland acted as if Ike's advice were an order.[1]

Westmoreland, who was forty-six when he became West Point's superintendent, was as competitive as Ike when it came to West Point football and every other aspect of Army life. His own career reflected his ambition and his ability to catch the eye of senior officers. Ever since World War II, when Westmoreland first saw action in North Africa in 1942 as a lieutenant colonel in command of the 9th Infantry Division's 34th Field Artillery Battalion, he had moved up quickly through the ranks.

After the 9th Division's campaigns in Tunisia and Sicily, Westmoreland was with the division as it fought its way through France, Belgium, and Germany following its D-Day landing on Utah Beach. He was decorated for his actions at Remagen, where the 9th Division held the last bridge standing on the Rhine despite two weeks of continuous bombardment. After the war, Westmoreland caught the attention of Major General James Gavin, one of the Army's rising stars, who appointed Westmoreland a regimental commander in the 82nd Airborne Division.

When the Korean War broke out, Westmoreland distinguished himself again, this time in the role of commander of the 187th Airborne Regimental Combat Team. In 1952 he was promoted from colonel to brigadier general. Then, in 1954, while still on active duty, he took a thirteen-week course in advanced management at the Harvard Business School. One year later, he was appointed secretary of the Army General Staff by Army Chief of Staff Maxwell Taylor, and by 1956, at the age of forty-two, Westmoreland was the youngest major general in the Army.[2]

Westmoreland looked the way a military leader is supposed to look. "The deep-set eyes and the heavy brows and clean profile give him the appearance of a goshawk on the lookout for prey, and he is invariably so immaculate that he makes other people feel a little grubby," *Life* magazine wrote after Westmoreland took command of American forces in Vietnam. At West Point, Westmoreland made the same impression on the players, even before he became their commander in Vietnam. "He was an impressive individual to have up there as superintendent when we were cadets," Rollie Stichweh remembered. "He looked the part. He acted the part."[3]

West Point in 1960 was a natural stopping point for Westmoreland. He had graduated from the Academy in 1936 as first captain of the corps, an honor bestowed on the cadet considered by the faculty and the corps as best suited for command. Returning to West Point after being away from it for nearly a quarter-century was another step up the career ladder, but it was also an assignment that Westmoreland wanted. He had thrived at West Point as a track and basketball star. Now he welcomed the chance to put his own mark on the Academy. In Westmoreland's judgment, West Point needed to continue the "modernizing" process it had begun in the late 1950s, and he was anxious to be part of that process. "I relished the assignment," he wrote in *A Soldier Reports*.[4]

As he settled into his role as superintendent, Westmoreland gave no indication in the fall of 1960 that he was about to make a sudden change in the football program. In the first letter that he wrote for *Assembly*, the West Point alumni magazine, Westmoreland stressed the improvements in academic life that his predecessor, General Garrison Davidson, had made. He only got around to football toward the end of his letter. "I have great confidence in our football team this year and in Coach Dale Hall and his staff. Since we lost through graduation our well-known star players, the keynote this year must be teamwork, which we hope will be of 'star caliber,'" Westmoreland wrote. "Our schedule is a tough one, but we welcome the challenge that it offers."[5]

By the end of the 1960 season, when the team finished a respectable 6-3-1 but lost to Navy 17–12, Westmoreland still seemed unworried about the football program: "During the last several months, the one thing that has made the greatest impression on me has been the spirit demonstrated by the Corps of Cadets throughout the fall athletic season. Even at a time when no spectacular success was anticipated by any of our teams, a high spirit was noticeable and built to a crescendo for the Navy game."[6]

It was the last time Westmoreland would take a wait-and-see attitude toward football. A year later, when despite a 6–4 season Army lost to Navy 13–7 in another close game, Westmoreland fired Hall while Hall still had a year left on his contract. The move was not one that caught West Point football fans by surprise. Days before the Army–Navy game, the *New York Times* had run a story under the headline "Army Fans Insist on Cadet Victory" that featured the players and Hall talking about the need to defeat Navy.[7]

Firing Hall required diplomacy on Westmoreland's part. A 1945 West Point graduate, Hall had excelled as a blocking back on the great World War II Army teams that featured Glenn Davis and Felix "Doc" Blanchard, and before succeeding Red Blaik as Army's coach in 1959, he had served as Blaik's defensive backfield coach. At West Point Hall had been an all-around athlete, playing on the tennis team and becoming the first Army player to be named an All-American in basketball.[8]

During his three years as Army's head football coach, Hall had compiled a respectable 16-11-2 record, and except for 1959, his first year as head coach, when Navy walloped Army 43–12, all his losses to Navy were by six points or fewer. With a shift of just a touchdown and an extra point, the well-liked Hall might have kept his coaching job. In the *New York Times*, Colonel Emory S. Adams Jr., West Point's director of athletics, justified Hall's firing with the observation, "We think football is a basic part of the academy life and an important part of the educational process. The sport hasn't developed as well as we'd like in the last three years." But Westmoreland knew that he could not hide behind a public statement from his athletic director.[9]

In a letter in the winter 1962 issue of *Assembly*, he spelled out his own thinking. Westmoreland began by praising Hall. "I have the highest regard for Coach Hall as a man and for his staff as individuals," he wrote. "We wish him well in the future." Letting Hall go, he went on to say, was a decision that he had personally struggled with: "Because of Coach Hall's high character, I regretted the need for my decision. However, in my opinion he has been treated fairly. He has been compensated for the one year remaining on his contract."

The particulars of Coach Hall's case, Westmoreland emphasized, stemmed from failures on the football field, not personal shortcomings: "It was evident to me during the course of the last season that a lack of full confidence, within the environment of West Point, developed in the ability of our coaching staff to bring out the best efforts of the team." But there was an even larger question, as far as Westmoreland was concerned, than the failings of Coach Hall's teams. In Westmoreland's mind, the overriding issue was West Point's status and its relationship to football.

"It is to the national interest, to the interest of the Army, and of the Academy that we, by our performance, create a public image of a winner," Westmoreland wrote. "Our outstanding young men, esprit de corps, and concerted efforts should cause us, with understandable exceptions, to be habitually victorious." There could be, Westmoreland concluded, no backing away from West Point's victory culture: "It is my conviction that West Point should strive for excellence in every endeavor. This applies to academics, military duties, extracurricular activities, and athletics—not to exclude football."[10]

Westmoreland had in mind not just finding a new coach for Army. He also wanted to change the fifty-year tradition that said a West Point graduate should be West Point's head coach. The last West Point head coach who had not been an Army alum was J. W. Beacham, a Cornell grad who had coached Army in 1911. Westmoreland wanted to be able to compete with any college in the country when it came to hiring the best football coach available. If tradition interfered with winning, tradition should go, he insisted.[11]

In January 1962, just a month after the firing of Hall, West Point announced that it had found the coach it wanted—Paul Dietzel, the head coach of Louisiana State University. In 1958—the same year that Red Blaik retired after leading West Point to an undefeated season and number-three ranking—Dietzel, just thirty-four at the time, won coach of the year honors when his LSU team went undefeated and was ranked number one in the nation.

The competition for the West Point coaching job was formidable. One plan even included approaching Vince Lombardi, who had been an assistant coach under Red Blaik for five seasons and was currently coaching the Green Bay Packers. Lombardi had earlier been thought of as a possible successor to Blaik, but Westmoreland, as military historian Thomas Ricks notes in his book *The Generals*, wanted nothing to do with Lombardi. He believed the story that Lombardi had slapped a player while coaching under Blaik. "This was not the kind of man I wanted around cadets," Westmoreland told his friend, General Phillip Davidson.[12]

In getting Dietzel, Westmoreland was getting a coach very much like himself. A World War II vet who at the age of twenty flew B-29 missions over Japan, Dietzel rose in the coaching ranks with the same speed that Westmoreland rose in the military ranks. At the start of his career, Dietzel caught the eye of two legendary coaches, Sid Gilman and Paul "Bear" Bryant, both of whom hired him to assist them and made it possible for him to get a head coaching job at an age when most of his peers were struggling to build their reputations.

Dietzel's college football career began in 1942 when he was recruited as an offensive lineman by Duke University after starring as the center at Mansfield High School in Ohio on a team that won the state championship. World War II quickly put an end to Dietzel's football days at Duke, and when he returned home in 1945, he did not go back to Duke. In 1944 he had married Anne Wilson, his high school sweetheart, who was enrolled at Miami University of Ohio, and after his discharge from the Air Force, Dietzel transferred to Miami to be near her and to play for Miami's Sid Gilman, who, while coaching at nearby Dennison College, had tried to recruit Dietzel for his team.

The return to Ohio worked out even better than Dietzel expected. He and Anne were able to live in her parents' house until summer school started, and at Miami, Dietzel, who played center on offense and linebacker on defense, thrived under Gilman's tutelage. It was the beginning of a lifelong friendship between the two men. Miami's 1947 team, which Dietzel captained, went undefeated, and then beat Texas Tech in the Sun Bowl. Miami's success in turn brought Gilman to the attention of Red Blaik, who offered him a job as West Point's offensive line coach for the 1948 season and the chance to bring along an assistant. The assistant Gilman chose was Dietzel, who quickly gave up his medical school plans to remain in football.

A year later, Gilman was offered the head coaching job at the University of Cincinnati, whose teams Miami had consistently defeated, and once again Gilman asked Dietzel to go with him. It was an ideal arrangement for both men. Gilman was free to concentrate on offense, the part of the game that he most cared about, and Dietzel had a free hand as the defensive coordinator. Taking a page from the popular World War II–era comic strip "Terry and the Pirates," Dietzel nicknamed his defensive team the Chinese Bandits for the take-no-prisoners style of play he wanted them to adopt.

The Chinese Bandits idea was, as Dietzel acknowledged, a gimmick, but over the course of 1949 and 1950, Dietzel was able to get the play he wanted from his defense so that it complemented Gilman's high-powered offense. Opponents took notice, and at the end of his second season at Cincinnati, Dietzel received an invitation from Bear Bryant to join him as his assistant at the University of Kentucky. Bryant had been impressed by the way Cincinnati's defenses kept Kentucky in check. The invitation was

Coach Paul Dietzel on the sidelines. (Courtesy Athletic Communications Office, USMA)

another step up in the coaching ranks for Dietzel, and in 1951 and 1952, he served as Bryant's offensive line coach.

Dietzel had now shown he could thrive under two very different coaches, and in 1953 he got yet another opportunity to ascend the career

Coach Paul Dietzel. (Courtesy Athletic Communications Office, USMA)

ladder when Red Blaik asked him to come back to West Point as his offensive line coach, the same position Sid Gilman had held in 1948. Dietzel's second stint with Army was the perfect jumping-off point for a move into the head coaching ranks. The move came quickly. After just missing out on being hired as head coach at Kentucky when Bear Bryant left to take over Texas A&M, Dietzel became head coach of Louisiana State University in 1955. Helping him get the LSU job was Biff Jones, a former Army and LSU head coach, who sat on the Board of Supervisors for LSU. Jones had known Dietzel since 1948 when he first arrived at West Point and had recognized his talent early on.

LSU was a university with a fan base that covered the entire state, but the football program that Dietzel took over in 1955 had been languishing for years. Dietzel was faced with a rebuilding challenge. In 1955, after winning its home opener, LSU won only two more games, finishing the season 3-5-2. In 1956 LSU was no better, winning three games and losing seven. It was not until 1957 that LSU managed to break even and finish the season 5–5.

But after 1957, Dietzel's coaching and tireless recruitment paid off. In 1958 LSU went 11–0, winning the Sugar Bowl and achieving the number-one ranking in the nation. At this time, Dietzel also introduced the three-platoon system he would become famous for. The best athletes on his squad, who played offense and defense, became the White Team because they always wore white jerseys. The White Team was backed up by the offensive specialists, the Go Team, and the defensive specialists, whom Dietzel again named the Chinese Bandits. The White Team played the first half of each quarter, and the Go Team and the Chinese Bandits were platooned in the second half of each quarter. The system kept fresh players on the field at all times, and the players liked it. More of them got into the game than would have under traditional, two-platoon football.

When the LSU fans began wearing coolie hats and the LSU band developed what became known as the "Chinese Bandit Chant," the strategy turned into a craze and Dietzel's popularity soared. He was on his way to making coaching history at LSU. In 1959 LSU turned in a 9–2 record and went to the Sugar Bowl for the second straight year. In 1960, however, LSU slumped to a mediocre 5-4-1 record, but in 1961, Dietzel's final year at LSU, the team bounced back. It finished 10–1 and closed out its season with a 25–7 victory over Colorado in the Orange Bowl.

By the end of his seventh season at LSU, Dietzel had compiled a 46-24-3 record. Fan support was at a fever pitch, and in addition to making LSU a national football power, Dietzel had helped develop All-American running backs Jim Taylor and Billy Cannon (the 1959 Heisman Trophy winner), who would go on to have sterling pro careers. For Westmoreland, getting Dietzel to return to West Point at this stage of his career was a real achievement. If there was a better young coach in college football, it was hard to say who he might be. The players also realized the significance of bringing Dietzel to West Point. "We recognized this was a guy who came with a big reputation," tailback John Seymour remembers thinking at the time.[13]

It was not salary that drew Dietzel to West Point, as opposed to such football giants of the 1960s as Ohio State and Notre Dame. The $18,500 that West Point offered him was exactly what LSU was already paying him, and at West Point he would not have such fringe LSU benefits as a sponsored radio and television show. For Dietzel, the appeal of West Point was that it allowed him to return to a place where he felt at home. "Deep in my heart, I've always wanted to come back to this place on the hill," he told the media. "My wife and I had long ago decided that West Point was where we would ultimately like to be. It's a wonderful place to raise a family." In an interview with *Sports Illustrated*, Dietzel revealed that he had been approached by West Point in 1958 when Red Blaik retired. He turned down the offer then, he explained, because he saw it as fatal to his coaching future: "I wasn't about to follow Blaik. Blaik is a legend. It is not healthy to succeed a legend."[14]

By 1962, with the firing of Dale Hall, the situation had entirely changed as far as Dietzel was concerned. He could now go to West Point without putting his football reputation in jeopardy. "I don't know of any way a football coach could better serve his country than by giving Army a winning team, and believe me I don't believe in losing," Dietzel said when he signed his new West Point contract.[15]

The importance that West Point placed in getting Dietzel as its new head coach was reflected in the celebrity treatment they gave him. "We are elated with the news," Colonel Emory Adams told the media at the start of his formal negotiations with Dietzel. Two days later, when Dietzel signed his Army contract, Adams made sure the signing was done at his West Point athletic office with reporters present. Even Dietzel's arrival in New York was turned into a publicity event by West Point. On hand to meet the train Dietzel took from Washington to Pennsylvania Station after New York's airports were fogged in by a storm were Colonel Russell "Red" Reeder, West Point's assistant athletic director; Joe Cahill, West Point's information director; and former All-American end Don Holleder, the coach of the West Point plebe team.[16]

The only downside to the hiring was that Dietzel arrived at West Point bringing with him the kind of controversy West Point always tried to avoid. Dietzel had four years left on his LSU contract when he agreed to coach Army, and many at LSU were opposed to letting him go. General

Westmoreland had formally called Troy Middleton, LSU's president, to get permission for West Point to negotiate with Dietzel, but LSU officials were still angry with Dietzel for putting them in a no-win position in which, if they held him to his contract, they were stuck with a resentful coach.[17]

Dietzel's defense was that, with the permission of Red Blaik, he had interviewed at LSU while under contract with Army. Those LSU officials who were angry with him for returning to Army were not being consistent, he insisted.[18]

The Dietzel-LSU controversy began just hours after LSU's victory over Colorado in the Orange Bowl when Dietzel announced that he would now give West Point his "full consideration." John Doles, the chairman of LSU's governing Board of Supervisors, quickly countered Dietzel, reminding reporters that Dietzel had "four years left on his contract." The following day, Jim Corbett, LSU's athletic director, told the media that Dietzel had not spoken to him about getting released from his contract. The debate over whether Dietzel should go or stay went up another notch when former LSU football star Tom Dutton, a key member of the university's Board of Supervisors, declared, "I don't believe Paul will be happy in joining the fiddle-footed coaches who walk off the job and have no respect for the sanctity of a contract."[19]

The showdown with LSU's Board of Supervisors came on January 5, when they voted on whether to give Dietzel the release he now said that he wanted. By an 8–5 margin, the Board of Supervisors opted to let Dietzel go, and then, to avoid more division among themselves, they took a second vote and made their decision to release Dietzel from his contract unanimous. Unchanged was the bitterness Dietzel's desire to return to West Point had caused. In August 1962, when the Senate agreed to authorize extra cadets for West Point and the Air Force Academy, Senator Russell Long of Louisiana proposed an amendment to the bill that forbade West Point from using any of the extra appointments for football players. In the *New York Times*, sports columnist Arthur Daley was outspoken in his criticism of West Point hiring Dietzel. "It's a sorry business to see an institution of higher learning persuade a man to violate his legal obligations," Daley wrote. "It's worse when the action comes from a school like the Military Academy, with its rigid code of honor."[20]

Westmoreland's expectations for Dietzel were dramatized early on at a birthday party the general and his wife hosted for him. As the Dietzels walked in, the general's wife, Kitsy, greeted them warmly. Then, looking directly at Dietzel, she announced, "There's one thing you'll need to understand right from the beginning." After a moment's pause, she turned around and flipped up her skirt to reveal a pair of black panties with "BEAT NAVY" printed on them in bright gold letters. Kitsy Westmoreland's gesture caught the Dietzels by surprise, but her gesture was not wasted on a coach who had already done two stints at West Point and came with a bag of tricks of his own.[21]

Dietzel told the media that it would take four years for him to turn Army's football program around, but he also knew that in the meantime he had to make sure that the West Point football team generated excitement and was seen by its supporters as moving in the right direction. Red Blaik had called Dietzel one of the great recruiters in college football, and on his taking the head coaching job at West Point, the *Dallas Times Herald* ran a cartoon that showed Dietzel, in the role traditionally assigned to Uncle Sam, telling a high school football player, "The Army Wants You!"[22]

In an era in which freshmen were not allowed to play on the varsity squad, the challenge for Dietzel was getting through two years of football in which nobody on his team was a player he had recruited. Dietzel's strategy was to build up interest in the football team regardless of what happened on the field. He had the West Point practice field nicknamed "The Army Proving Ground," and with his announcement that he would do at Army as he had done at LSU and platoon three teams, Dietzel generated heightened interest within the corps. Players realized that with Dietzel's system, thirty-three of them now had a good chance of getting meaningful playing time in every game.[23]

At the start of spring practice, there were not enough uniforms for the unexpected number of players (140) who tried out for the team, and even after the team shrank to ninety during the final stages of spring practice, interest remained high. Bleachers had to be set up for all those who wanted to watch Army work out. A crowd of two thousand showed up for the 1962 intrasquad game that concluded Army's spring football practice.[24]

As the fall season began, Dietzel continued to do everything possible to keep the team in the spotlight. On the sidelines, Dietzel was a conservative coach who insisted, "I would rather have a dull victory than a spectacular defeat," but when it came to promoting the West Point football team, he was a showman. To exploit the appeal of the Chinese Bandits, he sanctioned the distribution of straw coolie hats imported from Formosa. To emphasize that West Point now played three different teams in the course of a game, he sat each team on a different-colored bench—the Bandits on a red bench, the Go Team on a gold bench, and the Regulars (Dietzel's new name for his starters) on a black bench. In addition, on Monday nights Dietzel conducted a "Quarterback Club" in the West Point auditorium, answering questions on the spot, even supplying his audience with play diagrams that he drew on a blackboard.[25]

By the time of Army's 1962 football game against Navy, football fever at West Point was so high that prior to the game, 2,500 cadets staged a midnight rally in front of Dietzel's home and brought along a sixty-ton, M-48 medium tank for show. The next day, at a practice watched by General Westmoreland and the commandant of cadets, the cadets concluded their preparation by having the seniors on the team tackle a dummy wearing the number of Navy quarterback Roger Staubach. The hype did not seem misplaced. With a 6–3 record that included wins over Syracuse and Penn State, Army appeared poised to end its losing streak against Navy. "Flashy Paul Dietzel Gets Army Ready for Navy," declared the cover of *Sports Illustrated*, which featured a picture of Dietzel and Army's star lineman Dick Nowak.[26]

Navy quarterback Roger Staubach was not impressed with Army's high jinks, and by the end of the game, Navy had its fourth straight win. In a 34–14 route, Staubach ran for two touchdowns and passed for two more. During his postgame press conference, Dietzel took the blame for the lopsided defeat. "I'm not mad at my boys. They did all we asked them to," he told reporters. "Frankly, I don't think I prepared them enough for this game. I think that's obvious."[27]

It was not the kind of coaching debut that Westmoreland had brought Dietzel to West Point to have, and a second, much closer, loss to Navy in 1963 did not help. Two straight defeats were two straight defeats as far as Army's supporters were concerned. A third straight loss to Navy would make Dietzel's record against Navy no different from that of Dale Hall. By the fall of 1964, General Westmoreland, who that year would assume command of American forces in Vietnam, had been gone from West Point for over a year, but for Dietzel, there was no escaping his memory of the terse comments Westmoreland had made when Army lost to Navy in 1962. "Our efforts are pointed to next year," Westmoreland had declared. "We must, and we will, do better in football."[28]

The pressure on Dietzel to win was even greater than the pressure on the players, and when Army snapped its five-year losing streak to Navy with an 11–8 victory, Dietzel's relief was palpable. In his postgame interviews with reporters, Dietzel could not stop complimenting the players on both teams. Left for both Dietzel and the reporters to imagine were the words General Westmoreland would have used if Army had lost for a sixth straight time to Navy.[29]

3

DOUGLAS MACARTHUR'S FAREWELL

For the seniors on Army's 1964 football team, no event at West Point made a deeper impression on them than Douglas MacArthur's May 12, 1962, farewell speech. "It was one of the most profound experiences I have ever had," wingback John Johnson remembers. "You were in the presence of some kind of special person. There was an aura about the guy, the way he spoke."[1]

The speech that Johnson and the other seniors on the team were so moved by was not the MacArthur farewell speech that most Americans read about in their history books. That highly political farewell speech, with its memorable refrain, "Old soldiers never die. They just fade away," was delivered before a joint session of Congress on April 19, 1951, after MacArthur was relieved of his command in Korea by President Truman.[2]

MacArthur's West Point farewell speech, which came a decade later when he was eighty-two, was delivered without controversy. It was not even treated as a front-page story by most papers, but the speech that few outside the West Point community paid attention to at the time would never be forgotten by both the Vietnam-bound corps of cadets who heard it and their future commander, General William Westmoreland, then superintendent of West Point.

The occasion for MacArthur's West Point speech was his reception of the Thayer Award, given annually since 1958 by West Point for outstanding service to the nation. Previous Thayer Award winners included President Dwight Eisenhower and Secretary of State John Foster Dulles. When MacArthur's turn came to receive the award, West Point went all out to

General Douglas MacArthur reviews cadets on his 1962 return to West Point. (Courtesy Signal Corps Collections, USMA Archives)

mark the occasion. MacArthur was honored with a formal military review and introduced by, among others, General Leslie Groves, supervisor of the World War II–era Manhattan Project that resulted in the building of America's first atomic bomb.[3]

The entire corps of cadets assembled in the mess hall to hear MacArthur speak following luncheon, but for the football team, which was scheduled to close out its spring practice that day with an intrasquad game, the problem was how to hear MacArthur speak and still have time to get ready for the intrasquad game. The problem was one that Paul Dietzel solved by having the players sit in the back rows of the mess hall wearing their football pants and T-shirts, but it was also a solution that spoke to the deep ties MacArthur had to West Point football.

In Dietzel's case, those ties became deeply personal during his time at West Point. Before the start of the football season, MacArthur made a point of inviting Dietzel to his apartment at the Waldorf Astoria in New

General MacArthur, General Westmoreland, and their wives on MacArthur's 1962 return to West Point. (Courtesy Signal Corps Collections, USMA Archives)

York in order to discuss the team's prospects, and during Dietzel's coaching years the two corresponded, with MacArthur giving Dietzel advice on the importance of recruiting the best high school players available. In Dietzel's memoir, *Call Me Coach*, MacArthur figures prominently. Dietzel includes two letters and an autographed picture that MacArthur sent him, and he recalls how his Waldorf Astoria meetings with MacArthur followed a distinct pattern. "Precisely at 11:00 a.m., the apartment's French doors would open and out would stride General MacArthur, general of the Army, dressed in his West Point bathrobe with the letter *A* on its breast," Dietzel remembered. "He would address the superintendent and the athletic director tersely by their last names only and then indicate where we were all to sit."[4]

MacArthur's ties to Army football preceded Dietzel's arrival at West Point by decades. In his senior year, MacArthur, who briefly played baseball at West Point, managed the football team; for this service, he received the varsity "A," which for the rest of his life he wore on his bathrobe. The letter was such a source of pride for the general that, as William Manchester noted in *American Caesar*, during MacArthur's retirement, whenever the letter became frayed, it fell upon a delegation of cadets to travel down from West Point to MacArthur's apartment at the Waldorf Astoria and present him with a new one.

During his time as West Point's superintendent from 1919 to 1922, MacArthur made clear how seriously he took sports. Post–World War I West Point was a shambles. Much of the nation's military spending had gone into the war effort, and class after class of West Pointers had been graduated ahead of time in order to rush them to the battlefield. The leadership that older cadets provided younger cadets was gone. The class of 1918 graduated in August 1917. The class of 1919 followed in June 1918, as well as the classes of 1920 and 1921 in November 1918.

MacArthur took this disarray as an invitation to enact a series of reforms. He limited the hazing that could be done by upperclassmen, formalized the honor code system, and introduced political science and economics into the curriculum. The whole sports program, which (except for varsity teams) had been a hit-or-miss system, was similarly changed. Under MacArthur, cadets who were not on varsity teams were required to play intramural athletics, and greater emphasis was put on football. MacArthur wanted Army to recruit top-flight athletes, and he also realized that for West Point to get the maximum exposure and revenues from its football program, it could not play all its games, save for its one with Navy, on its home field. MacArthur instituted the policy of Army competing against teams besides Navy away from West Point, and his decision paid immediate dividends. Army's first two games in the Yale Bowl drew crowds of over seventy thousand and generated extensive coverage by the press.[5]

MacArthur's belief in the relationship between success in sports and success in war was summed up in the quatrain that he composed and ordered to be carved into the portals of the Army gymnasium:

> Upon the fields of friendly strife
> Are sown the seeds
> That, upon other fields, on other days
> Will bear the fruits of victory

Football epitomized this link between victory on the playing field and victory on the battlefield as far as MacArthur was concerned, and he made a point of saying so in public. "Football has become a symbol of courage, stamina, and coordinated efficiency. In war and peace, I have found football men to be my great reliance," he told the National Football Foundation and Hall of Fame when its members honored him.

In making sports, particularly football, more prominent at West Point, MacArthur was helped over the years by the friendship he developed while West Point superintendent with Red Blaik, Army's star end at the time. Soon after arriving at West Point, MacArthur showed his trust in Blaik by naming him chairman of a seven-cadet committee designed, as Blaik wrote in his autobiography, "to root out abuses from plebe hazing." Decades later, when Blaik became head coach of the West Point football team and led it through a golden age, MacArthur's thinking on sports and war was given still more prominence by Blaik's outspokenness on the same subject.

MacArthur took great pride in the victories of the West Point football teams coached by Blaik. In 1944, after Army beat Navy 23–7 to complete an undefeated season, MacArthur telegraphed Blaik from his headquarters in the Pacific: "THE GREATEST OF ALL ARMY TEAMS STOP WE HAVE STOPPED THE WAR TO CELEBRATE YOUR MAGNIFICENT SUCCESS."[6]

Two decades later, as he delivered his farewell address, MacArthur was again acknowledging the importance of West Point in his life, but this time the acknowledgment was tempered by MacArthur's awareness that the end of his life was drawing near. "The shadows are lengthening for me. The twilight is here. My days of old have vanished tone and tint," he declared in a voice filled with emotion. "Today marks my final roll call with you, but I want you to know that when I cross the river my last conscious thoughts will be of the Corps, and The Corps, and The Corps. I bid you farewell."

MacArthur's closing words captured his personal feelings about saying goodbye to West Point, but at the heart of his speech was more than a sentimental parting. In his farewell MacArthur also sought to emphasize for one final time his belief in the nobility of the soldier and the importance of military victory. Times had changed, MacArthur conceded, since he began his military career. "You now face a new world—a world of change," MacArthur told the cadets. "We are reaching out for a new and boundless frontier." But unchanged, as far as MacArthur was concerned, were the fundamental tasks of the soldier.

"The soldier, above all other men, is required to practice the greatest act of religious training—sacrifice. In battle and in the face of danger and death, he discloses those divine attributes which his Maker gave him when He created man in His own image," MacArthur insisted. "And through all this welter of change and development, your mission remains fixed, determined, inviolable—it is to win our wars. Everything else in your professional career is but corollary to this vital dedication."

MacArthur did not worry that such a focus narrowed the soldier's field of action. "All other public purposes, all other public projects, great or small, will find others for their accomplishment," he assured the cadets. "Let civilian voices argue the merits or demerits of our processes of government. . . . These great national problems are not for your professional participation or military solution." What remained for the soldier trained in the profession of arms to deal with was more paramount: "the sure knowledge that in war there is no substitute for victory; that if you lose, the nation will be destroyed."

In MacArthur's eyes, this knowledge made the professional soldier unique. "Serene, calm, aloof, you stand as the nation's war guardians, as its lifeguard from the raging tides of international conflict, as its gladiator in the arena of battle," MacArthur told his West Point audience in language that did not seem to him flowery or embellished. As the general whose military career reached its zenith in 1945 when he accepted the surrender of Japan to end World War II, MacArthur was sure that his views on soldiering were borne out by America's success in the two world wars he had been part of.[7]

As he listened to MacArthur, General Westmoreland was touched by the words he heard, as well as by the general's frail appearance. "The most memorable of all visits during my tenure at the Military Academy was that of an aging General MacArthur in 1962 to receive the Thayer Award," Westmoreland later wrote. "The general's physical condition, aggravated by a recent bout of the flu, disturbed me throughout his visit." Even more striking to Westmoreland than MacArthur's frailties, though, was how he rose to the occasion: "Speaking without notes, he was a man of composure and purpose. With unabashedly colorful rhetoric, he hypnotized his audience."

MacArthur's ability to rise to the occasion made Westmoreland want to visit with the general before assuming command of American forces in Vietnam, and in 1964 Westmoreland arranged to meet with MacArthur at the latter's apartment at the Waldorf Astoria. The meeting was in many ways a laying on of hands of two generals who would be remembered for their military leadership in the Far East. The advice Westmoreland recalled receiving from MacArthur followed closely upon what the general had said in his West Point farewell.

MacArthur, Westmoreland remembered, did not speak with him so much as lecture to him: "Characteristically, he expected a visitor to listen, not talk, although he would pause on occasion to solicit a nod of the head or an expression of understanding." Westmoreland came away from their meeting believing that MacArthur wanted him to play a very authoritarian role in Vietnam. In *A Soldier Reports* Westmoreland quotes MacArthur telling him, "Treat them as you did your cadets, be understanding, basic in your advice, patient, work with them to develop their sense of responsibility and their ability to make decisions," when he asked how he should deal with the officers in South Vietnam's army. "Do not overlook the possibility," Westmoreland then recalled MacArthur going on to say that "in order to defeat the guerrilla you may have to resort to a scorched earth policy."[8]

As a West Pointer who first made his mark as a young World War II officer, Westmoreland found MacArthur's advice consistent with his own combat experience, and in Vietnam he opted for a strategy based on the premise that the United States could inflict enough casualties on the North Vietnamese and the Vietcong to force them to stop fighting. As Westmoreland told *Life* magazine in a 1966 interview in which he sounded very much like MacArthur, "First we have to take the fight to the Vietcong and destroy them." Such a strategy, Westmoreland insisted, took advantage of America's strengths: "We have greater mobility and firepower; we have more endurance and more to fight for."[9]

For Westmoreland, what followed was a fateful decision about the path to victory in Vietnam. His war of attrition, which emphasized body counts and search-and-destroy missions, relied on American firepower and sweeps by big units. It also required, as in World War II, putting increasing numbers of soldiers in the field.[10]

Westmoreland's strategy came to affect the players directly. By Westmoreland's final year of command in Vietnam, American troop strength reached 536,100, but it reached this number without the victory that Westmoreland had said escalation would bring. As a result, the players, like everyone else in the military, were left in the worst possible position. They were caught up in a war Americans at home were tired of, but there was little they could personally do to change the direction of the war.[11]

The irony is that in reacting as he did to MacArthur's farewell speech and to their meeting at the Waldorf Astoria, Westmoreland was responding to only one side of a general whom he and West Point idolized. By the early 1960s, MacArthur was acutely sensitive to the limits America faced in waging a land war in Asia. A year before his farewell speech, he had spelled out his views in closed-door meetings arranged by President Kennedy, who, a month before his death in 1963, issued orders to withdraw one thousand American troops in Vietnam by the end of the year.[12]

In early 1961, President Kennedy, reluctant to get America more deeply involved in Laos and Vietnam, as many of his advisers wanted, had consulted MacArthur and found in him an unexpected ally. "He thinks," Kennedy wrote in an April 28, 1961, memorandum of his conversation with MacArthur, "our line should be Japan, Formosa, and the Philippines." To fight in Southeast Asia would be a "mistake." In the summer Kennedy invited MacArthur to Washington to meet with a select group of prowar congressmen, and at that meeting MacArthur repeated the advice he had earlier given Kennedy. "He said," wrote Attorney General Robert Kennedy, in the notes he took of the meeting, "that we would be foolish to fight on the Asiatic continent and that the future of Southeast Asia should be determined at the diplomatic table."[13]

MacArthur the military traditionalist was, when he spoke with the president, inseparable from MacArthur the military realist, who understood the danger of fighting an Asian land war that was likely to end without either an enforceable peace treaty or a decisive victory. In this light, it is clear that MacArthur's West Point farewell speech was tied to a far more complicated view of world affairs than Westmoreland or anyone else listening to MacArthur that afternoon realized.

A decade later, Red Blaik would capture the depth of MacArthur's thinking in the closing pages of *The Red Blaik Story*. He "advised Kennedy—as later when he was dying at Walter Reed Hospital, he vainly advised President Johnson—that no American soldier should be made to fight on Asian soil," Blaik wrote. "He stated his belief that the time might be dangerously near when many Americans might not have the will to fight for their country." Nobody at West Point on the afternoon that MacArthur delivered his farewell address could, however, have been expected to know what MacArthur had said to President Kennedy in confidence or to imagine what he would say to President Johnson. In his goodbye to West Point, MacArthur was speaking from the heart, not giving a carefully measured lecture on geopolitics and military affairs. Drama was his aim, and following his speech, MacArthur did not take questions.[14]

Running back John Seymour, who remembers once going with Dietzel to the Waldorf Astoria in order to brief MacArthur on how Army's football season was shaping up, captured the impact MacArthur was aiming for in his speech when years later he recalled that being in the presence of MacArthur felt like being in the presence of a god who had come down from Mt. Olympus: "He was iconic. This was living history talking to us." Under these circumstances, it was only natural for the players who heard MacArthur's farewell speech to recall, above all else, the importance he attached to military victory, just as three years later it was only natural for the 1965 West Point yearbook to contain a picture of General Westmoreland next to a caption that read, "We followed him before—we'll follow him again."[15]

Part II

Play by Play

4

SAFETY

Sonny Stowers

In 1962, in preparation for his first game against Navy as Army's head coach, Paul Dietzel more than lived up to his nickname, "Pepsodent Paul," by encouraging the kind of hype that he knew would make headlines. In the run-up to the Army–Navy game, Dietzel did his best to make sure there were plenty of photographers and reporters at Army practices and that they always came away with a story. To nobody's surprise, Dietzel's picture, rather than that of Navy coach Wayne Hardin, appeared the week before the game on the cover of *Sports Illustrated.* At the game itself, Dietzel continued his one-upmanship efforts. Army's players took the field at Philadelphia's Municipal Stadium in new white shoes, wearing "Beat Navy" emblems on their sleeves, and to make their on-the-field appearance still more dramatic, the players went without their customary pregame workout.[1]

By contrast, as the 1964 Army–Navy game got under way, Dietzel was all business. Two consecutive defeats at the hands of Navy had made him realize he could not afford to seem more showman than coach. He offered no reply when earlier in the week Navy coach Wayne Hardin said of him, "I've never heard a man talk so much and win so little." The last thing Dietzel wanted was a war of words with a coach whose teams he had never beaten.[2]

Dietzel's no-nonsense approach to the 1964 game reflected his strategy of asking five of his players to play both offense and defense. Dietzel knew how much he was risking, but he felt that he had no alternative, and his decision paid off immediately. The play that Dietzel later called the one that "opened our eyes" occurred with less than a minute gone on the game clock. On Navy's first set of downs, Army linebacker Sonny Stowers, one of the team's five two-way players, got free on an all-out blitz and barreled into Navy quarterback Roger Staubach, knocking him back into his own end zone, where he was tackled for a safety before he could regain his balance.[3]

The safety caught both teams by surprise. "In the other two Army games, I was caught behind the line only two or three times. Today, they were on me all the time," Staubach told reporters after the game. He was not exaggerating his previous success. Against Army, Staubach was Navy's leading rusher in 1962 and its third-leading rusher in 1963. Army's aim in 1964 was to use its blitzes to keep Staubach from breaking off long runs and having the time to set up long passes. The problem for Army was that catching Staubach was an altogether different matter from containing him. Behind Staubach's running and passing, Navy had scored five touchdowns against Army in 1962 and three touchdowns in 1963.[4]

In 1962, his first year at West Point, Stowers sat in the stands and watched Staubach dismantle Army. "We were outmanned. The team wasn't used to someone with that kind of talent," he realized. The next year, playing only on defense, Stowers saw the game in a wholly different light. He watched Army gain confidence as the game went on, and, like all of Army's players, he was sure that if time had not run out, Army would have scored on its final drive.

A year later, Stowers still felt that the 1963 game with Navy was one Army deserved to win, but he was also certain that if Army did not want to lose another close game, it had to put even more defensive pressure on Staubach than it had in 1963. He believed that Staubach was a great passer but that he was equally dangerous when he kept the ball himself and got into the open field. "He was faster than he appeared. He kind of glided when he ran," was how Stowers summed him up. From his inside linebacker position, Stowers saw his main job as making sure he kept track of Staubach, but as the 1964 game began, it became clear to him that Army's defensive line was much better than Navy's offensive line. On Navy's first play from scrimmage, Staubach threw a pass that was nearly intercepted, and on the second play Army stopped a run by Navy's most reliable back, Tom Leiser, for no gain.[5]

With third down and the ball resting on Navy's thirteen-yard line, the pressure was now on Navy to make a first down or else start the game by being forced to punt from deep in its own territory. As Staubach took the snap from center, he began looking for an open receiver. Finding none, he started drifting backward. With the line of scrimmage on his own thirteen-yard line, Staubach had plenty of room to avoid being trapped in his own end zone. The idea of throwing the ball away did not occur to him. He had too much past success in dealing with Army's rush to waste a down.

This time was different. As Navy's protection began to crumble in the face of Army's rush, Stowers, coming forward as fast as he could, saw Staubach was late in realizing how close he was. A brush block from one of Navy's running backs failed to slow Stowers down, and on the one-yard line, he crashed into Staubach, hitting him hard enough to send him tumbling back into his own end zone. "I stayed exceptionally low," Stowers recalls. "I got him in the head because he was ducking." Staubach, who had not expected Stowers could get to him as quickly as he did, suddenly found himself in the worst possible position for a quarterback who relied on his speed to get outside his opponents' rush. "They had good backside pursuit. I didn't think I was that far behind the line when they got me," he observed in his postgame interview.[6]

Just fifty-three seconds had elapsed, and Army was on the scoreboard with a safety. Two weeks of practices, during which the defense had worked on a seven-man rush in which they chased a player mimicking Staubach, had paid off. "I hit him with my shoulder like you would blocking somebody," was how Stowers explained why his tackle had sent Staubach reeling. In Stowers's mind, the safety was not even his best defensive play of the day. "I thought I made a better play in the same period just after Navy had made a first down," he told a reporter from the *Washington Post* who was asking him about the safety. "I moved through pretty good and dumped Staubach for a five-yard loss."[7]

It came as no surprise to Army's players and coaches that Stowers, a linebacker on defense and a guard on offense, was able to chase down the fleet Staubach. "I thought Sonny Stowers was the best football player I ever played with," John Johnson would say years later. "He could have lettered at any of the eleven positions." Stowers had run track as well as played football in high school, and, wanting to be in the starting lineup, he had settled for playing out of position at West Point because there were so many senior running backs ahead of him on the depth charts. "It was a matter of playing or sitting on the bench more," he realized.

The hard part for Stowers was being an offensive lineman while struggling to keep his weight around two hundred pounds. He was constantly faced with bigger opponents. In 1965, with Army's all-senior backfield of 1964 graduated, Stowers, now the team captain, played at 185 pounds and returned to his natural position at tailback, and for the second year in a row he starred in the Army–Navy game. This time, he led Army in rushing, gaining ninety-two yards in twenty-seven carries and scored Army's only touchdown in a 7–7 tie. It was a final-game performance that brought Stowers's total career carries to 204, then an Army record. The *New York Times* and *Washington Post* each featured him in their coverage of the game, and his hometown of Chesapeake, Ohio, declared January 16, 1966, "Sonny Stowers Day.[8]

Guard Sonny Stowers (61) leads quarterback Rollie Stichweh (16) on an end run against Navy. (Courtesy Athletic Communications Office, USMA)

For his defensive efforts in the 1964 Army–Navy game, Stowers was chosen as the outstanding lineman of the day, but as he left the field, his only thought was about making it on his own power back to the locker room. He was exhausted in a way he had never been before. When Army's cadets poured out of the stands to carry the team off the field, he realized that his strength was completely gone. "They knocked me down," he remembers. "I could barely walk."[9]

Being a star was not a new experience for Stowers. At Chesapeake High School in Ohio, he was captain of the 1961 football team, leading it to the first undefeated season in its history, earning all-state honors for himself and setting a school scoring record as a running back. Chesapeake was a town of just 1,200 residents across the Ohio River from Huntington, West Virginia, the home of the University of West Virginia, but Stowers's play was enough to attract the attention of colleges with big-time football programs. "I had it narrowed down to Ohio State, Kentucky, and Army," Stowers remembers.

As Stowers thought about where he wanted to go to college, the size of Ohio State, his logical choice, worried him. Columbus, the home of Ohio State, was only a 130-mile drive from Chesapeake. Stowers had visited there numerous times, but each time he did so, it occurred to him that he was likely to end up as a small cog in a massive football program. "I was just afraid it was too big for me," he recalls thinking of Ohio State. "It could take you thirty to forty minutes to walk from one part of the campus to the other, and you saw what kind of athletes they had."

For Stowers, who, despite his high school football honors, thought of himself as "a little, skinny kid from a river town," Army seemed a better fit in every way: "The biggest thing, I guess, was Coach Dietzel winning the national championship at Louisiana State University, and using the three-team system. That appealed to me because I loved to play."

In the end, Stowers believed there was more prestige in going to West Point than to the other schools recruiting him. "The honor of going to West Point was a factor. Getting a degree in four years was a factor," he recalls. Having a military career was not, by contrast, especially important. "War was not on my radar," he says of his thinking at this time. It was the combination of football and academics that tilted the balance for Army, despite Ohio State's nearness. The media attention that came with playing football for Ohio State was, Stowers felt, made up for by the all the tradition associated with West Point. As far as he was concerned, "Army still had a great reputation, and the Navy game was a classic."[10]

When he arrived on campus in the summer of 1962, West Point seemed at first sight everything Stowers hoped for. "It was one of the prettiest places I ever saw. I was most impressed with it," he remembers. The coaching staff also made him feel welcome. One of Dietzel's assistants met him and several other teammates at the Newark airport and took them to dinner before driving them to West Point.

What Stowers was unprepared for was the harassment of Beast Barracks, the summer ordeal that with its two months of hazing makes it clear to all entering cadets that their first year (plebe year) at West Point is one in which they are going to be treated as plebeians. "It was a shock, believe me," Stowers observed decades later. "Every minute was controlled. I started out at 185 pounds and lost ten or fifteen pounds before Beast Barracks was over." Stowers understood the aim of Beast Barracks: "It is designed to weed out those who are not mentally or physically talented enough to get through." But knowing that did not make Beast Barracks any easier.

"I wanted to go home about every night," Stowers remembers. It was a combination of pride and economics that kept him going: "I didn't want those 1,200 folks back in Chesapeake thinking I was a quitter." Even more important, there were his parents to consider. Stowers's father was a truck driver. His mother was a nurse. Neither of them had graduated from high school, and, like most families in Chesapeake, they were hard pressed for money. "Everybody in our town was poor then. The richest family in our hometown was the undertaker," Stowers recalls. If he dropped out of West Point, which provided a free ride for four years, he was, he knew, going to be putting a strain on the family budget. Stowers had signed a contingency agreement with Ohio State in case he did not like West Point, but it was not an agreement he was anxious to act on. West Point still seemed like the right place if he could make it through his plebe year.

For Stowers's two roommates, getting through plebe year proved more than they could handle. One had come to West Point after spending two years at Texas A&M and appeared to know what was expected of him. The second was from a military family and seemed destined to follow in his father's footsteps. But before Beast Barracks was over, both roommates had left the Academy. Stowers took pride in outlasting them:

"Thirty days later both these guys were gone, and the little kid from Chesapeake, Ohio, was still in the room."

As he adjusted to life at West Point, Stowers was helped by some of the older players. Don Parcells, the senior fullback on the 1964 team and the brother of famed football coach Bill Parcells, went out of his way to befriend Stowers: "He kept my spirits up. He was a great help getting me through plebe year." Stowers also remembers how eating at the football tables, where the older players did not harass plebes, provided him with relief at mealtime.

Stowers belonged to one of the last plebe classes at West Point required to remain on campus during Christmas vacation, and when his parents came to visit him for Christmas, their presence made an enormous difference. At the same time, he was also learning to adjust to West Point. Stowers found himself behind the curve academically. He compensated for his situation by learning how to speed read, and by his second year, when he was playing regularly on defense, everything seemed to gel. One night before a game, he even got a surprise visit in his room from General Westmoreland, who was going through the barracks meeting with cadets. It was the only personal contact he would ever have with the general, who would later be his commander in Vietnam, but the visit fed Stowers's growing sense of West Point as a place in which he could thrive, not merely get by. "Westmoreland was like the president almost," Stowers recalls feeling at the time.[11]

Stowers believes that his four years at West Point added up to one of the few times in his life when the challenges he faced were more difficult than they were reported to be, but he is grateful that West Point pushed him so hard. As far as Stowers is concerned, West Point puts a special mark on those cadets who can withstand the four years of constant pressure. The Academy leads them to bond with a special closeness. "You realize that you should not be selfish in life," is how Stowers describes what he learned from the help he got from other cadets. By the end of his senior year, Stowers's only regret about his four years of football at West Point was that in 1965, in the last game he ever played against Navy, Army settled for a 7–7 tie despite being the better team: "I was disappointed we didn't win. We had our chances."

With the American troop buildup in Vietnam rapidly increasing in 1966, Stowers graduated into a world in which he knew he would soon be facing combat, but by his own admission, Vietnam did not play a large role in his thinking during most of his time at West Point. There were, he recalls, some seminars on Vietnam, but nothing more: "It really didn't become a strong thought in my mind until probably my senior year."

What the prospect of Vietnam did affect, though, were Stowers's plans to get married. In December 1965, at the Blue–Gray college football game in Montgomery, Alabama, Stowers, a player for the Blue team, met his future wife, Charlotte Speigner. At the time, she was a sophomore at Auburn University and a big football fan. Her two brothers both played football at Auburn, and the connection between her and Stowers was immediate. They dated for the entire time Stowers was in Montgomery, and then continued a long-distance relationship after Stowers returned to West Point and began his Army career. "The real story is he asked me to marry him the night before he went to Vietnam," Charlotte remembers. It was a dramatic moment to propose, but from Stowers's point of view, the timing of his proposal also meant that in case he did not survive Vietnam, he would not be leaving a widow behind. "I purposely didn't want to try to get married before I went over," he remembers. "The chances of getting seriously injured or killed were there."[12]

At the end of his senior year at West Point, Stowers chose artillery as the branch of service in which he wanted to serve. His main reason for doing so, he realized at the time, was more negative than positive: "I did not want to go into the infantry. I was not a gung-ho type of soldier." In Vietnam, artillery turned out to be a good choice. It allowed Stowers to serve in an air defense unit in which the morale of the enlisted men and officers was high.

After finishing West Point, Stowers went to Ranger School and then to Airborne School. His final test at Ranger School was a grueling, long patrol, but after West Point and Beast Barracks, Stowers found that the challenges of Ranger School presented few problems. His transition into the Army was a smooth one. When he arrived in Vietnam, he was able to take an executive officer slot that had opened up in the 6th Battalion of the 71st Artillery.

With the 6th Battalion Stowers began by working in air defense and then moved on to serve as a security intelligence officer. "I pretty much was tending day-to-day staff duties with my unit," is how he describes his normal day. Neither Stowers nor the men in the 6th Battalion were involved in heavy fighting, but they were not safe from risk, either. They were subject to mortar attack and were constantly on guard: "We realized the enemy was out there. We just never knew where they were. You never knew who was a Vietcong and who wasn't."

Stowers still thinks about the death of a young sergeant whom he had sent out to take supplies to a nearby Chinese refugee village that the 6th Battalion was aiding. He had grown very fond of the sergeant, a young man who had, Stowers believed, everything to look forward to in life. On a mission that was supposed to be a routine civil-action project, not combat, the sergeant was killed in an unexpected firefight with the Vietcong when an enemy shell landed thirty yards from him and pierced his armor. Stowers had spoken with the sergeant almost every day for weeks on end, and he could not get over the suddenness of his death. "He was gone just like that," Stowers remembers. "That really struck home to me." Trying to imagine how the sergeant's family would take the news only made matters worse.

Stowers regarded the 6th Battalion as a good outfit. "From a straight military standpoint, it was one of the better situations for morale and attitude," he remembers. "I don't think there was a person there who wasn't trying to do his best." When the Vietcong's Tet offensive came at the end of January 1968, Stowers's unit was up to the challenge. Three battalions of Vietcong soldiers attacked the air base where he was stationed and were quickly thrown back. "It was a strong American military victory as far as the actual fighting," he recalls. "We kicked their butts pretty much from place to place." Only after he got back to the States did Stowers realize how much the Tet offensive had given the public a negative opinion of how the war was going. Far from being on the defensive, as the American military claimed, the enemy had shown itself capable of launching multiple attacks throughout Vietnam. "We didn't get all the news in the field that was available here in the States. From a political standpoint, I don't think most of us realized what the impact was of the Tet offensive," Stowers recalls.

Stowers never turned against the war while he was serving in the Army. "I was not political," he says. "My thoughts were we were fighting communism. Support what the country needs done!" Most of Stowers's energy was focused on doing his job and keeping everyone around him safe rather than worrying about the overall progress of the war. The attrition strategy of General Westmoreland had little impact on him or the men he served with: "As far as how you tell whether you're winning or losing via the body count situation, I don't know that we really gave that as much thought as people back home did." Stowers did, though, come to the realization that the war was likely to drag on for years. "A World War II–type victory," as he later put it, "was not going to happen." By the time he left Vietnam, Stowers had more questions than answers when it came to the progress of the war. "How much longer?" he remembers asking himself. "My thought at the time was I could not see the end of it. There were so many deaths."[13]

When his Vietnam tour of duty ended in October 1968, Stowers was happy to return to the States. "When I came back, I would wake up at night because there was usually a lot of artillery fire around the hills that would keep you awake all night," he remembers, but he was also ready to pick up the life he had left behind. While Stowers was in Vietnam, Charlotte had worried about him, but she had remained confident he would make it through the war intact. She wrote him every single day, even numbering her letters because they were so often not delivered in sequence. "I had an unwavering belief and was very certain that he would return from Vietnam," she says. There was nothing both wanted to do more now than have the wedding they had put on hold. On October 20, ten days after Stowers arrived back in America, he and Charlotte were married in Montgomery, Alabama, the town where they had first met and where her parents still lived.

Stowers's next Army assignment took him to Fort Bliss in Texas for training in a new air defense system, but when he got the offer of a three-year assignment in Germany that would allow him and Charlotte to have a stable life together, he jumped at the chance. The new posting added extra time to his Army service, but in addition to letting him and Charlotte live together, the assignment secured him from having to return to Vietnam.

The three years in Germany were a happy time for Stowers and Charlotte. They lived with a German family and had time to travel and raise their daughter, Margaret Elizabeth, who was two months old when they arrived Germany in 1970 (their son, Christopher James, was born in the States in 1974). Charlotte, whose degree from Auburn was in education, was able to teach at the American high school at nearby Bitburg Air Force Base, and Stowers was able to take enough courses to get his master's in business administration from the University of Arkansas, which posted faculty at military bases in Germany. The German assignment showed Stowers that a good life was possible in the Army, and he considered making a career of it. "They started recruiting me to stay in the service," he recalls.

It had been six years since Stowers graduated from West Point, and he had no regrets about having stayed in the Army as long as he did. "We both enjoyed the camaraderie and the social life and the sense of duty," he remembers thinking at the time. What turned Stowers against the idea of a military career was the Army's expectation that every third year an officer would take an assignment unaccompanied by his family. The thought of being away for a year or more from the young daughter he and Charlotte now had was horrible for Stowers. He and Charlotte found that whenever they went away together for a long weekend, all they could think about was getting home to their daughter. It was with absolute certainty that Stowers realized, "I did not want a military life."[14]

At the conclusion of Stowers's senior year, a scout from the New York Giants had driven up to West Point and asked him if he was interested in a pro-football career after his Army service was over. The scout said the Giants were looking at Stowers as a potential defensive player. The interest from the Giants was flattering, but Stowers asked the scout to drop him from consideration. Stowers believed that he was too small to play in the National Football League as a linebacker, and he thought that at twenty-six or twenty-seven, he was going to be too old and too slow to succeed as a defensive back. "I was pretty much resigned that this was the end of my football career," he remembers thinking at the time. "I couldn't imagine the four- or five-year interval and playing ball." As he began planning for life after the Army, Stowers found the doubts that he had as a West Point senior about the National Football League remained. He wanted a career, not a job that was iffy at best and would certainly end before his thirties were over.

On becoming a civilian, Stowers quickly found work that he liked after interviews with several companies. His first job was as a project engineer with Air Products and Chemicals, a firm based in Allentown, Pennsylvania. The engineering job marked the start of a business career that took him from Cincinnati to St. Louis, and finally to Georgia, where, after working for a Boeing Airlines subsidiary in Atlanta, he became the owner of a dealership in construction equipment that he ran until his retirement.

When Stowers looks back on his past, he has no second thoughts about the decisions he has made since he graduated from West Point. In Georgia, he and Charlotte made their home in Marietta. Charlotte, who in 1998 got her doctorate in educational leadership from the University of Georgia, worked in the Cobb County school system, serving as a principal in two different schools as well as working as an assistant supervisor for the entire system. Marietta turned out to be a good place to raise children, and Stowers was able to give his son and daughter the kind of comfort he did not have in Chesapeake, Ohio. The passage of time has reinforced Stowers's belief that he made the right decision in leaving the Army when he did.[15]

Stowers's thoughts about Vietnam are a different story. When he arrived at the San Francisco airport in 1968, he was met by a young reporter who shoved a microphone in his face and wanted to know if he had been involved in search-and-destroy missions. The accusatory nature of her questions caught Stowers by surprise. "I was really taken aback," he recalls. He had expected to be welcomed on his return to the States as someone who had done his duty. Stowers still looks back in anger at that airport encounter, but he has also come to view Vietnam through a very different lens than he did in 1968. "Did we really make a mistake in losing all those folks? I almost at this point in time have to say yes," he now says. "You look at Vietnam today. It is kind of a settled situation."

What has not changed with the passage of time are Stowers's memories of West Point and his Army teammates. As one of the four football captains to play under Paul Dietzel, Stowers was a key figure in welcoming back his former coach to West Point in 2009 at a dinner held in Dietzel's honor forty-five years after the 1964 Army–Navy game. Stowers was touched by how much the dinner and tributes from the players mattered to Dietzel, who became choked with tears several times, but he also saw the gathering as epitomizing what it meant to be part of a team that hung together and triumphed when winning mattered most. As he observes of himself and the players he has known for most of his life, "We've been close friends and will do anything for each other, pretty much forever."[16]

5

THE GANG'S ALL HERE

John Seymour

With Army leading by two points thanks to the safety that its defense had scored on Navy's first set of downs, the pressure now shifted to its offense to show what it could do. Army's defenders were confident that they could keep Staubach from dominating the game, but they knew they could not prevent him from eventually finding some way to get Navy on the scoreboard. Army's offense would have to do some scoring of its own as well as keep the ball out of Staubach's hands by running time off the clock.

On Army's side, nobody was more worried about the offense than tailback John Seymour. At the start of the 1964 season, Seymour was expected to be Army's featured running back, but a shoulder dislocation in summer training camp had sidelined him, and since his return, he had not been his old self. In the Syracuse and Pitt games leading up to Army's season finale against Navy, Seymour had carried the ball only nine times and never gotten off a long run. His ineffectiveness was a bad omen.

Early in the game against Navy, Seymour realized, however, that the two weeks' rest he and the team got after the Pitt game had made a difference. "They knew if they could stop the run, it was their ball game, and after the first couple of series, we knew they weren't going to shut the run down," he would later say of Navy. "So that was it. It was just a matter of could we break a big one. Could we catch a break?"[1]

Midway through the second quarter, Seymour provided the answer to his own question. After a Navy punt, Army took over the ball on its own forty-six-yard line, and on two straight counterplays Seymour changed the complexion of the game. On the first play, he swept right end for seventeen yards, bringing the ball to Navy's thirty-seven-yard line. Then, on the next play, again over right end, he broke loose for thirty-two yards, taking the ball down to the five-yard line on his longest run of the day. The forty-nine yards topped Seymour's total rushing yardage for his shortened 1964 season and set up Navy, now looking for a third straight run, for what followed—a quarterback option play on which Rollie Stichweh threw a short touchdown pass to Sam Champi.[2]

The early touchdown showed how much Seymour meant to the team. Just as Navy's offense was built around its passing attack, Army's offense was built around a running attack in which Seymour, the team's biggest back at 6'2" and 205 pounds, was expected to be both Army's workhorse and a breakaway threat. "We had a dozen plays with a dozen variations," Seymour recalls. "We had nowhere near the sophistication of

Tailback John Seymour (43) on a run against Navy. (Courtesy Athletic Communications Office, USMA)

any of the teams we played." The running attack was, nonetheless, highly effective, and at summer training camp in a full-contact scrimmage, the offense had shown what it could do at full strength, scoring repeatedly against a defense that knew what plays were coming. But without Seymour, who as a sophomore had led West Point in all-purpose yards, the offense became much easier to defend. Rollie Stichweh, the fastest man on the team, became Army's one serious breakaway threat, and opponents quickly learned that if they kept Stichweh bottled up, they could do the same for Army.[3]

With Seymour in the lineup, Army became more versatile again. As he puts it, "We could go back to what we intended to run from the very beginning. You couldn't just concentrate on Rollie." In 1964 the miracle was that Seymour was able to get over his summer camp training injury as quickly as he did. Normally, the kind of shoulder dislocation he experienced meant that a football player's season was over. At other colleges, an athlete was redshirted for a year when that happened and retained the year of NCAA eligibility that he might otherwise have lost.

Army did not redshirt. Varsity athletes who got injured did not get athletic dispensations that let them spend an extra year at West Point. Just as all varsity athletes were expected to attend Saturday classes when their team played home games, they were expected to graduate alongside the class with which they entered West Point. Seymour's big break was that a new operation using ligaments transplanted from the chest had just been developed for dealing with his kind of shoulder dislocation. With the aid of a surgeon who had been brought to West Point from Walter Reed Hospital in Washington, Seymour got the new operation from Army's regular orthopedic surgeon.[4]

Seymour still remembers how painful it felt seven weeks later to have the pin that had been used to help his shoulder heal removed: "It was agony and laughter at the same time." The doctor removed the pin in the team training room with two teammates holding Seymour down, and while Seymour was relieved to be on his way to resuming his starting role as tailback, equally vivid for him is the uncertainty he felt on the eve of the 1964 Navy game. Seymour was a good enough athlete to play offense and defense. At the 1964 North–South college all-star game at the Orange Bowl in Miami, Seymour started on defense, guarding future Dallas

Cowboys star and Olympic sprinter Bob Hayes, and under normal circumstances Seymour might have been another two-way player against Navy. But neither he nor Paul Dietzel wanted to take that chance. "I wasn't one of the two-way guys; I was still concerned about the shoulder, still concerned about the hits," he recalls. "I was still running around almost as a protected person at practice, much less getting smacked around, so I was concerned about my performance level."

As he broke off big runs, Seymour's confidence that he could play a full game at tailback grew, and so did Army's confidence in its offense. "We were able to look around and say, finally, finally, we have got the team we should have been playing with all year back together," Seymour remembers. The *New York Telegram* had made the same point in a pregame story: "Dietzel will be able to start his regular backfield for a change. . . . It is the first time all season that the quartet will be operating 100% physically, and it could make a difference." By the time the game ended, Seymour had caught a pass and rushed for 101 yards, and in the crucial final quarter, when Army's lead was just three points, Seymour reverted to his old status as a possession runner, keeping time-consuming Army drives alive by making tough yardage.[5]

"Vindicated" is the word Seymour uses to describe the satisfaction he felt as he walked off the field: "You realized that Staubach was a hell of a player, surrounded by good athletes, and you'd stopped them." By contrast, Seymour's memories of Army's 1962 and 1963 games with Navy are bitter ones. In 1962, as a sophomore, he had a good day as a runner in his debut against Navy, but Army was overwhelmed by Staubach, who was playing in his first varsity season. "It was an exceptional performance. He was the straw that stirred the drink," Seymour recalls. The next year, the game was closer but even more of a disappointment. Seymour played very little that day because of a hamstring pull, and he was on the bench when Army began its long fourth-quarter drive that ended with time running out just as it appeared that Army was about to score. Seymour came away from the 1963 game feeling sorry for Army's seniors. They had gone through four years of West Point without beating Navy. He did not want that for his class.

For Seymour, winning in 1964 took away much of the sting of the 1962 and 1963 defeats at the hands of Navy, but it also justified his view of the potential of Army's 1964 team. "We always felt we could play with anyone in the country if we had our players stay healthy," he recalls.

"I always said there were a dozen guys I played with who could have played any place in the country." For Seymour, beating a Navy team led by Roger Staubach confirmed his belief that Army was a top-tier team: "We didn't have to go through life wondering if we were B.S.-ing ourselves."[6]

As a high school senior, Seymour was not sure he wanted to go to West Point. At Royal Oak Shrine High School in suburban Detroit, Michigan, Seymour was a heavily recruited running back from a family in which football was king. His brother Jim became a first-team, All-American end at Notre Dame, and his brother Paul became a first-team, All-American tackle at the University of Michigan.

Florida State, Iowa State, and Notre Dame were among the schools that tried to recruit Seymour, but it was a visit to Michigan State that helped set him on the path to West Point. Before meeting with Michigan State head coach Duffy Daugherty, Seymour met with his assistant coach Bill Yeoman, the West Point center and 1948 football captain who coached at Michigan State from 1954 through 1961 before taking the head coaching job at the University of Houston. In his interview with Seymour, Yeoman never mentioned his West Point roots, but when Seymour said that West Point was interested in him, Yeoman told him that he ought to consider it. "I thought it was strange," Seymour remembers, but he took Yeoman seriously.[7]

Yeoman's advice met with the approval of Seymour's family. Seymour's father had served in World War II and been part of the famous Red Ball Express truck convoys that supplied the allied armies in the wake of D-Day. He held West Point in high esteem and encouraged his son's interest in the Academy. Seymour, a fan of the network television series *West Point*, which ran from 1956 to 1958 and focused on cadet life, was now primed for West Point

A visit to West Point with his father sold Seymour on the Academy. The visit was a memorable one for the two Seymours. They spent a day in New York City and watched Bing and Bob Crosby perform at the Copacabana night club. Then they drove up to West Point in the morning. Seymour was, as he recalls, especially impressed with the campus, and after meeting with Army's coaches, he saw how focused their recruiting efforts were: "I thought we would be a top twenty-five team."

Seymour had not, however, done much thinking about Beast Barracks and the difficulties that lay ahead during plebe year at West Point. After being a high school football star, Seymour's first months at West Point came as a shock. He saw how Beast Barracks made cadets feel as if they were children once again: "You are eighteen years old. You think, I'm a hot shit. I can put up with anything. Then by the third day you miss your mummy. You miss your daddy." Seymour still remembers that the starting halfback on his plebe team, a player he liked and thought had great potential, left because of the harassment, saying of the upperclassmen who were giving him a hard time, "I hate those assholes."

Seymour was part of a company in which the harassment was not as bad as in other companies, and his belief is that good fortune, plus being part of the football program, saved him. "I would not have graduated had it not been for the team. If I was just a cadet playing intramurals, I would have been long gone," he admits. For Seymour, the turning point came with the end of summer. "Once you got into the academic year and then into real football practice, it was wonderful," he recalls. "Nobody was yelling at us, and you didn't have to worry if your shoes were shined. It was a little enclave for two and a half hours." You could actually get to know somebody, Seymour discovered.

"We had a million dollar education shoved up our asses a nickel at a time," Seymour would later joke, but he also came to embrace the kind of personal change West Point was trying to bring about in all its cadets. Before his plebe year was up, Seymour told himself, "If I can get through West Point, I'll have something meaningful." Behind the pressure West Point was applying, there was, Seymour came to believe, a clear message: "We want to weed out the guys who can't handle the pressure. We are going to spend six months or eight months to get down to something we can work with."[8]

The result for Seymour is that the West Point from which he graduated in 1965 became a permanent part of his life. "It was a basis for the rest of your life. It was a foundation for the rest of your life," he says today. On the team, Seymour found a willingness to help anyone in trouble, and behind that reaching out, there was a sense of one's own limits: "You were part of something that was bigger than you. It was real simple. It wasn't about you as an individual."[9]

After graduation, Seymour had no hesitation about going to Vietnam. He hoped to be part of an outfit that saw combat and let him use his West Point experience. "I wanted to be with a front-line unit. I didn't want to be a general's aide. I didn't want to be on a brigade staff," he remembers thinking. Seymour eventually got his way, but with results that were far different from what he anticipated.

Seymour had little time for reflection after he finished West Point. "I got sixty days to have a great time. Then I've got to go to Airborne and Ranger school and figure out the rest of my life when we get through that sort of stuff," he recalls. "We were living in the moment," Seymour says of himself and his classmates. What was not rushed for Seymour was his decision to marry Donna Link. The two had been dating ever since Seymour's sophomore year in high school, and in November 1965, shortly after Seymour finished his Airborne and Ranger training, they married.

Seymour did not feel prepared for Vietnam. "We had instructors who had been over there as advisors," Seymour remembers, but they did not get him ready for what he calls "a different kind of warfare," in which punji sticks and booby traps were critical elements in the enemy's arsenal. Seymour went through Airborne and Ranger training without worrying about the unique challenges Vietnam presented. Don Parcells, the fullback on the 1964 team, was with Seymour at Ranger School at Fort Benning. Parcells was Seymour's Ranger buddy, and for the two of them, the physical challenges of Ranger School were easy to meet. The most memorable part of their experience was their survivalist training when their instructor killed a goat in front of their eyes, and they were then given rabbits to kill and gut. Seymour still remembers that the goat had blue eyes.

Following Ranger School, Seymour was sent to Germany for what he was told was going to be a three-year tour of duty, but after six months, he was levied back to the United States to get ready for Vietnam. The suddenness of the change in assignments worried him: "What you hoped for, at least in my case, was that you could get a year or two under your belt in the service before you went over there. You were then matured and had a little bit more confidence in your capability." Seymour's next assignment took him to Fort Lewis in Washington State, where he put draftees through their basic training. Then, in August 1967, just months after Matthew, his first son, was born, Seymour was ordered to Vietnam. The outfit he was assigned to was the 3rd Brigade of the 1st Air Cavalry

Division, and from Seymour's point of view, 1st Air Cavalry, with its reliance on helicopters, was well suited to dealing with the hit-and-run guerrilla tactics that distinguished Vietnam from the traditional wars he had studied at West Point.[10]

The 1st Air Cavalry was a crack outfit, and, as a forward observer who spent most of his time directing artillery fire from a helicopter 1,500 feet above the battlefield, Seymour saw constant action, often flying six and seven hours a day. Giving 1st Air Cavalry its distinctness was its ability to bring troops and firepower to the battlefield in a very short period of time. "We could get companies or platoons on the ground in a matter of ten or fifteen minutes, if necessary," Seymour remembers. "It was almost like a ballet." The same speed was true of the 1st Air Cavalry's ability to get artillery or planes into action: "Within minutes, you could bring all hell to bear on whoever had enough balls to hit you."

Seymour was glad to be part of what he called "a gung-ho type of professional outfit." He felt that being constantly exposed to danger helped discipline. "We never worried over troops having dope," he recalls. "The guys on the front line were pros. They recognized they had to count on the guy next to them to do his job. You can't get high in the middle of the bush." When Seymour later learned of the infamous My Lai Massacre that had taken place with a platoon led by Lieutenant William Calley, he was shocked. "We had been in that whole area," he remembers. "There had been lots of mines and guys got hurt, but we couldn't fathom reacting like that—wiping out kids in a village."[11]

The 1st Air Cavalry's professionalism did not, Seymour realized, come with a guarantee of getting through the war unharmed. Seymour recalls the time in Quang Tri that a rocket landed near him and a group of 1st Air Cavalry officers. The rocket killed the battalion commander and wounded three others. To Seymour's surprise, he escaped from the rocket attack unhurt except for a ringing in his ears. "There is no way I should have gone unscathed," he says. What the 1st Air Cavalry's professionalism did do, as far as Seymour was concerned, was show how it was possible to fight the war aggressively and still keep down American casualties.

"We felt we were the leading edge and couldn't understand why everybody didn't fight that way. We felt to some degree invincible," Seymour recalls. He was dismayed when other outfits did not adopt the 1st Air Cavalry's tactics. During the early part of the Tet offensive, a low cloud ceiling made it impossible for the 1st Air Cavalry to use its helicopters effectively, and the division suffered for it, engaging the enemy like a World War II army. As Seymour put it, "It was my father's war." The Marines in particular struck Seymour as regularly subjecting their infantry to needless casualties. "They would find an enemy force, surround it, and frontal assault it, getting half the Marines killed," he recalls. "We would find the same enemy, and we would surround them and blow the hell out of them and not expose our boys as best we could. It was a different mentality."

Seymour never underestimated the difficulties that the war presented for American commanders. "The Vietnamese are tough sons of bitches," he would say years later in admiration. But Seymour also believed that if America's overall military strength had been brought to bear in Vietnam, the war could have been won: "To this day, you can't convince me we couldn't have gone at least into North Vietnam, couldn't have gone into Haiphong, couldn't have gone into Hanoi." For Seymour, the government's failure to act decisively meant that American troops were caught up in a war of attrition that the average foot soldier paid for. "It was a war we always tried not to lose and never tried to win," he concluded.

Vietnamizing the war by having the South Vietnamese troops do more of the fighting was, Seymour believed, not a good alternative. "I'm watching it and knowing it's not going to work. We sit in our base camps and let the Vietnamese Rangers go out and do it, and they get horribly chewed up, and we have to go out and rescue them," he recalls. "Our morale as an army degenerated horribly."

After Seymour returned home in August 1968, he realized, to a degree not possible in Vietnam, how much America had changed. "There was no support from the home front. All you felt was abandoned. It was very difficult to be in the service at that point," he remembers. When, as a civilian, he tried to recruit football players for West Point, Seymour got, as he put it, "an education" in how unpopular the war was with the young. He was never able to come up with a great recruit from the Catholic school system in which he and his brothers had played. When he thought about what he called the "big picture," Seymour often found it impossible not to make fun of how expensive the war was for America to fight: "I would make jokes all the time about it. This is silly. It's costing us $500,000 for everyone we kill."[12]

For all his misgivings about the conduct of the war, Seymour continued to be loyal to General Westmoreland while he was serving as a junior officer in Vietnam. Westmoreland the commander seemed a larger-than-life version of Westmoreland the superintendent, whom Seymour had known at West Point. "I always gave Westmoreland the benefit of the doubt," Seymour says. "I always said he must know more than we do. He has the good intelligence. He is making decisions on a knowledge that we're not privy to."

In 1971, when Daniel Ellsberg, a former Marine who had worked in the State Department, provided the *New York Times* with the secret documents, later known as the Pentagon papers, that revealed the doubts the Johnson administration had about the war in Vietnam, Seymour's first reaction was anger with Ellsberg: "I thought they were going to take this guy out and shoot him." Seymour was dismayed when Ellsberg was lionized in the media for his actions: "I didn't have any empathy for Ellsberg, but I thought he was a real weather vane as to how the mood of the country had changed. He was basically treated as a hero for bringing that stuff out."[13]

"I just couldn't believe our government would deceive us," Seymour admits thinking during his time in the Army and in the years immediately following his return to civilian life. For Seymour, returning to the United States meant coming back to his wife and a young son whom he had not seen for a year and settling into a society in which everywhere he looked there were "constant protests." Seymour was never spat upon or harassed, but he found the antiwar mood of the country depressing, and he saw little chance of the country changing. As he later put it, "Vietnam was an experience I don't know how you teach."[14]

One of the reasons that he and the West Point classmates he knew did not suffer to the degree so many others did from post-traumatic stress disorder, Seymour believes, is that they did not immediately get discharged from the Army after they left Vietnam. Instead, they took on new military assignments that cushioned their return. "As such, we served with others who had done the same thing, and so we were able to talk through experiences and share experiences and realize life goes on."

Seymour was, however, very unhappy with the way the Army treated him after he got back to the States. When he reported to the personnel office at the Pentagon, he was told by the major doing the assignments for those in artillery, Seymour's branch of the service, that officers like him were expected to take the career course to advance their skills. It was an opportunity Seymour did not want because it extended his service obligation, but when he turned the career course down, Seymour was told that the alternative was for him to serve six months in the States and then expect to be sent back to Vietnam.

"Screw you," Seymour believed the Army was telling him when he refused to take the career course, and he immediately began searching for alternatives. He found one just down the hall at the Pentagon in the ordnance branch of the Army. At the Aberdeen Proving Ground in Maryland, there was an opening for an officer to teach combat assault, and the opening did not come with the threat of being sent to Vietnam in six months or the requirement to take the career course. It was the last assignment Seymour would have before leaving the Army, but it did not erase his anger at the events that led up to it. "I switched branches at that point just because I got a goofy major," he would later say.

The irony for Seymour was that as his time to leave the Army drew closer, he got better and better offers to stay. "When you did have the opportunity to resign, they were making these tremendous deals," he recalls. He was told that on the basis of his test scores, he would have no trouble getting into Harvard Business School. The Army would pay for him to start there with the next fall class, and after finishing Harvard he could return to West Point for three years of teaching before choosing his next assignment. "You crapped on me for four and a half years, and now you want to offer me this great deal," Seymour remembers telling himself as he turned the new offers down.[15]

In retrospect, Seymour does not think he would have stayed in the Army even if he had gotten better treatment on his return from Vietnam, but he does believe leaving the service would have been harder. "There would have been more discussion about it, a lot more thought about it," he acknowledges. For Seymour, the low pay in the Army was a worry once he had children. While at Aberdeen Proving Ground, his daughter, Heather, was born in 1969, and with two children to support (sons Daniel and Scott would arrive in 1970 and 1971), the Army increasingly seemed like the wrong place to be. The pay "was not a whole lot of money to raise a wife and a couple of kids on," Seymour thought.

As long as he stayed in the Army, Seymour was convinced that he was not going to be able to be as good a provider as his father, who, while not rich, had made life comfortable for the Seymour children as they grew up. "There were greener pastures on the other side," Seymour told himself. "I felt I had better economic opportunity in the civilian world." Donna left the final decision about going or staying in the Army to her husband, but she was relieved when he opted to leave the service. "It was frightening," she says of the time when Seymour was off in Vietnam and she worried about him daily.[16]

After he left the Army, Seymour found the Detroit Lions had not forgotten him. They had the rights to him if he wanted to play in the National Football League, and the team offered Seymour a tryout. He had grown up when the Lions were in their heyday and players such as Bobby Lane and Alex Karras led the team. He remembered watching the team practice at the Cranbrook Schools in nearby Bloomfield Hills. It was flattering to have the Lions call, but being away from football for so long made Seymour doubt that he could succeed in the pros. He wanted a job that he and his family could count on, and he found that job working in Michigan for Imperial Oil and Grease, a Beatrice Foods Company subsidiary in which his father was a manager and a shareholder. The National Football League would have to content itself with having Seymour's two brothers play for it.

Seymour's father died within a year of Seymour taking a job with Imperial Oil and Grease, but Seymour spent the next five years working in the company's Detroit office before moving on to California to manage sales on the West Coast. Seymour has remained in California ever since, working as a partner in a series of businesses. Today, he is an executive vice president with ProShot Golf, a company that develops and manufactures a GPS distance-measuring system for golf carts.

Like most of his teammates, Seymour is a regular at West Point reunions. "It was a singular experience that lasted four years that you wouldn't trade," Seymour says of his time at West Point on and off the football field. He has a very different memory of Vietnam, which he now views as a war in which the results do not, as far as he can see, justify the sacrifices that were made. Seymour traces the change in his thinking to getting distance from the war. "I'm sure that the realities of the war when viewed up close and personal had long-lasting effects on all the participants. In my case, the changes didn't manifest until later in life," he says. "We were there far too long. We prolonged it way beyond where we should have." In the 1980s a visit to Maya Lin's Vietnam Veterans Memorial in Washington made an impression on Seymour that has never gone away: "You look at the names on the wall. That's kind of a shattering experience the first time you see it. It was very difficult for me."[17]

6

TOUCHDOWN CATCH

Sam Champi

When Army broke from its huddle early in the second quarter with first down and five yards to go for a touchdown, Navy's defenders were sure that a run was coming. Army's tailback John Seymour had just burned them on consecutive sweeps of seventeen and thirty-two yards. A third straight run seemed like the obvious choice, especially for a team that passed as little as Army.

Sam Champi, Army's 6'4" tight end, was also expecting a run. He liked Paul Dietzel as a person and was sorry when Dietzel left West Point to coach the University of South Carolina ("He always had different things to say, always tried to pump you up," Champi remembers), but Champi was also convinced that Dietzel's coaching style severely limited what an end like himself could do when Army had the ball: "It always seemed to be 'Let's let the defense win the game.'" The offense was primarily designed to make sure Army did not turn over the ball. "Sweep one way, sweep the other. Off tackle, off tackle," was how Champi saw Army operating under Dietzel. But now, with the ball near Navy's goal line, it seemed like the perfect time to be consistent and avoid taking a risk. In the huddle Rollie Stichweh called a pass-run option play that nine out of ten times wound up as a run with Stichweh going over left end and Champi peeling back to seal off the defender nearest to him.[1]

At 225 pounds, Champi had the size to take on a linebacker as well as a defensive back. "I always had good hands. My speed was questionable," Champi would say of his offensive abilities. Champi was as big as most college tight ends ever got in the early 1960s, and he liked the contact that came from constantly being asked to block. In the past, he had had his nose broken several times, but he still wore only a single protective bar across the front of his helmet. "I didn't have the more extensive facemask because I needed the visibility," was Champi's explanation for his decision to risk more broken noses. On the play in which he scored Army's only touchdown against Navy, Champi had no qualms about being a decoy most of the time. "Typically, I'd block down for a few seconds, and then I'd go to the flag, but I was so used to the play ending up as a run that I was almost always trying to come back to block, which I normally did," Champi recalls.

This time the play did not go as expected. After Champi threw a brush block on Navy's defensive end and faded toward the left corner of the end zone, he found himself completely alone. "I don't think there was anyone within ten feet of me," he recalls. Navy had studied its game films of Army too well. Its defense had called a blitz against Stichweh, expecting that he would keep the ball, as he usually did, and when Stichweh saw the blitz coming, he had more than enough time to stop and throw a short pass to Champi. "I was probably the most surprised guy in the whole stadium when he actually threw it. To me that was fantastic," Champi remembered years later. "Thank God I caught it. If I had ever dropped the ball, I think I would have hopped a freighter and headed for Africa."

For Champi, the touchdown catch that put Army ahead 8–0 was not, as far as he was concerned, his most important play of the day: "In that 1964 game, the touchdown was nice and is something I will always remember, but the thing that I always think about was the catch that I made that set up a field goal." That catch occurred in the fourth quarter, with the score tied 8–8 and Army needing to keep a drive going.[2]

With the ball on its own forty-eight-yard line, Stichweh called a play that Army had practiced but not used in a game. The play was a long pass in which Champi faked a button hook and then kept on running, hoping to get behind the defensive backs guarding him. The play was designed to take advantage of teams that crowded the line of scrimmage against Army. "It was almost like a desperation play," as far as Champi was concerned.

This time, as Stichweh went back to pass, Navy's defenders were not caught by surprise as they had been on Champi's catch for a touchdown.

Tight end Sam Champi. (Courtesy Athletic Communications Office, USMA)

They stayed with Champi as he ran downfield, but Navy's defenders did not realize that their biggest challenge on this play lay in trying to outjump Champi for the ball.[3]

"He really lofted it, and it was slightly underthrown, which was probably a plus because I actually came back to the ball, where those guys were more or less standing there," Champi says of the pass. Once Champi went up in the air and got his body between Navy's defenders and the ball, he had made himself the only one who could catch Stichweh's pass. "It was thrown perfectly for the situation," Champi recalls of the thirty-three-yard completion that set the stage for Barry Nickerson's game-winning field goal.[4]

A year later, playing in his final game as a senior, Champi once again made headlines for his play against Navy, but this time the headlines were for his defense in a game that ended in a 7–7 tie. In the first quarter of the 1965 game, Champi recovered an errant pitchout deep in Navy's territory, and with good field position Army was able to score its only touchdown. Later in the game, he played a key role in breaking up a Navy field goal attempt from Army's sixteen-yard line.

In 1964, during his brief time on defense, Champi also played a strong game, helping to stop a fourth-quarter Navy drive by tackling Roger Staubach for a third-down loss that forced Navy to punt. But after the game, all the reporters wanted to talk about were Champi's two catches. Whatever the reporters wanted to talk about was fine by Champi. "I think I was still in a fog," Champi recalls of his postgame happiness over Army's victory. As a plebe, Champi had watched from the stands as Roger Staubach routed Army in their 1962 game. Champi was impressed by how poised Staubach was for a sophomore, but he was equally depressed by Army's inability to stop him.

The next year, when an improved Army team came close to beating Navy with a fourth-quarter touchdown drive, the loss was even more upsetting for Champi. "The 1963 game meant a lot to me because as a sophomore Paul Dietzel put me in a starting role," he recalls. Champi was on the field when Army mounted its final drive of the day, and he has a vivid memory of Army's struggle to get off a last play before time ran out. Watching the Navy players stall by getting off the ball as slowly as possible when a play ended made Champi think they, too, realized they were not going to stop Army. By 1964 Champi was desperate for Army to end its five-year losing streak against Navy, and when the team did, he felt the win more than compensated for the 1962 and 1963 losses.[5]

As a high school student at Seton Hall Prep in West Orange, New Jersey, Champi was a natural for West Point. He was a star end on the football team, the captain of the basketball team, and number one in his class academically. Seton Hall Prep did not throw the ball a lot on offense, which was fine with Champi. Defense was where he excelled, and it was always defensive players whom Paul Dietzel was looking to stockpile for his West Point football teams. "I was getting a lot of offers with different schools," he recalls. The problem for Champi was that his Seton Hall Prep coach wanted him to go to the University of Maryland. He did not think Champi had the right mentality for West Point. Champi still remembers the coach calling him into his office and telling him, "Sam, you're not mean enough to play for West Point. West Point is the toughest football team there is."[6]

Champi's reaction was not what his coach expected. He became more determined than ever to try for West Point. "When I walked out of the room, my mind was 110 percent made up. I'm going there," he told himself. Champi had visited the University of Maryland, and he had a good idea of how football players were viewed there: "I had been down there a few times for visits, and they told me during the football season that you can't take any serious courses." For someone who wanted to be an engineer after he finished college, being treated as a jock was demeaning: "I wanted something that was a challenge in addition to football, a way of life."

Champi's desire to go to West Point had started long before he ever got into Seton Hall Prep. "It was pure tunnel vision," he says. "This was something I wanted since I was ten years old." It did not matter to Champi that neither his father nor his uncles had ever been in the service. His desire to go to West Point was so strong that everything he learned about the Academy made him want to be a cadet. "The Army–Navy game has always been special," he says of the attraction playing football for West Point had for him. To this day, Champi remembers watching the 1952 comedy *Francis Goes to West Point*, starring Donald O'Connor, and the television series *West Point*.

Champi was one of the first players Paul Dietzel recruited after becoming head coach of Army, but far more compelling for Champi than his meeting with Dietzel was the time that he spent on his West Point visit with John Johnson, then a wingback on the plebe team. "I spent most of my time with Johnny Johnson, who was a year ahead of me," Champi remembers. "That was the real thrill, to get inside the buildings and meet the guys. I don't remember meeting that much with the coaches. It was being exposed to the cadets."

The one coach who may have done the most to help Champi settle on West Point was Joe Paterno, who, before he became Penn State's head coach in 1966, scouted New Jersey in his role as an assistant coach for Rip Engle. During dinner with Paterno, Champi told him that he had finally gotten the congressional appointment he needed to enter West Point and he wanted to go there. "You know, Sam, if it was any other school, I would try to talk you out of it," Paterno replied. "But not West Point. If that's where you want to go, then God bless you. I will not try to influence you in any other way." Champi was touched by Paterno's kindness. It reinforced his belief that he had made the right choice in setting his heart on West Point: "I always wanted to do something not everybody else could, and to me West Point provided that challenge."[7]

As someone for whom getting into West Point was "a dream," Champi arrived on campus in the summer of 1966 prepared to do whatever was asked of him. His first months at West Point were, nonetheless, a shock. "You are coming out of high school, and your whole world has changed," he remembers. Champi was so determined to succeed at West Point that he made sure that neither Beast Barracks nor the harassment that came his way as a plebe got the best of him.

"They considered it a game. If you try to fight it, you have a problem. Do what you have to do," was the way Champi came to terms with the hazing that was part of Beast Barracks. He was not sympathetic to cadets who wilted under the psychological pressure of Beast Barracks. He thought they lacked resolve: "If that drove you out, then it's probably best you left because it wasn't really a physical harassment."

Champi would later distinguish between his time at West Point and his time in the service. "My real allegiance is to West Point as an institution, not as a training area for the Army," he now says. It took time, however, for such a view to evolve. Despite his willingness to do whatever was asked of him, Champi still found that being a plebe at West Point was difficult. He sat at the football tables and was immune from harassment there, but the football tables did not protect him for the rest of the day. Like other plebes on the football team, Champi was the target of the "runts," the cadets who, often small in size, had it in for plebes who played football. Until Dick Nowak, the captain of the 1963 football team, learned Champi was a football player, he was hazed by him as well. Nowak would make Champi report to his room and go through "dress formations." It did not matter what Champi was wearing. As soon as he appeared, Nowak would tell him to go back to his own room and change into a different uniform. "He would drive me crazy," Champi remembers. As a plebe, Champi had dropped to 175 pounds, fifty pounds less than his playing weight two years later, and he recalls Nowak's astonishment at discovering who he was. "I had no idea you were a football player. You look like a ghost," Nowak told him.

Nowak's recognition of Champi as a football player and the apology by him that followed made a big difference to Champi. It confirmed his status as an athlete. Champi belonged to one of the last West Point plebe classes not allowed to go home for Christmas, but he remembers that being required to stay on campus turned out to be a pleasure rather than an ordeal: "All the upperclassmen are gone. You have the run of the place. No one is harassing you. It was like a little vacation. My parents came up on several days."

By his second year, Champi had adjusted to West Point life. The rigors of West Point suited him. "You were constantly on the go. You couldn't exercise many bad habits during the week," he recalls. "Basically, it was go to class, go to practice, and then go to bed. It was a pretty Spartan existence, which, I think, helped us all." General Westmoreland was still superintendent of West Point when Champi arrived, and he found Westmoreland to be the personification of West Point at its best. "I remember when he came into our locker room after a game and shook all our hands. That was a big thrill," Champi recalls. "He was a tough guy. He instilled that, and you saw it in him."

By his senior year, Champi had done nearly as well academically at West Point as he had at Seton Hall Prep. He graduated ranked number ten in the class of 1966. Especially for a cadet who had spent as much time on the football field as Champi, it was a singular accomplishment, and the Army rewarded him for his class standing. Instead of requiring him to begin his four years of military service immediately, the Army paid for Champi to attend Princeton and earn his master's degree in civil engineering.[8]

The degree would have a profound effect on Champi's life. He built roads and bridges while serving with an engineering battalion in Vietnam, and after leaving the Army, he worked for a series of construction companies before founding his own. At Princeton, Champi did not, however, spend all his time in the classroom. On a date a friend arranged, Champi met

Russi Bagott, a student at nearby Centenary College, and in 1967 the two married. It was a blissful time for Champi, but with the war in Vietnam now escalating, he felt uneasy about his own good fortune. "After a year and a half, I basically volunteered to go to Vietnam because many of my classmates had already been there," Champi remembers. "I really felt almost guilty that they were there and I was not." The birth of his first son, Sam Jr., who was just three months old when Champi left for Vietnam in July 1968, complicated matters, but becoming a father did not change Champi's feeling that it was time for him to face combat. "It's something you have to do," he recalls thinking at the time. Champi was fatalistic about the potential dangers that lay ahead: "My attitude was whatever is going to be is going to be."

As someone slated for an engineering assignment, Champi did not go to Airborne School, but the Army did send him to Ranger School. Ranger School pushed him to his physical limits, he acknowledges, but it had nowhere near the impact on him that Beast Barracks did in his first

Sam Champi (left) in Vietnam. (Courtesy Sam Champi)

summer at West Point. After West Point, dealing with long patrols and sleepless days was not a problem.

Being separated from his wife and child was far more worrying, but as he got ready to ship off to Vietnam, Champi's mind was on what kind of an officer he would be: "My greatest fear in going to Vietnam was not being prepared for the troops' sake." It was not a fear that he was given time to dwell on. In Vietnam, Champi was a member of the 577th Engineer Battalion. There he was put in charge of a company of two hundred men, but as he found out, he had plenty of support to go along with his new responsibility. The colonel he reported to was an officer he knew and admired from his time at West Point, and the 577th was a crack engineering battalion with good morale. The troops and the noncommissioned officers who commanded them took care of most of the discipline problems. Champi was free to do the engineering work that he had been trained for.[9]

With the 577th Engineer Battalion Champi worked on maintaining roads and bridges and was responsible for building what, he notes was for a week the longest bridge in Vietnam. During his time in Vietnam, the biggest threat to Champi and the troops he was working with came from land mines and an occasional mortar shelling: "You almost got the feeling that the Vietnamese, Vietcong, or whoever felt that we were building up the land for them. So why bother us? They used these roads and bridges to collect taxes." Champi found that some of the restrictions commanders placed on when and where the troops in the 577th Battalion could carry loaded weapons defied common sense, and he had no qualms about disobeying those restrictions when the situation called for it. "We were traveling roads unprotected every day, and I always kept a shotgun and a pistol," he recalls.

What Champi found difficult to come up with in the midst of his Vietnam tour was an overview of the war. "I was a young officer. I just got out of Ranger School," Champi remembers. "I didn't know the big picture." His instinct was to give those running the war the benefit of the doubt when it came to the demands they were making on troops like him. "They are doing the best they can. They don't want to sacrifice guys. That was my attitude," he says. Champi realized that the body count of enemy dead attributed to the Korean troops the 577th supported with engineering projects was often inflated, but he did not attach any special significance to the inflated numbers at the time that he became aware of them.

Later—he is not quite sure when—Champi found himself asking the question, "Are we really trying to win this war?" The Army's strategy, he began to realize, often seemed contradictory: "We occupy an area, and we pull out, and then we have got to go back and retake it. That to me didn't make much sense." It did not surprise Champi that by the early 1970s, more and more Vietnam vets began having doubts about the war: "I think there was a lot of disillusion with the government, with the military, for the guys who were in the service that led a lot of them to leave."[10]

When Champi's tour of duty ended in July 1969, he was happy to return to the States and to his family. His time away had been very hard on Russi, who was left on her own to take care of their baby. She had gone back to her parents' home in Chicago so she would not be alone, but being with her parents had not taken away her worries. She could follow the war on television, but she could never be sure of what was happening to her husband. Getting letters back from Vietnam, Russi remembers, was consistently difficult: "It was very spotty. You went for a stretch of time with nothing, and then I'd get like five letters." The good news for the family was Champi's next posting after he returned from Vietnam. He was sent back to West Point to teach in the Earth, Space, and Graphic Sciences Department. The result was a period when the Champis could lead a normal life as a young married couple. As a faculty member, Champi was free from the day-to-day pressures he had experienced as a cadet, and in 1970 the Champis' second son, Bill, was born at the West Point hospital.

The years at West Point were not enough to make Champi think that he wanted to make a career of the Army. By the time his teaching assignment was over, he and Russi agreed that it was time for him to leave the service. He had fought in a war that was ending without a victory, and they both wanted a large family, never easy to support on an Army officer's salary. Their daughter Cristine was born in 1973, their daughter Kim arrived in 1975, and in 1985 the Champis added a fifth child, Dana, through adoption. "My wife had a lot of difficulty when I was in Vietnam, and I knew there would be times like that again. I always wanted to establish myself in a community, and the Army does not give you that ability," Champi remembers thinking when he made the decision to resign his commission.[11]

For Champi, establishing himself in a community meant returning with his family to New Jersey near to where he grew up. Champi's first job as senior vice president of Engineers Incorporated lasted eight years from 1973 to 1981. Then he worked as senior vice president for Modular Structures Incorporated. In 1988, he founded his own company, Point Construction, where he worked as president until 2002, at which time he retired to do consulting work. It has been a very fulfilling professional life that has allowed the Champis to raise their five children in comfort. Champi was responsible for the construction of Johnson Stadium at West Point and the Yogi Berra Baseball Stadium and Yogi Berra Museum on the campus of Montclair State University. In New Jersey, Champi has been able to find the community ties he wanted. Regrettably, Champi did not make it to the 2009 West Point dinner honoring Paul Dietzel. The Little League players Champi was coaching were in a tournament, and he could not bring himself to disappoint them by missing their game.[12]

Champi still thinks about Vietnam. When he returned from the war in 1969, he never had any personal confrontations with antiwar demonstrators. His arrival in San Francisco after his long flight from Vietnam was uneventful. Neither reporters nor protestors were at the airport to ask him to explain what he had done during the war, but as Champi settled down in New Jersey, he found that the controversies the war had aroused when the fighting was at its peak were never far from the surface.

Champi remembers being at a party when military service in Vietnam became a hot topic of discussion after one of the guests began bragging about managing to avoid the draft. Champi kept clear of the argument, but he was fascinated by what it revealed to him. He and his teammates don't always agree on how the Vietnam War should be judged, but their opinions are always heartfelt and grounded in their own experiences. Champi has come to believe that the draft-age men of his generation who went out of their way to avoid service have their own consciences to deal with, especially if they pulled strings to get a deferment. "As far as I'm concerned, that's the guilt they have to carry. That's their punishment, so to speak. That's their Vietnam," he says. "I am not going to dwell on it with them."[13]

Champi remembers when he first saw the Vietnam Veterans Memorial in Washington with all the names of the dead on it. "It is a personal feeling you get when you look at the Vietnam Veterans Memorial versus the others," he says. "It was very emotional." As for Vietnam itself, Champi has a postwar knowledge of it shared by few who fought in the war. By his own count, he has been back to Vietnam thirteen times since he began making business trips there in the 1990s. The trips gave him a chance to see how the country had developed since the war ended and to think more about his years in the Army. Champi went back as part of an engineering group that had been invited to see if it could put together a massive housing program for the poor of Ho Chi Minh City, the former Saigon. Early on, Champi and his partners approached a series of banks to see if they could get financing. They were turned down, and the housing program, which came with an estimated $400 million price tag, eventually fell through because it could not get the financial guarantees it needed.

The trips to Vietnam did, however, open Champi's eyes to life in postwar Vietnam. Champi was nervous about how he would be received as an ex-Army officer from the United States. Would he still be looked on as the enemy? Much to his surprise, Champi found that he was welcomed. "People in Saigon were very friendly. I was taken aback by how nice they were to us. There was no bitterness," he remembers. Champi walked through the city's markets without any difficulty. A "mutual respect" also prevailed among the government officials he met with in Vietnam. There was no desire on their part to rehash old battles. "The people we dealt with at the government level were all officers or soldiers with the Vietcong or with the North Vietnamese Army," Champi recalls. "They certainly weren't gloating."[14]

7

ON A HIGH

Peter Braun

It was the perfect time for Army's coaches to call for another blitz. Peter Braun, one of Army's five two-way players, thought so, too. He believed it was crucial to keep the pressure on Roger Staubach. With twenty-five seconds remaining in the second quarter, Staubach had just led Navy on a long drive that ended in a touchdown. A two-point conversion would tie the game at 8–8, erasing the lead Army had held since it scored on a safety in the first minute of play.

Navy's touchdown had come on a disputed, fourth-down run from the one-yard line by halfback Tom Leiser. Army's defenders were so sure that they had stopped the run that even after the game, they were talking to reporters about how they had kept Leiser out of the end zone. "We honestly didn't think he had made it," Rollie Stichweh insisted. With the ball now sitting on the two-yard line, it was hard to imagine that Navy would try a second straight run for the two-point conversion that it needed to tie the score. A quick pass from Roger Staubach seemed like Navy's best choice. A passing play put the ball in Staubach's hands from the start and set up the option of a run if his receivers were covered.[1]

From Army's perspective, an all-out rush was better than playing it safe and giving Staubach time to improvise. That decision suited Braun. At 6'1" and 215 pounds, Braun was the classic West Point lineman and linebacker of the early 1960s. He was fast enough to catch a running back and strong enough to handle an opposing lineman. What Army and Braun

Army guard and linebacker Peter Braun. (Courtesy Athletic Communications Office, USMA)

had not counted on, however, was that with Staubach at the top of his game, even the perfect defensive call could fail to stop him. As *Philadelphia Inquirer* sportswriter Frank Dolson observed in his account of the pass Staubach completed for a two-point conversion, "Facing a stiff rush, Roger went back to the fifteen, where linebacker Pete Braun, who was in for all but one play, tackled him. With Braun clutching him around the legs, Staubach, falling backward, heaved the ball into the end zone. End Phil Norton reached as high as he could and pulled it down."[2]

Years later, Staubach's account of the play makes it clear that Dolson's reportage was, if anything, understated. "I have probably never been involved in a more unbelievable play," Staubach wrote in his memoir, *Staubach: First Down, Lifetime to Go*. "I was trying to pass but was chased all over the field. A guy grabbed both my legs and another reached for my passing arm so I moved the ball over to my left hand. Then as I was going down, I moved the ball back to my right and threw it about fifteen yards into the end zone. Phil Norton jumped up and caught it for two points and it was 8–8 at halftime."[3]

Staubach never saw the pass completed, and neither did Braun. All they heard were the cheers from the Navy side of the field, but for Braun the cheers were devastating—the low point of the game for him. He had been in on the safety against Staubach that set the tone for the first half. "We all swarmed," he remembers. "Navy's line and blocking backs just broke down. We went right through them." Braun was counting on Army's line to continue to stymie Staubach. The safety had proven contagious. "When we got the safety that was the spark. Everybody was frothing at the mouth when that happened," Braun recalls. Now the worst had occurred: Army's coaches had called the perfect defensive play, everyone had executed his assignment, and Staubach had still scored. It was a painful reminder of how good Staubach could be.

In 1962, in his plebe year at West Point, when NCAA rules still prevented freshmen from playing in varsity games, Braun had watched the Army–Navy game from the stands. Navy dismantled Army that day, and Braun had been impressed by how good Staubach for a player at the start of his college career. It was clear to Braun that with Staubach leading them, "Navy was going to be one of the top teams in the country."

In 1963, as a sophomore, Braun was a starter on Army's offensive team, and he became even more impressed watching Staubach up close. "He was a triple threat," Braun recalls thinking at the time. "He had the leadership, the running ability, and the passing ability." After Army's 1963 loss to Navy, Braun came to see beating Navy as no longer just a matter of beating an archrival. For him, "Navy became a campaign" as well as a way of redeeming the 1964 football season in which injuries had dimmed Army's hopes for being one of the best teams in the country.

"Our record was disappointing given the talent we had on the field," Braun still believes.

As Army went into its locker room at halftime with the score tied 8–8, there was little for the players to say to each other. They were all mindful of the five straight defeats at Navy's hands. From his perspective as left linebacker on defense, right guard on offense, Braun was thinking that there would be extra pressure on the defense to keep Navy in check during the second half. Braun was right about the need for the defense to assert itself after Navy tied the score. The only points Army scored in the second half of the game came on a field goal. Army won because it shut out Navy for the rest of the afternoon. The following year, Braun would play even better as a senior. He made honorable mention on the All-East football team, and he was chosen co-captain of the Blue squad in the 1965 Blue–Gray Game. No game, though, gave Braun as much satisfaction as Army's 1964 victory over Navy. "That game," he has no doubt, "is by far the most significant of my football career."

Braun was instrumental in the second half in preventing Staubach from getting Navy's passing attack going, and at the conclusion of the game, he took as much pride in how Army won as the fact that it did win. "I was on a high that we were playing as well as we were against them," he recalls thinking at the time. Playing offense and defense did not tire Braun. Playing two ways was a repeat of what he had done in high school. "I did not get worn out, not at all," he remembers. "There was an adrenaline kick from someplace."[4]

Braun still recalls the only time he came out of the game. It was late in the fourth quarter, and Coach Dietzel decided to give seniors who had not been in the game a chance to get on the field: "It was a very risky move. It was only a three-point game. I give Dietzel credit for that." Braun's replacement was Mike Berdy, a right guard, but for Braun the memory of standing on the sidelines and watching Berdy substitute for him has little to do with football. Berdy's death in Vietnam makes Braun think of that moment in the game. Berdy was getting ready to go home after finishing his tour of duty, and just before leaving, he took a last-minute helicopter ride to an outpost where Bob Hope was entertaining the troops with his comedy act. On the way to the outpost, the helicopter crashed, killing Berdy, who had escaped injury while he was in combat.

Berdy's death was not the first time the personal and political had come together for Braun. During his time at West Point, Braun was aware of how much the outside world was affecting him and his classmates. He remembers the 1962 Cuban Missile Crisis and the "sick jokes" that were made about what would happen if there were a nuclear war between the United States and Soviet Union. Even more vivid for Braun was the shock he felt at getting the news of President Kennedy's assassination. Worried about morale on the team, which still had its 1963 game with Navy left to play, Dietzel tried to get the players to relax by taking them to New York for dinner and a movie. Braun still recalls the movie—*How the West Was Won*—Dietzel chose for the team to watch. For Braun, what makes Berdy's death in Vietnam stand out from these other events is that it is so inseparable from the satisfaction he takes in the 1964 victory over Navy.[5]

As a high school football player, Braun was an ideal prospect for West Point. At Westfield High School in New Jersey, he won first-team, all-state football honors two years in a row, and in his senior year, he made the *New York Herald Tribune* All-Scholastic team. The coaches at Duke and the University of Iowa were both interested in Braun, but his recruiting visits to those schools filled him with doubt. He did not feel comfortable with the fraternity life that was so important on both campuses. "I said to myself," Braun recalls, "I don't know if I can survive in this kind of environment. I need somebody to kick me in the butt."

Braun's problem with West Point was altogether different: he was not sure he could make it there in terms of grades. "This is totally out of my reach academically," he remembers telling himself. Braun had grown up admiring West Point. He was a fan of the television series *West Point*, and he carried with him a vivid memory of Army's undefeated 1958 football team, which featured Bill Carpenter as the "Lonely End" and Pete Dawkins and Bob Anderson as running backs.

A visit to West Point with his Westfield High School coach added to Braun's desire to be a cadet. "I went up with my coach in the spring," Braun recalls. "It was a gorgeous day. I had never been to West Point before. It blew me away." A second visit to West Point, this one the official visit the NCAA sanctions on a one-time-only basis for athletes, made the prospect of becoming an Army football player still more appealing. The four-year service commitment that came with going to West

Point did not worry Braun. "Everybody was going to get drafted and have military service anyway," he thought.

The cadet who escorted Braun around West Point was Al Vanderbush, an Army football co-captain, later West Point athletic director, and the coach he met with was Tom Cahill, who after the 1966 season became Paul Dietzel's successor at West Point. Cahill and Braun got along well, but he wasn't the only one in the Cahill family to make an impression. Mrs. Cahill and Braun's mother also established an immediate bond.

The result was the perfect West Point trip, and after Cahill paid a return visit to Braun at his parents' home in New Jersey, all that remained was to see what could be done to improve Braun's SAT scores, especially in math, his weakest subject. An extra year of high school, this one at the Manlius School in Upstate New York, where Cahill had coached from 1947 to 1957, did the trick. In the fall of 1962, Braun and two other Manlius grads entered West Point.[6]

Manlius had not, however, prepared Braun for the trials of plebe year. "Beast Barracks came as a shock," he recalls. He and his roommates got through Beast Barracks by sticking together, but the experience took a toll on Braun. He dropped thirty pounds and got a look at a side of West Point that he did not like. "Some of the behavior of the upperclassmen at Beast Barracks wasn't classy," Braun would later say. What sticks in his memory is the case of a plebe who was forced to drink water until he wet his pants. "The kid was totally humiliated," Braun remembers.

After Beast Barracks, there was still a lot of harassment that went on during his first year, Braun discovered. In the company he was part of, the upperclassmen seemed to have it in for the football players. "I took some crap from people I thought were out of line," Braun recalls. There was some relief at Christmas, when all the other classes were allowed to go home and the plebes were the only ones left, but that was the only peaceful time in Braun's first year at West Point.

It was not until his second year began with summer football practice at Camp Buckner that Braun felt truly comfortable at West Point. His memory of his first practice at Camp Buckner is very distinct: "You are not a plebe anymore. It is a beautiful setting. It's like going to a nice camp." From this point on, Braun was able to enjoy his West Point experience without looking over his shoulder. General Westmoreland was West Point's superintendent when Braun arrived, and he remembers the impression the general created: "You couldn't construct someone physically to be more impressive than this guy. He was handsome. He was tall. I was in awe. He was very impressive to me as a cadet."

Coach Dietzel was utterly different in Braun's eyes, but the coach also, Braun recalls, made everyone around him feel special. "I have never seen anybody as organized as Dietzel," Braun says. The practices and the trips the team took were always designed by Dietzel with the players in mind. It was not just after President Kennedy's assassination that Dietzel showed his ability to bring the team together. He did so on numerous other occasions as well. Braun remembers the coach once taking the players for dinner at the 21 Club in New York, and then allowing them to stay afterward and watch the popular comedian Henny Youngman do his routine in the 21 Club's upper room.

Most of all, though, what Braun thinks of as key to his four years at West Point was that as a football player he was not separated from the rest of the cadets. "In looking back, I'm very glad we even had Saturday classes when we played at home," he says. For Braun, those classes symbolized how being a football player did not exempt him and his teammates from the larger responsibilities they were expected to fulfill.[7]

Braun took in stride the four years of required service that were expected of all cadets after they finished West Point. He did not resent losing out on the chance to play pro football. He had made his decision on the pros before he entered West Point, and with the draft a two-year requirement for all 1-A men, as far as Braun was concerned, his service requirement simply amounted to two extra years in the military.

The "hives," the highest-ranking West Point cadets, got first choice of whatever branch of the Army they wanted to enter, and most of them chose the corps of engineers. That was fine with Braun. He wanted a combat branch. He chose the artillery and was happy to get his preference. The two months between his West Point graduation and his reporting date for the Army were a happy time. Braun spent most of them at Cape Cod, where Martha O'Neil, whom he had dated in high school, was also vacationing. By the time the two months were over, he and Martha had made plans to marry.

With more and more troops being sent to Vietnam, Braun was sure that he would be going there soon, but like most of his classmates, he went through a period of extensive stateside training. First, there was Airborne School and Ranger School; afterward, he spent over a year as an artillery battery commander with the 5th Infantry Division (Mechanized) at Fort Carson, Colorado. Nothing that happened in this pre-Vietnam period was especially memorable for Braun. During Ranger training he was deprived of sleep and pushed to the point of exhaustion, but after Beast Barracks, Braun found the challenges of Ranger School could be handled without too much trouble. "It was macho, macho, macho," he would joke years later, but for Braun the most important event in the period before Vietnam was his marriage to Martha O'Neil in December 1966.

When his time to go to Vietnam began in July 1968, Braun was more than ready. He was also aware of the social turmoil going on in the country at the time. "Even before I went over there, Martin Luther King had been killed. The country was in a state of unrest," he recalls. With Vietnam on the horizon, it was, however, difficult for Braun to think of too much else. "I was more worried about my own skin, going over there and doing a decent job," he admits. In 1962, when he entered West Point, Vietnam was, Braun remembers, Indochina, nothing more, but as the American war buildup began, Vietnam increasingly assumed new importance at West Point. "Our tactical courses became more and more counterinsurgency based and not Normandy-invasion based," Braun recalls. "I saw the progression."[8]

In Vietnam, Braun was part of a Military Assistance Command, Vietnam (MACV) to South Vietnam's 1st Division stationed in I Corps, the northernmost area of the country and an entry point for North Vietnamese regulars. His first months with the 1st Division, were, Braun remembers, marked by the American Army's growing commitment to the Vietnamization of the war, which meant more and more of the actual fighting being turned over to units like the one he was advising. Braun's experience with the 1st Division was excellent. "I was with a very good unit," he says. "They were motivated. They had some of the very best officers." Braun's biggest regret about the time he spent with the 1st Division was that he did not make more of an effort to know them better as individuals: "We were nearby an American unit, and every chance I got, instead of eating with my Vietnamese counterparts, I went over and got good old U.S. food."

The South Vietnamese 1st Division was part of Operation Dewey Canyon, a massive offensive in the A Shau Valley undertaken during the first three months of 1969. The aim of Operation Dewey Canyon was to stop the flow of North Vietnamese troops and materiel into South Vietnam, and Braun was impressed with how well the 1st Division troops reacted in combat. His personal fondness for the South Vietnamese troops and officers he worked with made him worry years later about their survival after the North Vietnamese took control of the country in 1975. He was sure that a South Vietnamese colonel he was close to and who had a family in Quang Tri was someone who would have been marked for execution.

During his tour of duty, Braun often had qualms about the way the war was being fought on a day-to-day basis. "It was frustrating," he remembers. "We would go into a battle, take prisoners, then go somewhere else, and a week later we would take the same area again. It was hard to see progress." The constant rotation of troops was also a liability in Braun's eyes. Soldiers no sooner got good at their jobs than they found themselves getting replaced because their tour of duty was up. The change was very disruptive to unit cohesion, Braun found, and adding to his frustration was that, from his perspective, America never seemed willing to bring its full military power to bear in Vietnam: "I always felt that we were capable of leveling North Vietnam from the air, and I never fully understood why we didn't."

"My attitude on the Vietnam War was that it was part of the Cold War. That was the rationale for our involvement in Southeast Asia," Braun says of his postwar thinking, but he has also come to believe that, especially for his generation, the war is destined to be continually debated and refought: "I don't think it will ever be resolved what we could have done, why we did it."[9]

When Braun's tour of duty in Vietnam ended, he was eager to return to the United States. His daughter Christina was born in 1969 while he had three months left on his Vietnam tour, and after her birth he began to worry that he might not live to see her. "I said I hope I don't get knocked off before I see this child alive. I got paranoid about this," he remembers. When Braun arrived back in the States at Travis Air Force Base near San Francisco, he was met by his West Point roommate and friends, who were waiting for him at the airport. He was, as he later put it, "high as a kite" knowing that in a few more hours he would get to see Christina. The high did not last long. At Travis Air Force Base, Braun's return was marred by antiwar protestors, who spit at him and the other arriving vets. It was a

Peter Braun (right) and a Vietnamese colonel in Vietnam eating dried squid. (Courtesy of Peter Braun)

jarring experience and made Braun realize that, like it or not, he was going to have to defend his service in Vietnam as long as he was wearing a uniform.

While in Vietnam, Braun had secured a final assignment he was looking forward to: assisting Tom Cahill, now the head coach at West Point. The chance to work for the coach who had recruited him to West Point and to be reunited with his family seemed almost too good to be true. At West Point, Braun would be working with Rollie Stichweh, who also had secured an assistant coaching position after his tour in Vietnam ended. Braun could think about football again, but, as he soon realized, the West Point assignment came with challenges that were not present when he was a cadet. One of Braun's chief duties was going on recruiting trips for Cahill and meeting high school football players and their parents. "I was literally on a recruiting trip when Kent State occurred," Braun remembers. For Braun, the Kent State antiwar demonstrations of May 1970, which resulted in Ohio National Guardsmen killing four Kent State students, turned out to be the tip of a political iceberg that would make his job at West Point especially difficult.

Throughout Braun's time as assistant coach at West Point, the news was dominated by antiwar protests, and when he spoke to students who were being pursued by schools such as Alabama and Notre Dame, Braun found himself at a distinct disadvantage. Joe Namath's lucrative contract with the New York Jets had changed how college football was now viewed by the best high school players. "My stories versus their stories and the potential to go into the pro ranks were an inhibiting factor for us," Braun says of the football programs against which he was competing. Even among students who were not overly political, Vietnam was still a problem, Braun realized: "I didn't sense they were antiwar. I just sensed they didn't want to be killed." Braun did his best as a recruiter, but there was, he concluded, no denying how much the appeal of West Point had diminished in just a few years.[10]

Braun also had to make a decision about whether he wanted to remain in the Army after his assignment at West Point ended, and the longer he thought about staying in the Army, the more returning to civilian life became the right choice for him and his family. Braun learned from a contact he had at the Pentagon that he was certain to be sent back to Vietnam if he extended his time in the service, and he thought being away again would make life very difficult for his daughter, whom he was just getting to know after missing her birth.

For Martha Braun, the prospect of her husband going back to Vietnam on his next assignment was also daunting. She did not like the thought of him being in danger again, and the idea that, as a future Army wife, she would have to move every few years was especially unappealing. Braun had no good answers for these problems, and when he considered what his future in the Army looked like, he did not like what he saw. In Vietnam, he had witnessed career officers, desperate to get promoted, take on the most boring assignments in order to fulfill their duties: "I would see majors, field grade officers, putting tacks in maps. I said, 'Is that what I have in front of me?'" Braun believed that there was no guarantee that even if he did all that was asked of him, promotion would come any time soon. "Promotion was grinding to a halt," Braun realized as America began to reduce its force in Vietnam. "They had all these field grade officers who were clogging up the promotion line."

When his coaching assignment at West Point ended in 1970, Braun left the Army. He would, he knew, miss being at West Point and being part of its football program, but as soon as he resigned his commission,

Braun realized that he had made the right decision for himself and his family. Braun wanted to find work that would let him live near the New Jersey area where he was born, and he was able to do so. After leaving the Army, he took a job with Exxon, and he subsequently moved on to the investment firm of Bear Stearns, where he focused on marketing Bear Stearns products to institutional investors. His work allowed him to be present when his daughter Heather was born in 1972, as well as his daughter Lindsey in 1979, and to help raise his three daughters.[11]

For Braun, who still works two days a week at Financial Partners Capital Management, it has been a good life, but it has not been a life in which he has left Vietnam behind. He was very moved by Maya Lin's Vietnam Veterans Memorial in Washington when he first saw it, and he makes a point of going back to the memorial when he is in Washington. Braun's closest friends remain those from West Point, and it was on one of his visits to West Point, where he still has season tickets for the team's home games, that he began wearing his Vietnam veterans pin for the first time. In the company of West Point teammates and classmates, the pin seemed neither boastful nor an act of defiance—just a symbol of being true to himself.

Since coming back from the war, Braun has had Vietnam nightmares. He has come to accept the nightmares as one of the costs of the Vietnam War, and so has his second wife, Lucille, whom Braun married in 2005 (Braun's first marriage ended in divorce). "It has affected his life," Lucille says of the toll the nightmares have taken. Braun recognizes that some parts of his Vietnam experience will never go away and that his service in the war will always make him a target. Braun once had an antiwar demonstrator shout "Baby Killer" at him. It was an accusation that Braun, whose time in Vietnam was spent with South Vietnamese troops, not South Vietnamese civilians, felt was completely off the mark, but it has not been possible for him to forget the "Baby Killer" incident or the anger behind it.

Braun found Oliver Stone's Vietnam War film *Platoon* to be "far-fetched," but he is an avid reader of Vietnam histories, and he expects those writing about the war to take it as seriously as he does. At a lecture given at the Union League Club in New York by Lewis Sorley, author of *A Better War: The Unexamined Victories and Final Tragedy of America's Last Years in Vietnam*, Braun found himself incensed by Sorley's criticism of General Westmoreland and went out of his way to let Sorley know how angry he was after the lecture ended. "I had to say something," Braun remembers telling himself.

Braun's point was not that Westmoreland's Vietnam War strategy of trying to achieve victory by wearing down the enemy deserved to be defended uncritically. "Westmoreland made a lot of bad decisions," Braun concedes. What caused Braun to lose his temper with Sorley was his belief that Sorley was criticizing Westmoreland without taking sufficient account of the pressures Westmoreland was under and the World War II and Korean War cultures that shaped him. From Braun's point of view, there is no easy answer as to why America fought the Vietnam War the way it did.[12]

8

IRON MAN

John Johnson

As the second half of the Navy game began, John Johnson was not feeling tired as a result of playing wingback on offense and cornerback on defense, but he was having a hard time forgetting the two-point conversion that Roger Staubach had made while being tackled by Peter Braun. "He was falling on his back, prone on his back, and he completes the two-point conversion," Johnson remembered. "I couldn't believe it, and I was just thinking, what does it take to beat this guy?"[1]

All year long, Johnson had played both offense and defense for Army—just not at the same time over the course of a full game. Johnson did not think of himself as an iron man, but he still felt comfortable being a two-way player for the season's final game with Navy. With tailback John Seymour healthy for the first time all year, Johnson knew he wasn't going to get a lot of carries on offense, and that made him more confident in his ability to play without taking a breather. "I do think I needed to play on the corner. On offense, we played the wing T. I wasn't going to make a huge difference there," he recalls thinking after Paul Dietzel announced to the media that five of his starters would play offense and defense for the entire Navy game.

Johnson was happy with Dietzel's decision to rely on a core of two-way players. "We had gotten down to the nucleus of players we needed to have out there to win," he was convinced. "We needed to do that. We needed to sell out." Being cautious was not going to work. Johnson did not mind being the fourth back to carry the ball on offense. From his point of view, the key to winning was keeping Navy from doing too much scoring. He knew Army's run-oriented offense was not going to generate a lot of points, even on a good day. The offense was doing its job if it took time off the clock and ground out a touchdown or two. "It was pretty close to three yards and a cloud of dust. That was pretty much our standard approach," Johnson recalls. It was when Army got so far behind that it had to pass that the team got into trouble. In their 1962 and 1963 games against Navy, West Point had scored fourteen and fifteen points in losing efforts, and the team's conservative coaching staff had done nothing that was likely to get them more touchdowns in 1964.

Johnson was convinced that Army could defeat Navy this time around. "It was the best two weeks of practice we had all season reaching back into the preseason. The mindset was 'We can beat those guys!'" Johnson remembers. Among seniors such as himself, the confidence level was especially high. After five consecutive years of losses, the team was determined not to have another senior class graduate from West Point without experiencing a football victory over Navy: "We felt we could not go back and face a roommate or a classmate if we did not win."[2]

As he got ready for the 1964 game, Johnson was deeply aware of how special an opportunity it was to play against Navy. In 1962, as a sophomore, he started the game against Navy as cornerback and was shocked by how deftly Staubach, playing in his first Army–Navy game, handled Army's defense: "It was just a debacle from the first series on. He had great presence. He didn't play like a sophomore." The next season, when Army almost beat Navy, Johnson was not on the field. He was sitting in the stands. In the 1963 opening game against Boston University, Johnson was tackled in the back and experienced a kidney tear so severe that the doctors would not let him risk further contact, even in scrimmages, for the rest of the season. For Johnson, the injury was a devastating personal setback. "Not playing with that team is really to this day one of my great regrets," he says.[3]

Two years later, Johnson felt fortunate to be getting a second chance to play against Staubach, and he was determined to make the most of his opportunity. He admired Staubach's running and passing abilities, but he thought Staubach's greatest strength was his grasp of the game. "He had a good arm. He was a good runner, but his overall feel for the game was his strong point," Johnson believes. "He just knew how to win." As the 1964

Wingback John Johnson (22). (Courtesy Athletic Communications Office, USMA)

game began, Johnson was not, however, intimidated by the prospect of facing Staubach. It was not until late in the first quarter that he realized how zoned in he was. An errant Staubach pass bounced off Johnson's hand as he tried to intercept it, and, much to his surprise, the ball stung. Only then did Johnson realize the weather was colder than he thought and Staubach threw a much harder ball than he remembered.

The play from the 1964 game that Johnson recalls most vividly, though, had nothing to do with Staubach. The play occurred in the second quarter when Navy fullback Pat Donnelly, who the year before had scored three touchdowns against Army, broke through a huge hole that had suddenly opened up in Army's line. Seeing nobody else near Donnelly, Johnson took a chance on bringing down the much bigger back on his own. He tripped Donnelly up enough for Peter Braun to come over and finish the play, but his decision to meet Donnelly at the line of scrimmage made Johnson aware of how much winning or losing against Navy depended on very small differences between the teams. "I think he'd still be running if I had slipped," Johnson would later say.[4]

In the second half, Johnson and Army's defense were pressed even harder than in the first half. Unable to move the ball on the ground, Staubach repeatedly tested Army with his passes, getting Navy close enough for a field goal try in the third quarter and moving the team to Army's twenty-eight-yard line in the fourth quarter. Finally, late in the game, when Army got the ball on offense, the coaches gave Johnson a breather, but the breather was for an offensive series that lasted only three plays. Without time to recover, Johnson was back on defense again.[5]

When, on the last play of the game, Army stopped Navy for a meaningless two-yard gain, Johnson was only too happy to leave the field. "It was the first game I played that I started to get a tinge of dehydration," he remembers. The crowd of cadets pouring out on the field makes up Johnson's memory of what happened when the gun went off. Army's on-the-field celebration was quickly followed by a second, and longer, celebration in the locker room. "I remember my parents and my wife-to-be were there," he recalls. "That was probably the sweetest postgame gathering we ever had."

Back at West Point, spontaneous rallies broke out in the mess hall during dinner that evening. "There was a terrific impact, if you will, on cadet life for a year," Johnson recalls. A season that from the start had been plagued with injuries to key players and games the team believed it could have won at full strength had been redeemed. "We all felt this was our day," Johnson thought when Army first took the field. Now he could say that out loud.[6]

If Johnson had followed family tradition, he would have stayed in the South rather than go to West Point. His father was a Clemson graduate, and Johnson, a star fullback and linebacker on his Winnsboro, South Carolina, high school football team, was recruited by Clemson, as well as North Carolina, South Carolina, and Tennessee. But from a young age, West Point had captured Johnson's attention. He first become aware of West Point by watching home movies that his father had taken of the football team practicing when Doc Blanchard and Glenn Davis were leading it to undefeated seasons in the 1940s.

Johnson soon found himself fascinated by all things West Point. "I was hooked," he would say of his admiration for West Point. The last West Point team that Red Blaik coached, the undefeated 1958 Army squad, showed Johnson that Army was still capable of great football a decade after his father had taken home movies of the team. Reading Colonel Red Reeder's *The West Point Story*, with its tales of history and heroism, and in the mid-1950s becoming a devoted follower of the television series *West Point* did the rest, convincing Johnson that West Point had an aura few other colleges could match.[7]

"It was the fulfillment of a boyhood dream," Johnson remembers thinking on the day he was accepted to West Point. "I just had a special regard for West Point." By contrast, Johnson's visit to Clemson, even though it was his father's school, failed to impress him: "When I went up to Clemson, I never felt anything special." Johnson did not, however, just follow his heart when it came to choosing West Point. He was practical as well. Army, he felt, had a better football program and was stronger academically than Clemson: "I elected to go to West Point to play football and get a good diploma."

West Point took some adjusting to on Johnson's part when he arrived in the fall of 1961. "They treat you like a fifth-class citizen," he later observed of his plebe year. "Beast Barracks was totally different from anything I had experienced," he remembers, but getting through Beast Barracks was not the problem for Johnson that it was for many of his classmates. Johnson found that going along with whatever was asked

The 1964 starting backfield for Army: John Johnson (22), Rollie Stichweh (16), Don Parcells (31), and John Seymour (43). The 1964 Navy game was the first time all were healthy. (Courtesy Athletic Communications Office, USMA)

spared him from being singled out for additional rough treatment. "I didn't fight the system; I did OK," he recalls.

Behind Johnson's thinking about surviving the ordeal of Beast Barracks and the hazing of plebe year was his determination not to let anything drive him out of West Point after he had worked so hard to get in: "I never considered leaving. I had made the decision to go to West Point." As his plebe year went on, Johnson discovered more and more to like about West Point. In the company he was assigned to, the football players made life easier for him, shielding him from extreme hazing and allowing him to say of the hazing he got, "I rolled pretty much with the punches. I can honestly say I probably escaped a lot." Forced by the rules of the Academy to remain on campus, along with the rest of his class, over Christmas vacation in his plebe year, Johnson missed going back home, but he enjoyed the free time, and he got to play squash with General Westmoreland when the general's regular squash partner failed to show up at the gym.

"I was not a particularly good cadet," Johnson says of his dislike of the spit and polish expected of him, but the values that West Point sought to inculcate and the camaraderie that grew out of cadet life were embraced by Johnson. "The solid values that you learn there," Johnson believes, shaped his life. "I always felt like at West Point I was prepared pretty much to participate in and contribute to just about every type of situation I encountered in the service." Johnson especially liked that being an athlete did not isolate him from the rest of West Point. The thought of going to a college with athletic dorms was anathema for him. "The great part of being a football player at West Point," he recalls, "was the fact that your classmates appreciated that you were out there and pretty much meeting the same standards and going through the same regime that they were." By the conclusion of the 1964 football season, Johnson was, however, content to have played his last game. Pro football held no special appeal for him. "Most of us," he would later say of himself and his teammates, "left West Point satisfied that our football aspirations had been met."[8]

In the spring of his senior year, Johnson chose the infantry as the branch of the Army in which he would begin his mandatory service. In contrast to the more popular service branches, engineers and armor, infantry had plenty of slots available, and Johnson was at ease with the risks that went with getting sent to Vietnam as a junior infantry officer: "I fully anticipated that I would go to Vietnam, that our class would go. I accepted that."

In his senior year, Johnson recalls that counterinsurgency doctrines were introduced into the curriculum in his military instruction classes, and he has a vivid memory of Bernard Fall, the French historian who, as a young reporter, covered the French Indochina War of the early 1950s, coming to West Point to lecture. It was also at this time that Johnson had his most direct contact with antiwar protestors. On May 15, 1965, he was in New York City with a contingent of cadets marching in the city's Armed Forces Day parade when it was stopped by demonstrators. Johnson was singled out by West Point officials for provoking the demonstrators by pointing at them and smirking. Johnson still denies the charge. His only remembrance of the Armed Forces Day parade is that while marching, he felt contempt for the demonstrators. "I thought at the time that they were fruitcakes," he says. The charge of provoking the demonstrators, nonetheless, stuck. Just weeks before his West Point graduation,

Johnson found himself put in confinement, unable to leave his room except for classes, dinner, and exercise at the gym.[9]

In the wake of his confinement, Johnson was only too happy to be set free by graduation, but his immediate plans after graduation had nothing to do with West Point or the Army. On June 19, exactly ten days after graduation, he married Mary Coleman, his high school sweetheart, in a ceremony in South Carolina. "She joined the Army, too," Johnson would later say of the many moves she made with him during his twenty-four-year Army career. Although John and Mary had known each other since their teens, it had not been an easy relationship to maintain during their college years. Mary was attending Columbia College in Columbia, South Carolina, and getting to see her future husband meant taking the train to New York City, then catching a bus at New York's Port Authority Bus Terminal to West Point. During the football season, Mary usually got north for the Army–Navy game, but she was not a regular at Army's home games.

For Johnson, the sixty days' leave he got after finishing West Point was his time for a honeymoon. At the end of summer, he began what was routine for West Point grads in the 1960s—Airborne and Ranger training. Airborne School was a breeze for Johnson, and getting his airborne wings added to his monthly salary. Ranger School took longer and was harder, but it also presented no trouble for Johnson. As someone who was in good shape, he had no difficulty dealing with the physical challenges of Ranger School. Rollie Stichweh was, by coincidence, in the same Ranger class, and so Johnson was able to have a teammate for a "Ranger buddy" in all the exercises that required a partner.

After completing his Ranger training, Johnson spent additional time in the States. Then, in 1967, as part of the Military Assistance Command, Vietnam (MACV), he was sent to Vietnam as an advisor to a Vietnamese airborne battalion. It is a period that Mary Johnson remembers well. Her husband left for Vietnam in March, and she learned in April that she was pregnant. Johnson would be away from home when his daughter Martha was born in November 1967, but while the timing of his assignment was bad, the assignment itself was excellent as far as Johnson was concerned. "From the standpoint of professional experience, it was a very good and positive one," Johnson says of his posting. He found the Vietnamese battalion he was working with to be a first-rate combat unit. He especially admired the forty-year-old major who commanded it. The major was a

Cambodian who had fought in the French Army a decade earlier, and he had the respect of his troops and the noncommissioned officers under his authority. "It was just an extraordinary experience to be with this person and around this person," Johnson thought.

Johnson stayed with the battalion for ten months and was awarded a Silver Star. He would have remained in Vietnam for a full year, but he had his tour cut short when he came down with hepatitis. Johnson remembers the Cambodian major visiting him before he was evacuated. It was a moving goodbye for them both. Johnson was glad to be going back to the States, where he could recover and at last see his daughter, but he was dogged by the feeling of heading back to safety while the major and his battalion continued to fight on. Johnson's regret over his early departure to safety in the States was deepened years later when he learned that after the North Vietnamese took control of Vietnam, the major was among a group of South Vietnamese officers who were executed.

With the passage of time, Johnson, now fully recovered from his hepatitis, began to see the Vietnam War differently than he had in 1967. General Westmoreland, a South Carolinian like himself, remained a leader Johnson personally admired. "He had the utmost integrity," Johnson would say years afterward when Westmoreland was accused, in a CBS television documentary, of exaggerating the body count of dead enemy soldiers. Johnson believed that Westmoreland would never deliberately distort the information before him, but as a result of his service in Vietnam, Johnson came to believe Westmoreland was out of touch with events on the ground: "He was a product of the great leaders who came out of World War II with the attitude if we go on it, it will come out all right."[10]

In Johnson's eyes, Westmoreland's confidence in America's ability to dictate the outcome of the war in Vietnam by virtue of its firepower and resources was misplaced. "Probably he misunderstood the resolve, the commitment of the North Vietnamese. They were skilled and good fighters," Johnson found himself thinking at the time. "Their patience exceeded any we had," Johnson would say of the North Vietnamese and Vietcong.

By 1970, when Johnson returned to Vietnam for a second tour, this time with the 173rd Airborne Brigade, Westmoreland was gone. He had been appointed Army chief of staff in 1968, and taking his place was General Creighton Abrams, who in 1972 would go on to succeed West-

John Johnson in front of the compound of Advisors to the Republic of Vietnam Airborne Division. (Courtesy John Johnson)

moreland as chief of staff. The change of Vietnam commanders was significant in terms of Army leadership, but on his second Vietnam tour, Johnson did not see the American military position improving. As far as he could tell, America was caught in a war that it could not win. "I think it became obvious that there wasn't any way this was going to be a victory," Johnson recalls.[11]

"I don't think any of us put much stock in the protests," he now says, but at the same time he did not see the military having an answer to the protestors. "Everybody kind of understood that we were looking for a way out of this thing." As a junior officer, Johnson continued to do his best. "I soldiered then as I would have under any other circumstances," he says. For Johnson, there was, however, no denying that he personally no longer saw the war as he once had. "I had lost my zeal and enthusiasm, frankly, for serving up front," he came to realize.

Johnson's initial reaction to the doubts he had reached about the war was to conclude that his best alternative was to submit his resignation as soon as his required service was over. He had put in his papers to do so when he learned that Rollie Stichweh, who was on Coach Tom Cahill's football staff at West Point, was about to leave the Army. The chance to return to West Point had enormous appeal for Johnson. Cahill, who had replaced Dietzel as Army head coach, had been Johnson's plebe coach, and he was happy to have Johnson as one of his assistants. The only condition he made was that Johnson stay with the team for three years. Johnson would have to withdraw his resignation from the Army. The decision was one that Johnson had no trouble making, but, as it turned out, the decision meant more than just a return to West Point. Going back to West Point was the real start of what became a twenty-four-year military career. Johnson is not exaggerating when he says that Cahill "kept me in the Army."

The period Johnson spent coaching at West Point was a happy one for him. "We had three wonderful years at West Point," he recalls. Everything balanced out. Johnson was back with the West Point football team, and he was back with his family. They could now lead a life free from the worries that came with a combat assignment. Johnson took special satisfaction in getting to know a new generation of West Pointers, and later on in following their careers. Among the players he remembered coaching for the plebe team were future Army chief of staff Ray Odierno and future West Point superintendent Lieutenant General Robert Caslen Jr.

Johnson had been away when his daughter Martha was born in 1967, but he was present when his second daughter, Helen, was born at West Point in 1971. The war, though, was still having an impact on him. When he tried to recruit high school football players who in the past would have jumped at the chance to go to West Point, Johnson often found himself getting turned down. "It was terribly disappointing," he remembers.[12]

Johnson's time at West Point did, however, convince him that he should stay in the Army rather than return to civilian life as he had planned. He decided that it was important for vets like him to try to undo the damage Vietnam had done to the military. When his coaching stint at West Point ended, Johnson spent the next year taking the Infantry Officer Advanced Course at Fort Benning. From there, he went to Fort Bragg to fill a staff position with the 82nd Airborne, and following his time at Fort Bragg, he did a three-year tour in Germany. The Johnsons now had a third child, John, who was born in 1974 (like his father, he would go on to West Point), and Johnson was steadily moving up through the post-Vietnam Army ranks. After his tour of duty in Germany was over, he took the Army General Command Staff Course at Fort Leavenworth in Kansas. His training there paved the way for his work with the special operations planning at the Atlantic Command and his final assignment at the Pentagon before he retired in 1989 as a colonel.

Throughout his service, Johnson was sensitive to the difficulties the Army had finding its identity as it recovered from the shock of a war that had become unpopular and ended without a military victory. Johnson still remembers the personal horror he felt on learning of the My Lai Massacre and the role that Lieutenant William Calley had played in the killing of Vietnamese women and children: "It was just terrible." There was, Johnson knew, no getting away from such a story. "We had a terrific challenge coming out of Vietnam," he recalls, and all too often, he found the Army did not seem up to meeting the issues before it: "The approach was that the Army ought to be like a regular job, and those of us who were in supervisory positions could see that it was obvious that the Army just doesn't work that way."

Sometime between the late 1970s and early 1980s, Johnson became convinced that the new volunteer Army had halted its downward slide. "It was starting to come back," he recalls thinking at the time. The discipline that had been lost over the course of the Vietnam War returned, and with that change, the training of recruits quickly improved. By the time he retired in 1989, Johnson believed that "the volunteer Army was really on its feet."

After leaving the Army, Johnson stayed in Washington and worked as a defense contractor for seven years before returning to South Carolina, where he now lives in retirement in his hometown of Winnsboro. Johnson is happy that he stayed in the Army for as long as he did. He takes pride in having played a role in its revival. Thinking retrospectively about the legacy of Vietnam has been more difficult for him. Like so many other vets, Johnson found the 1971 publication of *The Pentagon Papers* unsettling, but as a practical matter, the publication confirmed feelings he already had about America's military failures. "That wasn't wasted on any of us," he says of the information *The Pentagon Papers* conveyed to him and everyone he served with. "We were all aware. We weren't babes in arms."[13]

The much larger question Johnson faced in the 1970s was what to do with his disappointment over how the Vietnam War had been conducted. Johnson had entered the Army believing that "West Point is the ideal," and the challenge he faced, given his loyalty to that ideal, was how to judge the Vietnam War on grounds that were appropriate to the realities of the war. "Most of us found out that it was different from what we thought it would be," Johnson says of the war he and his classmates inherited. In Johnson's case, the result was a predicament that was compounded by his South Carolina roots: "Being a Southerner, you take the cause and do your best." As Johnson sorted through his thinking about Vietnam, he realized that he was able to acknowledge the full range of feelings he had about the war. "I was not bitter," he says of his mindset at the time. It was this lack of bitterness that allowed Johnson to stay in the Army as long as he did and still speak candidly about his Vietnam experience to anyone who asked.[14]

9

GAME CHANGER

Rollie Stichweh

As the scoreless third quarter drew to a close, Army's players had reason to worry. Despite getting the first points of the game and dominating the line of scrimmage, they had not been able to put Navy away. Just before halftime, Roger Staubach had brought Navy back into contention with a long touchdown drive, followed by a pass for a two-point conversion. With a little over fifteen minutes to play, it looked as if the game might end in an 8–8 tie.

Nobody felt the urgency of the moment more than Rollie Stichweh. Army's offense depended on Stichweh, who led the team in scoring, rushing, and passing, but despite his versatility, Stichweh was not the kind of quarterback who could engineer a quick scoring drive. From the first start of his junior year, when he took over the quarterback duties for Army, Stichweh was a player who ran first and passed second. "I was a converted halfback who didn't pass much," he freely admitted.[1]

Stichweh's skill set fit perfectly with Paul Dietzel's conservative approach to football, which emphasized defense over offense. The fastest runner on the team, Stichweh excelled at pass-run option plays that usually ended with him keeping the ball, but what gave Stichweh an extra dimension at quarterback was his leadership. Army's players and coaches had such confidence in him that there was never any doubt that in his senior year he was going to captain the 1964 team.[2]

The media's reaction to Stichweh was a different matter. With his blond, good looks and six-foot height, he fit the Hollywood image of a quarterback, and he was widely regarded as the best athlete on the team. But there was widespread doubt among the reporters covering the Army–Navy game that Stichweh had the ability to beat Staubach in their head-to-head quarterback competition. In 1963 the *Philadelphia Inquirer* referred to Stichweh as the "other quarterback" in the Army–Navy game, and in 1964 Navy officials took special delight in portraying Stichweh as someone who did not deserve to be on the same field as Staubach. At a press conference held on the day before the game, Navy athletic director Rip Miller pretended not to remember Stichweh's name, and in the team introductions at John F. Kennedy Stadium, Navy continued the same theme. The public address announcer, a member of the Navy athletic staff, deliberately mispronounced Stichweh's name, calling him Stee-which rather than Stich-way.[3]

Stichweh and Dietzel never publicly responded to Navy's gamesmanship, but it bothered them both, and in his second quarterback encounter with Staubach, Stichweh did not just show the reporters covering the game that they had underestimated him. He also departed long enough from his run-first, pass-second script to change the course of the game.

The break that Army needed to mount its final scoring drive came in the closing minutes of the third quarter when Navy missed a field goal attempt from the thirty-two-yard line and the ball rolled into the end zone for a touchback. With the ball deep in its territory, Army began its drive cautiously, with Stichweh handing off three straight times to tailback John Seymour for a first down on Army's thirty-one-yard line. Then Stichweh himself took over and, in the words of the *New York Times*, became "the man of the hour." Earlier in the game Stichweh had a long drive stopped when a pass of his was intercepted in the end zone, but on this drive, he refused to think about anything except the moment that he was in.[4]

Two plays after Seymour's run, Stichweh broke loose around left end for seventeen yards, bringing the ball to Army's forty-eight-yard line and setting up a Navy team, more geared than ever to stopping the Army's runs, for a pass. "Navy was cheating on trying to stop running plays," Stichweh remembers telling himself as he went back into the huddle. Now he thought was as good a time as any to see if Army could take advantage of Navy having so many men close to the line of scrimmage.

Quarterback and team captain Rollie Stichweh (16). (Courtesy Athletic Communications Office, USMA)

Rollie Stichweh (16) throwing a pass in the flat to John Seymour (43). (Courtesy Athletic Communications Office, USMA)

"I'm just going to put it up high. Go up and get it!" Stichweh told his end Sam Champi, who towered above Navy's defensive backs. Champi had already caught one touchdown pass from Stichweh when Navy was expecting a run, but that pass was for just five yards. A long pass from midfield on a play that relied on Champi's leaping skills presented Stichweh with a different set of challenges. He would need extra time to get off his pass, and he would have to make sure he did not throw an interception.[5]

"In the midst of any play, you have at most a microsecond to be thinking about that particular moment," Stichweh would later say. As he threw his pass to Champi, Stichweh remembered feeling confident as soon as the ball left his hand: "I felt good about getting the ball to the right place with some height on it." Champi, Stichweh believed, would make the most of the situation: "My feeling was that if the ball was within his grasp, he would pull it down at this critical point in the game." Stichweh was right about Champi's ability to catch a pass in traffic. The thirty-three-yard completion was Stichweh's longest of the day and justified the risk he had taken with his play call.[6]

Army quarterback Rollie Stichweh (16) skirts left end. (Courtesy Athletic Communications Office, USMA)

Army was suddenly on Navy's nineteen-yard line, and Navy was again forced to worry about the threat of a pass. It could not just call defenses designed to stop the run. The change in momentum was the opening that Army needed to move the ball close enough to the goal line for Barry Nickerson to kick a short field goal to break the 8–8 tie. With nine minutes and thirty seconds left on the clock, Army was in front to stay.

Stichweh was not done for the day. He was doubling as a defensive back, and with Staubach still capable of mounting a Navy comeback with his passing, there was no time to relax on the bench and celebrate the scoring drive he had just engineered. After the kickoff to Navy, Stichweh continued playing defense as well as quarterback until the game ended. The dual role was one that Stichweh relished. "The thing that I felt best about was having made the tackle on the last play of the game," he would later say. "I remember on that play Roger dealing the ball off to a back with a flair pass. I felt so good chasing the guy down, and then the game was over."[7]

As he headed toward the Army locker room, Stichweh's thoughts turned to his parents. This was, he knew, the last Army–Navy football game they would ever see him play, and he had desperately wanted it to be a happy occasion. His parents had suffered along with him when Army lost to Navy in 1963. In the media, much of the blame for Army's failure to get off a final play had fallen on Stichweh.

"On what turned out to be the last play of the ball game, Stichweh seemed as helpless as a boy caught with an inadequate alibi," Dan Jenkins wrote in *Sports Illustrated*. Jenkins caught the anguish that Stichweh felt in coming out on the losing end of the 21–15 score. Years later, Stichweh can still picture the sequence of events at the close of the 1963 Army–Navy game that led to Army failing to score. He even remembers the name of the referee—Barney Finn—who moments earlier had granted Army a timeout when the crowd noise made it impossible for Army's signals to be heard but refused to grant another timeout when the situation repeated itself.[8]

At this point in the game, Stichweh believes that he and Army were left with only bad choices. "I was aware of the clock toward the end, knew we were running out of time, but I was torn with my guys up and out of their stance. Do we bark out commands and get one snap to go?" he recalls thinking. In hindsight, the answer to the question is clear to Stichweh: "If I had it to do over, knowing the way it ended, I would have done that rather than try to get things under control with the cooperation of the referee."[9]

The loss was infuriating for Paul Dietzel. "In a situation like that, the officials have to use common sense. We couldn't even pull off an automatic because our boys couldn't hear the count," he observed in an angry postgame interview. There were, however, limits to the criticism Dietzel could level without seeming like a poor sport. Two days later, at the weekly meeting of the New York Football Writers Association, Dietzel made it clear that he was not blaming Army's defeat on the referee.[10]

Stichweh understood Dietzel's anger just as he understood his own and his teammates' frustration with how the game ended. Beating Navy in 1964 did not ease Stichweh's disappointment over the 1963 game, but the victory did put the loss in a different perspective. What is paramount for Stichweh is that he and his teammates did not lose confidence in themselves after their defeat. Instead, they set about planning for their next encounter with Navy. "On the way back and in the weeks and months leading up to the '64 game, I have never seen such determination," Stichweh recalls. "We were not under any circumstances going to leave that field in this head-to-head rematch without a win."[11]

That Stichweh became such a key figure in Army football during the early 1960s was no surprise to anyone who knew him. At Mineola High School on Long Island, Stichweh was a heavily recruited athlete. Princeton wanted him as a running back and made a strong effort to reach him through one of its assistant coaches (later its head coach), Bob Casciola, a Mineola grad and All-Ivy tackle in the 1950s.

Stichweh's choice of West Point over Princeton was in part a football decision. He wanted to be on a team that played a national rather than an Ivy League schedule. But the other part of his decision had nothing to do with sports. Stichweh's father had been a captain in World War II and admired the West Point officers under whom he served. He was very enthusiastic about having his son go to West Point, exerting what Stichweh later called "friendly pressure" for him to make West Point his top choice. In addition, Stichweh knew that his parents, both of whom worked, were going to have a hard time paying for any expenses that financial aid at Princeton did not cover. The prospect of going to West Point, where he would have no expenses, eliminated his family's money concerns completely. Stichweh would be able to compete against the best teams in the country without worrying that he was a burden to his parents.[12]

Nonetheless, during Stichweh's first year at West Point, his plans for starring on the football team almost came undone. The hazing and constant pressure on first-year cadets at West Point got to Stichweh. In the basement of his barracks, there was a pay phone, and it became a regular stopping point for Stichweh after dinner. "I was making collect calls home every night about how tough it was. I was very unhappy, very sad," he recalls.

It was a visit by his high school football coach, Bruce Gehrke, a Columbia University grad who in the late 1940s had played football for the New York Giants, that finally convinced Stichweh to stay at West Point. Stichweh's parents, fearing he was going to drop out before Christmas arrived, called Gehrke to let him know of their son's troubles, and Gehrke, who years later would be the best man at Stichweh's wedding, took it upon himself to drive up to West Point. There he and Stichweh spent the afternoon driving around the West Point grounds, and in talking together, they reached an agreement. Stichweh would stay in school for the rest of the year, and if by June he still wanted to leave West Point, he would—no questions asked.

Like the handwritten notes Gehrke sent him after their visit, Stichweh remembers their conversation distinctly. "The Rollie I know is not a quitter," Gehrke told him. "Here is the deal. Finish your plebe year. You'll be able to hold your head high. If at that point it makes sense to consider going another route, that's one thing. But not now." Gehrke's talk settled Stichweh down, and he was able to get through the rest of the term.[13]

By the beginning of spring football practice, Stichweh was convinced that West Point was the right place for him, but he would never forget the experience of those first months away from home. He believes Beast Barracks taught cadets the need to rely on others to get through the rigors, but he still gets angry when he thinks about the "runts" who made a point of harassing plebes. "They seemed to take delight in having this opportunity to really sock it to so-called tough football-player types," he recalls.

Stichweh never again questioned what he was getting out of his West Point education. During his remaining three years, his athletic prominence made him a campus figure to be reckoned with, but he never isolated himself as a jock. His close friendships with future generals Dan Christman, who years later would return to West Point as its superintendent, and Eric Shinseki, who would become Army chief of staff, began at this time. In his senior year, when Dwight Eisenhower returned to campus for his fiftieth class reunion, Stichweh was one of four cadets chosen to have lunch with the former president. The lunch is one that Stichweh has never forgotten, and it was made even more memorable for his parents when the *New York Times*, in its coverage of the reunion, noted that Ike made a point of congratulating Stichweh for the game he had played against Navy.[14]

If Stichweh had not been playing for a service academy, a pro football career would have been a real possibility. In 1964 Texas coach Darrel Royal called Stichweh "the finest back in America" after watching him lead Army in a close game against his first-ranked team, and pro scouts across the country had Stichweh in their sights. The Oakland Raiders and the New York Giants were both interested in him as a running back who could double as a kickoff and punt returner, but nothing ever came of their interest. When Stichweh finally got out of the Army, he had a wife and three daughters to support. Trying to pick up his football career from where he had left off seemed foolish. "My feeling was it was time to move on," Stichweh remembers.[15]

Stichweh's first stops after graduating from West Point were Airborne and Ranger schools, followed by a year of a year of duty with the 82nd Airborne Division at Fort Bragg in the position of artillery forward observer. It was a military assignment that Stichweh felt good about. The 82nd Airborne was a storied division with a long history, but with more and more soldiers being shipped off to Vietnam, Stichweh also knew that his time in the States was limited.

Stichweh was at another crossroads as well. He had been dating Carole Burmann for many years. They had known each other since the age of two, when their families became neighbors in Williston Park, Long Island. They had even been high school prom king and prom queen. But after high school, they decided to try dating others rather than continue an exclusive relationship. They thought it was important to make sure their romance had staying power. Carole visited Stichweh at West Point, but she never became a regular at Army football games. She watched the 1964 Army–Navy game on television rather than in person. Now, with Vietnam and the prospect of being away from Carole for still another year looming, Stichweh concluded that it was the time to make a decision on where their future was headed. In April 1966 while on leave from the 82nd Airborne, he proposed to Carole, and in July the two were married.

Stichweh's next Army assignment was serving as a general's aide at the headquarters of the Northeast Region of the Air Defense Command at Fort Totten in Queens, New York, and for the first year of their married life, the Stichwehs were able to live together on base housing near the town in which they had grown up. Before the year was over, Carole had become pregnant with Jennifer, their first daughter. It was a joyous occasion for the Stichwehs, but in the spring of 1967, the Vietnam War took over their lives. Stichweh got his Vietnam assignment—forward observer with the 173rd Airborne Brigade. Stichweh could have remained in the States until Jennifer was born, but he and Carole decided it was best to get his Vietnam service over with as quickly as possible. Carole moved back home with her parents and had her baby while Stichweh was in Vietnam.[16]

The year of separation was hard on both of them. Carole was able to rely on her family to get through her pregnancy, but, as she later recalled, "It was always a worry waiting for the next letter to come." Stichweh's Vietnam assignment was an especially tough one. It meant a year in which he was constantly involved in combat. In November 1967 the 173rd Airborne Brigade was ordered into the Central Highlands, where the brigade faced North Vietnamese Army regulars infiltrating into South Vietnam.

Rarely did a day go by when the brigade was not on high alert. For Stichweh, whose duties as forward observer meant setting up the artillery to protect his unit each time it moved to a new location, there was no relaxing. "It was draining emotionally and physically. I lost a lot of weight," he remembers. The isolation of the brigade was so complete that Stichweh learned of the birth of his first daughter, whom he did not see until she was ten months old, from a message written on a shoebox dropped from a helicopter delivering supplies.[17]

Stichweh was never wounded, but the year of combat, in which he was awarded a Bronze Star and the Air Medal with a V for valor, changed him. He came to appreciate the fighting ability of the 173rd Brigade, especially the leadership of its veteran noncommissioned officers. "Militarily, we kicked butt," he remembers. But the more time Stichweh spent in the field, the more he began to question the Army's search-and-destroy strategy, which struck him as an anachronism from World War II and Korea, where there were front lines and a massed enemy.

Stichweh was very aware of the evolution of his own thinking while he was still a junior officer. "At first, you are focused on what do I have to do today. You are in the immediacy of the moment and not thinking more broadly, certainly not thinking strategically. But then things start to raise questions. You are moving through the jungle with steel helmets and seventy-pound packs," he recalls. The heavy equipment made no sense, given the enemy's approach to combat: "It was more cowboys and Indians, hit and run. So you start to say, what is it we are doing? If we are trying to engage the enemy and defeat it, they are not presenting a whole lot of opportunities to do that." There was, as Stichweh later put it, a "disconnect" between America's Vietnam strategy and events on the ground.

At West Point, Stichweh, like most cadets, had been a great admirer of General William Westmoreland, but in Vietnam his memory of the impressive figure the general cut as West Point superintendent was undermined by the battle tactics that Westmoreland championed. "I think our military leadership, starting with General Westmoreland, had very strong and confident beliefs that our firepower could dominate the battlefield," Stichweh realized. The problem, as Stichweh discovered in the Central Highlands, was that enemy refused to be drawn into large firefights, preferring to remain elusive. "They had the staying power and the patience, and they could outlast us," he would later say of the North Vietnamese and the Vietcong. Making for more doubts was the contact that Stichweh had with South Vietnamese troops. Their soldiers struck him as far less impressive and far less motivated than those in the crack North Vietnamese army units he was fighting. "You wondered about who you were helping," Stichweh remembers thinking to himself.[18]

In the years since Vietnam, Stichweh has come to believe that David Halberstam's *The Best and the Brightest* and Stanley Karnow's *Vietnam*, both highly critical books of America's role in Vietnam, are two of the best accounts of the war, but it was not the postwar analyses of Vietnam or *The Pentagon Papers* that made Stichweh a critic of the war. His firsthand experience of combat did that. As far as Stichweh was concerned, "*The Pentagon Papers* to me and others were confirming of what we suspected rather than a revelation."

When Stichweh returned to the United States after Vietnam, he recalls feeling isolated from normal life: "I didn't have anybody spitting on me, but people were averting eye contact. The whole atmosphere was very subdued and negative." Nonetheless, Stichweh was relieved to have Vietnam behind him. He was with his family again, and he got the chance to end his military service as an assistant football coach at West Point when Tom Cahill asked him to join his staff.

"I quickly jumped on that," Stichweh says of Cahill's offer. He was back doing what he enjoyed, and despite his qualms about the Vietnam War, he was willing to go on the road and recruit players for West Point. Stichweh remembers asking himself, "Do I really want to encourage a young man to get into a situation where his life literally is in jeopardy?" But the longer he thought about his own question, the more convinced Stichweh became that "West Point remained for the right young man a wonderful opportunity."

In the end even a prized coaching assignment was not enough to convince Stichweh to remain in the Army. He and Carole had long talks over what they would do when his period of required service was over, and the more they thought about it, the more leaving the Army seemed like the right decision for their family. The Stichwehs' second daughter, Lisa, was born in 1969, and their third daughter, Kathy, was born in 1970. Especially for Carole, the thought of being separated again from her husband was unbearable. "We needed to be together to raise our children," she remembers thinking at the time. She had also seen the toll the war took on her husband. "We didn't talk very much about the war. He was very quiet," she says, but she remembers how when Stichweh returned home, the war was still with him. The incident that to her is most telling occurred in her parents' home when someone accidentally let the handle on the record player slip and the needle striking the record made a loud, booming noise. The next moment her husband, who had been sitting on the couch holding their daughter, was on the floor covering her with his body.

Returning to civilian life was not, when Stichweh reflects back on it, a decision that was inevitable. He had graduated from West Point with, as he recalls, a "positive bias" toward a lifetime Army career, but in reaching the conclusion that he did not want to stay in the Army any longer than he had to, Stichweh never thought of himself as out of step with the times. The Vietnam War left him with many doubts about the country's political leadership.[19]

Deciding to leave the Army has turned out to be a good choice for Stichweh. His first civilian job was as the director of Camp Dudley, the oldest continuing camp for boys in the United States. He had been a scholarship camper there, and for him and Carole, who was a school teacher, the camp provided an undertaking that they both believed in. Stichweh remained director of the camp for five years. Then he moved into the business world, finally retiring after serving as a senior executive and managing director of Towers Perrin, one of the largest management consulting firms in the world, with ten thousand employees and ninety-five offices worldwide.

Retirement has not, however, made Stichweh willing to forget the events that shaped his and his teammates' lives while they were in their twenties. He has been a constant supporter of West Point. He ranks high in his class in career giving to the Academy, and he has put in long hours as an advisor to the search committees responsible for hiring West Point's recent football coaches. There is no happier time in Stichweh's life than when he is surrounded by his former teammates at a West Point reunion. Years after they played their final game, Stichweh is in many ways still the captain, worrying about his teammates' welfare as any team captain should.

The passage of time has also not lessened Stichweh's anger over the Johnson administration's conduct of the Vietnam War. "War is war, but so much of the loss of fifty-six thousand to fifty-eight thousand dead, not to mention the wounded, was so unnecessary," Stichweh long ago concluded. What infuriates him even more than President Johnson's and Secretary of Defense McNamara's bad judgment about Vietnam is that after they concluded the war could not be won, they failed to take the steps that would have saved troops' lives. This lack of courage was their worst failure as leaders as far as Stichweh is concerned: "They didn't have the political will or the political courage to step up."[20]

In the wake of Vietnam, the challenge for Stichweh has been to keep his feelings about the war in balance. The kind of massacre that occurred at My Lai cannot be excused, Stichweh believes, because the troops doing it were under pressure or angry. "It was totally unacceptable," he says. But Stichweh believes it was possible to fight the war honorably, as the 173rd Airborne Brigade that he served with did in the Central Highlands. Stichweh walked out of Oliver Stone's film *Platoon* because he thought Stone's portrayal of American troops in action all too often made them seem like thugs and sadists.

After leaving the Army, Stichweh had a final meeting with General Westmoreland, who remembered Stichweh from his time as a West Point football star. The two had run into each other at a West Point football game, and Westmoreland made a point of reaching out to Stichweh the next week. It was the mid-1980s, shortly after Westmoreland failed to win his libel suit against CBS for its highly critical 1982 documentary of him, *The Uncounted Enemy: A Vietnam Deception*, and the general telephoned Stichweh at his Towers Perrin office in New York, asking him to lunch at the exclusive Brook Club. Stichweh accepted the invitation without knowing what to expect. At lunch he found that Westmoreland wanted to talk about Vietnam with someone whom he thought would provide a sympathetic ear. "He wasn't backing off. He was not making any apology," Stichweh recalls. "I also sensed he was at a point in his life when he had been hurt badly. There was a certain sadness there."[21]

Their Brook Club lunch was Stichweh and Westmoreland's last meeting. Stichweh has no regrets about being a listener rather than a talker during their meal, but he deals with his own Vietnam memories far differently. Every Memorial Day, Stichweh travels from wherever he is to the West Point cemetery to honor his classmates, including two players from the 1964 team, who died in Vietnam. He and Carole go so early in the morning that they are usually the only ones in the cemetery. Stichweh prefers it that way. He wants, as he says, the "solitude to visit with my friends."[22]

10

THE MARINE

Bill Zadel

Like everyone else on Army's team, Bill Zadel admired Roger Staubach. "We wanted to hold the ball as long as we could to keep him off the field," he would say of Army's need to run a ball-control offense that ate up time in its 1964 game against Navy. After Army went ahead 11–8 in the fourth quarter, Zadel knew it was no time to relax.[1]

As one of Army's five two-way players, Zadel was happy with Coach Paul Dietzel's decision to ask nearly half the team to play close to sixty minutes. West Point's lack of depth mandated such a strategy, he believed: "I used to say we had seventeen players who could play with anybody, but after those seventeen, there was a drop off that you didn't see at Michigan or Notre Dame or Nebraska." The downside to Dietzel's decision was minimal as far as Zadel could see. "If they get hurt," Zadel would say of himself and the four other two-way players, "you were not going to lose them for the rest of the season." Zadel was a big man at 235 pounds, but he did not imagine getting tired against Navy. Playing both ways for sixty minutes was an extension of what he had already done throughout the season. "I played all the offense at right tackle and defense whenever the opponents got inside our twenty-yard line. That was my routine," he recalled.

Zadel was hungry for a win over Navy. In 1962, as a sophomore, he had started against Navy in a game that Staubach turned into a rout. "We got beaten pretty bad," he remembered. "I felt bad, but nowhere near as

Tackle Bill Zadel (76), one of Army's five two-way players against Navy. (Courtesy Athletic Communications Office, USMA)

bad as I felt in 1963." At the end of the 1963 game, Zadel could not bear being praised for his play: "When we got back to West Point, the whole Academy was saying great game, great game, and all of us just felt empty. It was not the way we wanted to end the season."

The 1963 game convinced Zadel that Army did not have to fear Navy. The following year, as summer football practice began, he was sure that Army had the potential to be one of the best teams in the nation. "We had the best athletes, the best team of the three varsity teams I played on," he told himself. "I thought we had a chance to be 9–1 or undefeated." Soon, however, injuries and illness began taking their toll, and by the time of the Navy game, a thinned-out Army team had fallen to a 3–6 record. Over the course of the season, six different players had started next to him at guard, Zadel remembered.

The two weeks of practice between Army's November 14 game with Pittsburgh and its final game with Navy were a godsend for the team. Zadel, who had sustained a thigh injury against Pittsburgh, had time to recover without being rushed back into practice. John Seymour also had time to get healthy, and as the game drew near, Zadel liked Army's chances for ending its five-year losing streak to Navy: "Partly because we were healthier and partly because we had played them so tough the year before, we felt we could beat them."

In believing that Army could defeat Navy, Zadel was realistic about the effort it would take. Army was not, he knew, going to go on a scoring spree, and if it got far behind, the team did not have the capacity to score quickly. "We were not as good on offense as we were on defense. Stopping Navy was a high priority," he recalled the coaches and players all thinking. The players had bought into assistant coach George Terry's plans for blitzing Staubach even more intensely than they had in 1963, when he had led Navy to three touchdowns.

Everything began well for Army in the fourth quarter after it kicked off following its go-ahead field goal. Navy was forced to start out on its own four-yard line when its kick returner and starting halfback, Tom Leiser, slipped fielding Army's kickoff. Whether Army's defense could hold Navy in check when it mattered most now became the issue. "Early in the game, we did get that safety. We had kept them pretty well bottled up," Zadel remembered. Staubach seemed unfazed by Navy's poor starting position, however. Two straight running plays gave Navy a first down. Then Staubach began to take over the game as he had in the past.

After an eleven-yard completion followed by a seventeen-yard completion, Navy had the ball on its own forty-four-yard line. A Staubach run for seven more yards brought Navy to Army's forty-nine-yard line with plenty of time left on the clock.[2]

Then Army's defense stiffened, and on a key third-down play, Zadel and Sam Champi, now playing defense as well as offense, trapped Staubach for a loss that forced Navy to punt. But what seemed like good news for Zadel and Army turned out to be short-lived. A roughing-the-kicker penalty gave the ball back to Navy on Army's thirty-eight-yard line. "We helped them. We kept that drive alive," was all Zadel could think at that moment. There were still five minutes to go, and with a fresh set of downs to work with, Navy was back in the game. Staubach completed a ten-yard pass that brought the ball to Army's twenty-eight-yard line.

After losing yardage on first and second downs, Navy faced the same pressure it had earlier in the quarter when Zadel and Champi tackled Staubach for a loss as he attempted to pass. This time, Staubach tried to buy himself the extra time for a pass that he needed to complete to the eighteen-yard line for a first down by going into a shotgun formation. "He never had a chance," Frank Dolson wrote in his *Philadelphia Inquirer* account of the game. "Zadel led a blitz that threw Roger on his own forty-seven."[3]

Navy was forced to punt, and when it got the ball back for a last drive, Staubach did not have the time to mount a serious threat. For Zadel, who had been in on the two big stops Army made when Navy was trying a fourth-quarter comeback, it was the moment he had been waiting for. As cadets swarmed the field, Zadel was thinking about what it meant to be part of the first Army team to beat Navy since 1958. For Zadel, the victory he called "the sweetest of my college career" was above all else a shared triumph. "I have been able to relive that feeling every time the class of 1965 congregates," he later wrote. "It was our last chance. It was very, very important. It is still something we can say we did."[4]

As a high school football and basketball star in the northwestern Chicago suburb of Mt. Prospect, Zadel had a number of colleges interested in him. Coaches saw immediately that he had the size and speed to play at the college level. "Every school in the Big Ten recruited me," Zadel remembered. "I got offers from probably thirty colleges in total." It was a situation that was very different from the one his parents had faced when they were growing up. Zadel was aware early on of how much easier college was going to make his life than that of his parents: "My parents were high school graduates who didn't have a chance to go to college. My father worked in a factory, and my mother worked in a bake shop."

The first time Zadel was on an airplane was when Stanford paid for him to fly to the West Coast. The trip was a memorable one, but Zadel wasn't easily impressed by the recruiters he met, even at Stanford. He was very clear on his college priorities: "I wanted to go to a school that had good academics, and I wanted to go to a school that played good football." Zadel lost interest in Princeton because he thought that by 1961 its football program, like that of the entire Ivy League, had sharply declined, and he turned down offers from a number of football powerhouses because he thought they saw him only as a football player. "They had a reputation of being football factories that didn't let you take the curriculum you wanted," he would say of a group of colleges that he did not even bother visiting. If he had not opted for West Point, Zadel believed he would have gone to the University of Michigan, but for him West Point stood out: "It wasn't a very hard decision. The big question was, 'Was I going to qualify for West Point?'"

It had been just three years, Zadel recalled, since Pete Dawkins, playing for an undefeated Army team, had won the Heisman Trophy. That was good news, and the challenges that West Point presented in the classroom corresponded with Zadel's idea of what college should be like. He did not worry about the limits West Point put on a future pro football career. "I didn't think beyond college football," he remembered. His father, a World War II Marine vet, was, Zadel knew, proud of him for getting into West Point, and there was the added bonus that came with being able to go to West Point for free. Zadel's parents were not going to have to dig into their savings for him to complete his education.

In the fall of 1961, Zadel arrived at West Point eager to prove himself in the classroom as well as on the football field. What he was unprepared for was the harassment that during his era at West Point shaped Beast Barracks and plebe year. "I think a lot of that was unnecessary," Zadel would recall. "Sadistic cadets could really make it miserable on young cadets." At one point, Zadel got so fed up with the harassment that he called his parents and told them he was thinking about returning to Chicago, but he soon realized that the best way to deal with Beast Barracks was to avoid fighting back: "I just made up my mind that whatever they did, I was going to take it and learn from it."

After Beast Barracks ended, Zadel's plebe year went well. He made the dean's list during his first semester at West Point, and on the football field he had no trouble establishing himself as a sure bet to be a starter at tackle in his sophomore year. Later, Zadel even came to believe that the ordeal of plebe year, if kept within bounds, served a good purpose. It set the tone, he thought, for the kind of discipline that cadets needed to internalize in order to get through West Point. In the summer following his second year at West Point, when Zadel was made a squad leader for Beast Barracks, he did not, however, try to duplicate the harsh treatment he had received. During a class on military decorum, he even joined in a skit designed to give "the humor-starved plebes," as he called them, a break from the demands of Beast Barracks.

"There was no downtime at West Point over four years," Zadel found, and for him, that lack of downtime was a plus. "The whole plebe system and the academics put a lot of pressure on you, and you got used to dealing with pressure as a result. Then as you go on in school, you get more leadership responsibility, but you end up filling your days from beginning to end," he recalled. "It really determines how you are going to live the rest of your life." By his senior year, Zadel had immersed himself so deeply into West Point life on and off the football field that he was elected the 1965 class vice president. Zadel had surprised himself by how thoroughly he took to West Point after arriving there with only a vague sense of the demands of a military career: "I went there for the prestige and really underestimated the developmental power of the program. West Point is the beginning of a bonding that goes right into war."

At graduation, Zadel had a surprise for his classmates. While they were choosing which branch of the Army to go into, he took advantage of the rule that allowed a limited number of West Point grads to select their commission outside the Army. Following in his father's World War II footsteps, Zadel joined the Marines.[5]

Zadel was equally decisive when it came to his personal life. On June 12, 1965, just three days after his graduation, he married Betty Nickla, whom he had met during his sophomore year at West Point when she visited the Academy to watch her brother, Raymond Nickla, a member of the West Point class of 1963, wrestle. Their courtship, as Zadel put it, was initially

Bill Zadel and Betty Nickla, soon to be Betty Zadel, at the 1965 West Point graduation ceremonies. (Courtesy Betty Zadel)

a "rocky" romance, and not one that seemed likely to lead to the forty-six-year marriage that followed it. "I like to tell the story that Betty dated every cadet at West Point in the class of 1963, 1964, and finally when she got to the 'Zs' of 1965, she got serious," Zadel later joked. By the start of his senior year, the two were serious enough about each other to get engaged. Zadel's decision to get married and join the Marines reflected his determination to begin his post–West Point life as much as possible on his own terms. A four-year service commitment lay ahead of him, but he did not view the four years as a burden. "When I got out, I thought I would be a career military officer," Zadel recalled believing when he left West Point.

After graduation, Zadel did his training at Quantico Marine Corps Base in Virginia and then completed a six-month tour of duty at Guantanamo Naval Base in Cuba. It was a different set of assignments from those Zadel would have served if he had taken the commission he was offered in the Army Corps of Engineers, but by May 1967, when Zadel's one-year Vietnam tour began, he faced the same challenges and issues he would have encountered in the Army.[6]

"I graduated and was looking forward to going to Vietnam," Zadel would later say. Betty Zadel, who would take their son Bart (born in April 1966) and move back to her parents' home on Long Island during the time that Zadel was away, remembers how her own fears about her husband going off to war contrasted with his calm. "Don't mourn for me long," she recalls Zadel telling her when they discussed what could go wrong in Vietnam. "I'm doing exactly what I was trained to do. I am happy to do it."

Zadel's combat assignment was as an advisor to the 39th Vietnamese Ranger Battalion, in I Corps, the northern part of Vietnam. There, the enemy that Zadel and the other Marines advising the Vietnamese Rangers encountered most of the time consisted of North Vietnamese regulars. Compared to the Vietcong, "they were better trained and had better equipment," Zadel soon discovered. He also quickly realized that in Vietnam, unlike on the football field, his size was a disadvantage. "At 6'4", I was surrounded by Vietnamese Ranger counterparts who stood between 4'8" and 5'4" tall. I was a big target, to say the least," Zadel recalled. His way of compensating, he later joked, was to learn how to "run full speed in a duck walk." Zadel's tour in Vietnam was anything but easy. He was involved in intense fighting in I Corps, and when he returned to the United States in May 1968, he came back with two Bronze Stars, a Purple Heart, and the Vietnamese Cross of Gallantry with a Silver Star.[7]

Zadel's combat experience left him convinced that both the Marines and the Vietnamese troops he served with were doing everything that was asked of them. "The war continued to intensify from the time I got there to the Tet offensive in 1968," Zadel remembered, but in his judgment that intensity worked in America's favor: "Every time we were able to get the bad guys into a battle, we had so much superior firepower that we would take casualties, but nothing like what we dished out." The classic case of bringing that firepower to bear came for Zadel during the massive Tet offensive launched by the North Vietnamese and Vietcong. "The Tet offensive surprised us in terms of how strong of an attack it was," Zadel remembered, but everywhere he went, he found that American and South Vietnamese troops had recovered quickly enough to inflict heavy damage with counterattacks of their own. "It was a devastating defeat for the North Vietnamese and the Vietcong," in Zadel's eyes. "They got their butts kicked royally, even though they temporarily held Hue City and did other things to press the battle."

Only when he returned to the States did Zadel realized how negative the reaction to the news of the Tet attacks was in America, where the country had been told the North Vietnamese and the Vietcong had been severely weakened as a result of the American troop buildup. "I didn't have any idea of what was going on back in the States," Zadel recalled. He was shocked to learn that so many people viewed the Tet offensive in exactly the opposite way he did: "I never had that insight when I was over there." Coming back home after his Vietnam tour ended immediately cleared up any doubts Zadel had about the strength of the antiwar movement. When Betty went to pick him up at McGuire Air Force Base in New Jersey, she had to drive through a crowd of protestors just to get on the military base. It was an experience Betty never forgot. She had her mother and her son in the car with her, but their presence did not lead the protestors to back off. She drove through the crowd surrounding her car, despite being told by one of the policemen at the entrance to McGuire to come back the next day. "You're doing it at your own risk," she remembers the policeman shouting at her as she drove past him.[8]

Zadel was unfazed by the antiwar demonstrators he encountered at McGuire and throughout the 1960s and 1970s. The Oliver Stone history of Vietnam, as Zadel called the views of the director of the 1986 movie *Platoon*, was not his: "I think the mood of the country was sad, but it didn't have an influence on my beliefs." The antiwar movement, especially when it took to the streets, both dismayed and angered Zadel. "We have got this segment of society that has gone crazy," he recalled thinking at the time. "They are demonstrating against what is right for the country." Away from the battlefield, but still in the Marines, Zadel never wavered in his belief that America had made the correct decision in undertaking the Vietnam War: "My belief that we were doing the right thing remained the whole time. I never questioned what we were doing."

"I felt betrayed," Zadel later admitted when he learned of the doubts that President Lyndon Johnson and Secretary of Defense Robert McNamara had kept hidden about the war. McNamara in particular infuriated Zadel: "What really bothered me was when McNamara came out and said, 'It was a mistake.' My whole argument on which I had built my feelings about the war were totally devastated by this guy who was running the war." Zadel was never persuaded that Johnson and McNamara saw the war in its full context. As far as he was concerned, "they were just thinking narrowly." To make matters worse, from Zadel's perspective as a Marine, Johnson and McNamara's skepticism limited how America fought in Vietnam: "Obviously, if they didn't feel what they were doing was going to be successful, they didn't have their whole heart in the game." Zadel believed that a more intensive bombing campaign against North Vietnam would have made a difference in the outcome of the war and that General Westmoreland should have been listened to when he asked for more troops. For Zadel, the bottom line was clear: "Those policymakers on high could have prosecuted the war to a successful conclusion."[9]

Years later, Zadel would look back on the Vietnam War and conclude that it at least had a positive effect on countries that sought to remain neutral or side with America in Southeast Asia: "If we lost the war, we still won a significant political objective—to stabilize that part of the world." As he took up his post-Vietnam duties for the Marines, Zadel had more practical problems to worry about. He was put in charge of a series of Marine recruiting stations in and around Chicago. The job was part administrative and part ceremonial. In addition to overseeing the personnel in recruiting stations as far away as Iowa, Michigan, and Wisconsin, Zadel was expected to speak to various groups on behalf of the Marines.

It was a difficult time to be a Marine recruiter. Zadel was in uniform all day long and frequently met with hostility as he was going about his business. "Often people would flip me the bird as I was driving down the street," he remembered. Even at parties, the atmosphere could be chilly, Zadel found out. There, too, it did not take much for him to become the center of attention: "Everybody was complaining about the unnecessary war." Zadel's response to the situation in which he found himself was to devote himself to his job. He even managed to pull off an induction ceremony for one hundred new Marine recruits at the Chicago Civic Center Plaza during the same summer week that the 1968 Democratic National Convention made headlines when thousands of antiwar demonstrators clashed with the police in Chicago's parks and streets.[10]

For Zadel, who had left West Point thinking that he wanted to make a career in the military, the big decision, as his required service in the Marines drew to an end, was what he wanted to do next with his life. His thinking was not changed by the hostility that had come his way as a result of the Vietnam War. "I didn't change my feeling about the military," he remembered. "I still thought that it was a worthwhile pursuit and the hippies and the yippies and all the protestors had it wrong." But staying in the Marines also involved practical decisions, especially since the Zadels' second child, Elizabeth, was born in May 1969.

The Marine Corps had enormous personal appeal for Zadel: "I loved the camaraderie. I liked the idea of serving your country." But Zadel worried about how much of a career he could have in the Marines. The corps had expanded quickly during Vietnam, but with the war in Vietnam already showing signs of winding down, Zadel thought Marine Corps promotions would come very slowly in the future. In addition, there were his wife's feelings to consider. Betty never asked her husband to leave the Marines, but he knew Vietnam had been emotionally hard on her, and he also knew that if he stayed in the Marines, he was sure to be sent back for a second Vietnam tour. "She went through those thirteen months like I did," Zadel recalled. "I knew what was going on, but she didn't. It was not easy for her."

When he added up the pros and cons, the civilian world, with its greater stability and the likelihood of a job that would make it easier to support his family, seemed like the right choice, Zadel concluded. Betty, who had made up her mind to accept whatever decision her husband made, was immensely relieved. "Inside I was very happy," she recalls. "I remember so distinctly wanting him to get out of the service." Zadel, however, was more divided in his feelings. "The decision to leave the Marine Corps was one of the most difficult of my life," he would later say. He had not been a civilian since his last year in high school, and exactly what he would do for work was impossible to know. The good news, Zadel felt, was that he was re-entering the civilian world at an opportune time. "We were leading the baby boomers," he recalled thinking of himself and his classmates with their World War II–era birth dates. "In the workplace, that was a benefit, because there was still a high demand and not a lot of supply."[11]

Zadel did not wait for his Marine Corps service to end before he began searching for work. "Toward the end of my time in that recruiter job, I started looking for a civilian job," he recalled. For a brief time, Zadel thought about pro football. In his senior year, he, along with Rollie Stichweh, John Johnson, and John Seymour, had played in the North–South game and met players from all over the country who were headed for the National Football League. Zadel knew his skills matched up with theirs, and before he shipped off to Vietnam, he received an invitation from John Rauch, the Oakland Raiders head coach from 1966 to 1968, to try out with the Raiders when his Marine Corps service ended. Later, there was also an opportunity to see what he could do closer to home with the Chicago Bears. Paul Dietzel wrote George Halas, the longtime coach and owner of the Bears, about giving Zadel a tryout and got a favorable response back. But as his time for leaving the Marines drew closer, Zadel decided that trying out for the Bears after such a long time away from college football was too risky. "I didn't want to stake my family's welfare on football," he decided.

Zadel's alternative was to reach out to Donold Lourie, the chairman of the board of Quaker Oats from 1962 to 1970 and a Princeton football star in the 1920s. Zadel had met Lourie during his senior year at a banquet in New York, when Zadel was among the college players receiving the National Football Foundation's Scholar-Athlete Award. Lourie remembered their earlier meeting and the encouragement he had given Zadel to look him up if he decided to leave the service for private industry. What followed was a job offer in the Chicago office of Quaker Oats. For Zadel, who would earn a master's in business administration from the University of Chicago in 1974, it was the start of a career that took him from Quaker Oats to Johnson and Johnson, to Abbott Laboratories, to Corning, and, finally, to CEO positions at Millipore Corporation and Mykrolis Corporation. The family made eighteen moves in all during these years, Betty recalls.[12]

Zadel was living in retirement when, in the fall of 2011, at the age of sixty-eight, he suffered a fatal heart attack at his summer home on Cape Cod. He had long since achieved a level of comfort for himself and his family that was beyond the reach of his parents, and he was grateful for his good fortune. "I made and spent a lot more money in my life than I thought possible growing up in a middle-class suburb of Chicago," he wrote in the 2011 report he did for a history of his West Point class of 1965. In the years following his departure from the Marine Corps, Zadel had not spent a lot of time thinking about what would have happened if he had pursued the military career he once planned on, but he had, he was convinced, done everything that West Point expected of him. He saw no reason to second-guess the decisions he had made after returning from combat. He was especially proud that his younger son, David, a 6'5" and 255-pound linebacker at Wake Forest, had done the unexpected following college—turn down a chance to play for the Dallas Cowboys after making the team in training camp. Instead of cashing in on a lucrative pro-football contract, David did what he wanted: he joined the Marines and served two tours in Iraq. It was a decision that added to Zadel's belief that his own year in Vietnam was not wasted. His tour in Vietnam had, with the passage of time, become a continuing link in a family tradition that had its roots in his father's World War II service with the Marines at Guadalcanal.[13]

Part III

Aftermath

EPILOGUE

In the Wake of Vietnam

1973

In the same year that the last American combat troops left Vietnam and the nation moved to an all-volunteer military, John Johnson was on his way to a twenty-four-year Army career that would conclude with him working at the Pentagon. By contrast, the 1964 team's four other two-way players, as well as Sam Champi and John Seymour, were just beginning successful business careers. They had already made the decision to resign their Army commissions.[1]

The statistic represented by six out of seven West Point football players opting to leave the military when their period of required service ended was the kind that alarmed Army officials. The figure was far in excess of the rate with which the players' classmates had taken that option while the Vietnam War was going on, and that figure, too, was high. Out of the 596 graduates of the West Point class of 1965 (the seniors on the 1964 Army football team), 148, a quarter of the class, had resigned by 1970. Out of the 579 graduates of the West Point class of 1966 (the juniors on the 1964 team), 23.1 percent had resigned by 1970, and by December 1971 over a third of the class of 1966 was gone.[2]

By comparison, in the class of 1950, only 11 percent of West Pointers had resigned after five years, and from 1950 to 1961, an era that included the Korean War, the average resignation rate after four years was 15.5

percent. A Pentagon-commissioned study, "Why They Leave: Resignations from USMA Class of 1966," which was published in July 1970, told the Army much of what it might have learned directly from the players. The study showed that, measured by an intensity index, the top reasons for leaving the Army after four years were family separations and the prospect of another Vietnam tour, but close behind were complaints over the slowness of promotion and the presence of too many uninspiring senior officers.[3]

Rollie Stichweh thought that if he and his teammates had felt about their Vietnam War service the way their fathers felt about their World War II service, more of them would have made careers in the Army, but he did not see his decision or those of his teammates to leave the Army as taking the easy way out of a tough situation. Like Stichweh, Army's 1964 football players had returned from Vietnam frustrated by the way the war was being conducted, but their frustration did not leave them at loose ends. It came with a clear sense of what they would and would not do next with their lives. The players were not comfortable with the antiwar movement or the counterculture that had become part of it.[4]

Those who made the decision to leave the Army and become civilians again saw themselves acting with the same discipline and sense of duty that had characterized their lives at West Point. They were convinced that they could do more for their families and better by society if they went to work in the private sector.[5]

For the West Point football program, 1973 was also a turning point. The players had been on Army teams that regularly scheduled games with national football powerhouses, and they had been unfazed by the challenge posed by these bigger schools. "I was proud that Army played the schedule it played," Bill Zadel recalled. He, like his teammates, always believed that, when healthy, Army had a core of players who could compete against any college team in the nation. In 1973 Army officials declared that time was over.[6]

Central to West Point's football problems was the fallout from the Vietnam War. Before 1973, the war had begun to take a toll on West Point's standing with the public. One of the sharpest blow came on March 17, 1970, when Major General Samuel Koster resigned as the forty-eighth superintendent of West Point in order to defend himself against charges that, when he headed the Americal Division in Vietnam, he had failed to investigate adequately reports that American troops under his command had massacred unarmed Vietnamese, many of them women and children, in the small village of My Lai. An angry Koster announced his resignation at noon from the poop deck of the West Point mess hall, telling the cadets eating their lunches, "Don't let the bastards grind you down."[7]

Koster's defiance of the bastards—whether he meant the Army brass or the liberal media was unclear—prompted the cadets to give him a standing ovation when he finished speaking, but the applause amounted to a last hurrah. Koster was found guilty of "commissions and omissions" in his response to the My Lai Massacre and was demoted to brigadier general. Koster was allowed to stay in the Army and became deputy commander of the Army's Test and Evaluation Command at the Aberdeen Proving Ground in Maryland, but his defiance, in combination with the backing he got from the cadets, was damaging to the image of West Point. Later in the year, a *New York Times Magazine* story titled "West Point Cadets Now Say, 'Why Sir?'" looked at the difficulty of dissenting at West Point. Then, in 1972, another *New York Times* feature story, this one on the resignation from West Point of thirty-three teachers, most of them captains and majors with Vietnam combat experience, added to the perception that West Point was an institution stuck in the past.[8]

The result was the kind of bad publicity that spilled over to the football program. In the late 1960s the players from the 1964 team who completed their Army service by returning to West Point to work as assistant coaches had gotten a firsthand look at the problem. Increasingly, the high school football players they were trying to recruit did not want to join an Army that was mired in Vietnam. For a while, West Point was able to avoid the full consequences of these problems. In 1966, with a team Paul Dietzel had recruited in earlier years, Tom Cahill guided West Point to an 8–2 record and was named college coach of the year, but by the 1970s the impact of the war had caught up with the West Point team. A *New York Times* story, "Law Cripples Army Recruiting," which appeared just as the 1973 football season (in which Army lost all its games) was drawing to a close, highlighted Army's difficulty in getting the players it wanted. The story centered on interviews with college players who had turned Army down because they were unwilling to put up with the new five-year service requirement that had begun with the class of 1968.[9]

At the end of the 1973 season, Cahill's contract was not renewed. "Is this because the football team hurt the image of the Army?" Cahill asked Major General William Knowlton, who had replaced Koster as superintendent. "Yes," Knowlton answered. Their exchange, which was reported in the *New York Times*, rather than kept confidential, seemed like a page out of West Point's traditional, no-substitute-for-victory past, but there was more to the exchange than that. Cahill's reply to Knowlton was telling: "The problems with the football team are that it is suffering from the image of the Army," he told the superintendent. There is no record of Knowlton's response to Cahill, but in 1973 and 1974 Knowlton and West Point officials made a point of acknowledging that the problems with Army's football program went well beyond its coach. The team was in over its head when it played the top college football powers.[10]

In letters to alums that appeared in *Assembly*, Knowlton spelled out the challenge West Point had to overcome. "When I arrived in the spring of 1970, it was apparent that the 1970 and 1973 schedules were more than we should ask cadets to face. In 1970 we played four away games in a row, three of them against bowl teams," he pointed out. Army was up against football teams that were "a feeder belt to the professional version of the sport"; it was too much to expect the cadets to hold their own when they faced such opponents, Knowlton concluded. Colonel William Schuder, Army's director of athletics, left no doubts about West Point's next move. "We can do something about the schedules. We will take a realistic look at some of the major teams, but we are not going to play lots of bowl teams," he promised. Army's schedule for the 1970s, he explained, had been made in the early 1960s and represented the assumptions of a different era: "Generally, when these schedules were made, there was a feeling here that Army could be number one in the nation sometime. That is not the case now, and it is not realistic."[11]

It took a while for Army to remove from its schedule the teams that it could no longer compete against, but there was no escaping the meaning of Knowlton's and Schuder's pronouncements. Army football as the 1964 players knew it was over. Like the draft Army, the 1964 team was now part of an era that was not coming back anytime soon.[12]

2003

The players would, over time, reconcile themselves to watching the brand of football Army played after 1973, but reconciling themselves to their Vietnam experience was a different story. Especially after the publication of *The Pentagon Papers* in 1971, the military's Vietnam strategy was put under the microscope, and so were the political motives of Lyndon Johnson and his secretary of defense, Robert McNamara. Even John Kennedy was not immune to scrutiny over the role he had played in sending military advisors to Vietnam. For the players, it often seemed as if they were being asked to relive their Vietnam War experience on the media's terms.[13]

In 2003 the event that made the players revisit their Vietnam experience was unexpected—it was the highly publicized clash between the George W. Bush administration and Army Chief of Staff Eric Shinseki over the number of troops needed in Iraq. Shinseki, who, like the seniors on the 1964 team, is a graduate of the West Point class of 1965, was the last person in the world the players imagined getting into a public battle with the president of the United States and his secretary of defense just as the country was going to war. At West Point Shinseki was a cadet Sunday school teacher for four years. He had a reputation for going out of his way to protect plebes from undue hazing, and in the Army he had quietly moved up the career ladder without ever being thought of as a dissident.[14]

Confrontation was not Shinseki's style. Toughness and hard work were. He was guided by the belief that "you take every assignment the Army gives you, and you do it to the best of your ability." In 1966, during his first tour of duty in Vietnam, he had been wounded so badly in a helicopter crash that he took seven months to recover, and in 1970 he was wounded even more seriously. After stepping on a land mine, he lost his right foot and part of his lower leg. The Army wanted him to retire. Because of his injuries and the time he lost recovering from them, Shinseki fell nearly two years behind his West Point class in career advancement, but he fought to stay on, promising to rehabilitate himself through physical therapy. He went to graduate school at Duke and earned a master's degree in literature. Then he taught for three years at West Point, and at last in shape to meet the Army's physical requirements, he quickly made up for the promotions he had missed. In the 1980s he served in the Cold War army that America kept in Europe against the prospect of a

Soviet invasion, and in the early 1990s he commanded a peacekeeping force in Bosnia before getting the call in 1998 to go to Washington as vice chief of staff for General Dennis Reimer.[15]

The following year, President Clinton appointed Shinseki Army chief of staff. Shinseki seemed like the perfect, noncontroversial choice, and so did his plans for turning the Army into a more mobile force by making it increasingly reliant on medium-weight, armored vehicles that could fit into a C-130 cargo plane. Shinseki's vision for the Army featured Stryker Brigades that could be moved to anywhere in the world in ninety-six hours.

Shinseki's problems began in 2001 when Donald Rumsfeld, secretary of defense in the new George W. Bush administration, took office. Rumsfeld, too, wanted modernization, but his idea of modernization was directly opposed to Shinseki's. Shinseki's aim was to get boots on the ground as rapidly as possible. Rumsfeld's ideal of modernization was a high-tech military with long-distance striking ability that relied on smart bombs and air power. Rumsfeld's way of paying for this new, high-tech military was to reduce troop strength, which, by his calculations, would no longer be needed at its previous levels.[16]

The differences between the two views of the Army were so great that by 2002, when Shinseki still had more than a year to go on his term as Army chief of staff, Rumsfeld announced his replacement. The clash that made 2003 such a pivotal year in how the players looked back on their Vietnam experience came months later on the eve of the Iraq War. On February 25, during a hearing before the Senate Armed Services Committee, Shinseki was asked by Senator Carl Levin, a liberal Democrat from Michigan, how many troops would be needed in Iraq. "Something on the order of several hundred thousand soldiers," Shinseki replied after first insisting that in order to provide more specific figures, he would have to rely on what combat commanders in the field told him.[17]

Shinseki's estimate was far in excess of that of the Bush administration, which a month later sent a ground force of 145,000 troops into Iraq, but there was nothing surprising in his testimony. His figures were consistent with the 250,000 troop estimate that General Tommy Franks, the head of Central Command, had been using all along in projecting how big a force the United States would need in Iraq by the time it began stabilizing the country. In Bosnia, the Pentagon had used a formula of one soldier for every fifty civilians when it came to carrying out an occupation. Shinseki's timing was especially infuriating to the president and secretary of defense. They were busy selling the Iraq War to Congress and the public as an undertaking that could be done in short order without the need for raising taxes. Shinseki's estimate of the troops needed made it look as if the administration was trying to wage war on the cheap.[18]

Two days later, during hearings before the House Budget Committee, Deputy Secretary of Defense Paul Wolfowitz made a point of disparaging Shinseki's testimony. "I am reluctant to try to predict anything about what the cost of a possible conflict in Iraq would be," Wolfowitz declared. "But some of the higher-end predictions that we have been hearing recently, such as the notion that it will take several hundred thousand U.S. troops to provide stability in post-Saddam Iraq, are wildly off the mark . . . it is hard to conceive that it would take more forces to provide stability in post-Saddam Iraq than it would to conduct the war itself." Rumsfeld used virtually the same language in attacking Shinseki. "The idea that it would take several hundred thousand U.S. forces I think is far off the mark," he told reporters.[19]

History soon proved Shinseki correct in his estimate of the number of troops needed in Iraq, but his being right was only more infuriating to Bush and Rumsfeld. They would make a point of conspicuously absenting themselves from his Pentagon retirement ceremony in June 2003. In his retirement speech Shinseki indirectly noted their absence when he thanked by name many of the generals and congressmen who did show up. Then he went on to describe the danger of trying to modernize the Army while failing to give it the troops it needed. "Beware the twelve-division strategy for a ten-division Army," he warned.

At the heart of Shinseki's speech was his Vietnam experience. "The current war brings me full circle to where I began my journey as a soldier—the lessons I learned in Vietnam," he observed. "Those were hard-earned lessons—lessons about loyalty; about taking care of the people who sacrifice the most for the good of the nation; about uncompromising readiness."[20]

What the public heard in Shinseki's reference to Vietnam was how much the men he soldiered with mattered to him. The players, who, like Shinseki, had experienced combat in Vietnam, heard that and more. As far as the players were concerned, in his Senate testimony and in his refusal to change his position in the face of criticism from the Bush administration, Shinseki was looking out for the troops in Iraq in a way that Lyndon Johnson and Robert McNamara had failed to do for soldiers like them in Vietnam. Shinseki was also making it clear that history did not have to repeat itself. Instead of remaining silent, he was speaking openly about the problems in America's Iraq War strategy before a single shot was fired.

"I was among a number of classmates who went down to Ric's retirement ceremony in Washington, D.C.," Rollie Stichweh remembers. "I and others developed some tremendous concerns about Rumsfeld as a personality and an advisor to the president. I think they treated Ric very badly." As far as Stichweh was concerned, the failure of the president and secretary of defense to show up for Shinseki's retirement ceremony was more than a sign of disrespect. It was their way of turning their policy differences into a vendetta. Stichweh wanted to make certain that, on one of the most important days of his life, Shinseki was surrounded by friends and classmates who had known him for a long time.[21]

Bill Zadel, like the other players, was struck by how much Bush and Rumsfeld were repeating history. It was "like the Vietnam leadership all over again," Zadel thought, and from his perspective that link with the past made supporting Shinseki especially crucial. "They were wrong. He was right," Zadel declared. There was no way that Shinseki or anybody else could bring back the soldiers who had lost their lives in Vietnam, but Zadel believed it was possible to keep a new generation of soldiers from needlessly dying in Iraq.[22]

The players were aware that in defending Shinseki they were reacting to their own Vietnam experience, but it did not occur to them that anything Shinseki said was unsound military policy. His sobering words about the troop strength needed in Iraq reflected the thinking of someone who took a cautious approach to battle. Shinseki was at the end of his military career when he testified before Congress. He had nothing to gain from becoming more of an outlier to the Bush administration than he already was. "Ric's words were boots on the ground," was the way Zadel summed up Shinseki's testimony. It was the very absence of fanciful schemes for winning the Iraq War that Zadel found the most compelling aspect of Shinseki's testimony, and in the months that followed, Zadel and the other players placed special stock in Shinseki's refusal to go on the Sunday talk shows to take credit for being right about Iraq. John Seymour, who admired Shinseki for taking a stance that was "going to do nothing but piss off his bosses," admired Shinseki even more for not gloating over how wrong his critics had been. "He never made a public comment about it, has never written about it," Seymour observed of Shinseki's refusal to widen his battle with the Bush administration after being savaged by Defense Department officials.[23]

It was no accident that Seymour and the other players so often came back to Shinseki's character—Seymour calls him "down to earth, very capable, very real." The players' criticism of Johnson's and McNamara's failures to disclose their doubts about the Vietnam War always returned to the idea that they had put political expediency ahead of candor. By virtue of his example, Shinseki showed that it made sense for the players to feel as they did about the way Johnson and McNamara had let them down. Shinseki's priorities were clear—the lives of the men under his command were more important than his career.[24]

2009

Two years after his Pentagon retirement, Shinseki's clash with Bush and Rumsfeld made news again when one of Shinseki's classmates distributed "Ric Was Right" baseball caps at the fortieth reunion of his West Point class of 1965. It was not the kind of symbolic protest Shinseki wanted. It did not seem dignified to him, but the timing of the gesture gave his classmates who had been unable to get to Washington for his retirement ceremony a chance to express their support. The "Ric Was Right" symbolism of the caps dovetailed with the reassessment of the Iraq War that was gathering steam in 2005, and *Newsweek* made Shinseki's class reunion central to a feature story it did about the military's dissatisfaction with Rumsfeld's Iraq War strategy.[25]

By contrast, in 2009, forty-five years after Army's 1964 victory over Navy, the decision by Army's players to bring Coach Paul Dietzel back to West Point for a reunion created no controversy, although here, too, Vietnam was very much part of the players' minds when they remembered the classmates whom they had lost in Vietnam. The timing of the reunion caught many players by surprise. The fiftieth anniversary of the most important win of Dietzel's Army coaching career was the logical time to honor him, but waiting another five years seemed risky to many on the team, given Dietzel's age. One year earlier, Dietzel had published his autobiography, *Call Me Coach*, and it did not seem wise to count on him continuing to be in good health (he would die in 2013 at the age of eighty-nine).

The idea for the Dietzel reunion came from Rhesa Barksdale, the assistant football team manager in 1964 and the team manager in 1965. Barksdale had served in Vietnam with an armored cavalry unit, but when his four years of required service were up, he resigned his commission and went back home to Mississippi to live. His mother, father, and brothers were all graduates of Ole Miss, and Barksdale, following their example, entered Ole Miss law school in 1970. It was the start of a distinguished legal career that included a clerkship with Supreme Court Justice Byron White in 1972–1973; private practice in Jackson, Mississippi; and, beginning in 1990, service on the Fifth Circuit Court of Appeals after the Senate confirmed his nomination by President George H. W. Bush.

As a cadet, Barksdale was one of more than one hundred members of his graduating class to volunteer for combat duty in Vietnam, and the *New York Times* made a point of quoting him for its story, "West Point Class of '66 Eager to Fight." "I don't look forward to going to Vietnam," a somber Barksdale told the *Times* before going on to say, "I wish there wasn't trouble there, but there is, and we have to do something about it." The other side of Barksdale was the jokester. At West Point he became well known for the parody he did—with a white towel draped around his neck and a whistle and clipboard in hand—of Dietzel. The parody reflected the close bonds that Dietzel and Barksdale shared and even led Dietzel to do a parody of Barksdale at the West Point talent show of 1965.

"Rees is very sharp and understood Paul. He was Paul's right-hand man, really," Anne Dietzel would say of the relationship her husband and Barksdale had at West Point. Afterward, the two remained close. When Dietzel and his wife retired to Baton Rouge, Louisiana, Barksdale, who was living in nearby Jackson, Mississippi, and periodically commuting to New Orleans for his work on the Fifth Circuit Court of Appeals, was able to see Dietzel more frequently. In 2008, after a book-signing trip to Jackson, Dietzel spent the night with Barksdale and his wife. During that visit, Barksdale learned the University of South Carolina, where Dietzel had coached after he left West Point, was planning to honor him, and he asked Dietzel how he would feel if West Point did the same. "I would love that," Dietzel replied. It was all Barksdale needed to hear.[26]

Honoring Dietzel was not, Barksdale knew, a decision that would sit well with everyone. In his four years at West Point, Dietzel had been at the center of his players' lives, but his departure in April 1966, just as spring football practice was about to start, came as a shock. Dietzel still had a year to go on his five-year contract with Army, and his announcement that he was taking the head coaching job at the University of South Carolina left West Point in a difficult position. "The entire move caught us by surprise," Colonel Ray Murphy, Army's director of athletics, announced as he postponed the start of spring practice by a week. "We had been completely satisfied by his performance and were looking forward to a long, profitable relationship." The press echoed Murphy's perspective, portraying Dietzel as a coaching opportunist. "The latest to flout a contract is Paul Dietzel," Arthur Daley wrote in his *New York Times* sports column. "Although he had several years to go on a document binding him to West Point, he figuratively tore it up to accept a fancier bid at the University of South Carolina."[27]

From Dietzel's point of view, nothing was further from the truth than Murphy's surprise or Daley's disdain. He knew how their criticism made him look, and in a personal essay, "I Have Never Broken a Contract," that appeared in *Sports Illustrated* at the start of the 1966 football season, Dietzel went to great lengths to defend himself, providing a detailed account of his difficulty dealing with the constant rotation of West Point's brass. With the arrival in early January 1966 of Major General Donald Bennett, Dietzel found himself answering to his third West Point superintendant in four years (there were also three commandants during this period), and with the announcement in February that Murphy was going to be replaced as athletic director in June, Dietzel saw his coaching situation becoming more precarious by the minute. Dietzel was not looking for a raise in salary after four years at West Point, but he wanted assurance from the new superintendant that the Academy was committed to the kind of football program he had been asked to put in place by General Westmoreland in 1962.[28]

Red Blaik, for whom Dietzel had twice served as an assistant coach, had possessed the kind of power that Dietzel knew he did not have. As a coach who never graduated from West Point, Dietzel lacked the old-boy connections that Blaik, who had played Army football, could count on. "Colonel Blaik had great power at the Academy," Dietzel recalled. "He had all these friends scattered around. He could always call up someone in authority and get what he wanted for his football program." For Dietzel, the only alternative to Blaik's power was gaining the assurance of the officials to whom he reported, and with the arrival of Bennett, Dietzel saw himself on thin ice. When he met with Bennett and told him about his worries, he got a response that seemed like a barely disguised invitation to leave West Point. "When I talk with Army people, they are almost evenly divided about Paul Dietzel. I would strongly recommend that you talk with the South Carolina people and listen very seriously to what they have to say," Dietzel recalled Bennett saying before he concluded their meeting with the following observation: "Paul, I've always had this credo. If I don't think that I could add something to a place, I would leave."

Dietzel took Bennett's response as a vote of no confidence in him and his staff. "When I walked out of the supe's office, I felt about as high as a thimble," he remembered. Dietzel now felt free to pursue the coaching offer he had received from South Carolina at the end of the football season. The coaching job at South Carolina was not one that Dietzel saw as a step up on the career ladder. He was not anxious to leave West Point, and years later, he still felt hurt by the way he was treated. "I really loved the Academy. Both of our children were born at West Point, I admired the place so much," he would say. What Dietzel did not see in 1966 or years later was an alternative to his decision to go to South Carolina. "There was no one I could go to. I was in a vacuum," he reluctantly concluded.

The timing of his departure added to Dietzel's worries. He knew that he was leaving the team in a bad spot for the 1966 season, but he did not think that there was any way to tell his players all that had happened without it seeming as if he were trying to turn them against the new West Point administration.[29]

Dietzel was right to worry about all the questions his sudden departure would raise among his past and present players. John Johnson, who was home on leave in South Carolina when he got the news, remembered his first reaction: "I was flabbergasted. I just didn't expect that." Johnson was coming out of church when a state senator, who was a member of the congregation that Johnson's family belonged to, stopped him and said, "Guess what? We just hired your West Point football coach." Johnson did not know the story behind Dietzel's departure, but he was sure losing Dietzel meant bad news for Army. He thought that Dietzel had taken the football program up a notch and that the high school players Dietzel had recruited were getting better each year.[30]

Bill Zadel had a similar reaction to learning that Dietzel was headed to South Carolina. "I was surprised. I thought Paul Dietzel would be there a long time," he recalled. "He did say a number of times that he came back because he thought this was the best job in the country." It was not until many years later that Zadel realized the position that Dietzel had been put in by West Point.[31]

For Paul Dietzel, coming back to West Point to be honored forty-five years after the victory over Navy that marked the height of his Army coaching career was not a time for settling old scores or for getting the record straight. In his return to West Point, he wanted to focus his attention on the players who had come back to see him. "I had no idea what to say to them in advance. There was no way for me to prepare," he would later say. "It was strictly extemporaneous."

"Tall, broad-shouldered, and handsome, the blue-eyed, sandy-haired coach makes a fine appearance," was how the *New York Times* described Dietzel in 1962, and his players often saw him as someone who enjoyed the spotlight. "He liked to pose a little on the sidelines when reporters were around," John Seymour recalls. But in meeting with his former players in 2009, Dietzel had an audience that he did not have to win over. They had made their feelings about him clear by coming from across the country to West Point. In his speech at the dinner in his honor, Dietzel limited himself to telling stories that harkened back to his days at West Point.[32]

Dietzel's stories went over big, and his decision not to explain why he had left West Point in 1966 was exactly the right one. His players were beyond worrying about old controversies. At the time of his 2009 reunion with his players, Dietzel was older than General Douglas MacArthur had been in 1962 when Dietzel made sure the team was present in Washington Hall to hear MacArthur deliver his farewell address to West Point. It was impossible for the coach's age not to weigh on the minds of his players. "Kind of a last hurrah. I guess that was unspoken," John Johnson thought at the time.[33]

Sonny Stowers had the same feeling. When asked, he was unable to recall exactly what Dietzel said in his speech, but he remembered how deeply the coach was moved by his players' wanting him to come back to West Point. "I think probably the biggest thing really was to see the smile on his face and hear the cracking of his voice and the tears he fought back

Rollie Stichweh (16) fakes a handoff to John Seymour (43) as Peter Braun (50) and Sonny Stowers (61) pull out to lead blocking against Navy. (Courtesy Athletic Communications Office, USMA)

during his presentation," Stowers recalls. Stowers, like most of the players, was able to talk personally with the coach before the evening was over. He was astonished by the detail with which the coach remembered the past. To Stowers, the coach's recollection was a sign of not only how sharp he still was but also how much his time at West Point had mattered to him.[34]

New York Times sports columnist George Vecsey, in his account of the reunion with Dietzel, began with an opening paragraph that took his readers back to 1964. "They beat Navy. They beat Roger Staubach. Forty-five years later, that is worth celebrating, all over again," Vecsey wrote. Vecsey's lead made Bill Zadel uneasy when he read it. The way Vecsey described the reunion made it seem as if the players on the 1964 team had really returned to West Point to celebrate their own past triumph. In Zadel's mind, that kind of return was very different from one in which the message the players delivered to Dietzel was, "We enjoyed playing for you. Thanks for coming back."[35]

The problem for Zadel was that the more he thought about Vecsey's interpretation of the reunion, the harder it got for him to say that Vecsey did not have a point. Zadel had to admit that he and his teammates had mixed motives in honoring Dietzel. "It is just very hard to describe how much beating Navy mattered," he found himself thinking. Had Zadel and the seniors on the 1964 team lost to Navy, it would have meant that during their four years at West Point, they had experienced only defeat in the football game that mattered most to them. In the years that followed, they would still have remained close friends, but their closeness as players would have been shaped by their failure on the field. It would have been consolation, as opposed to accomplishment, that they shared when they talked about their rivalry with Navy.[36]

Dietzel, too, would have left West Point as a coach with a very different reputation and a very different set of memories. Army's 7–7 tie with Navy in 1965 would have marked the only time that a West Point football team he coached was not defeated in the game he had been hired to win. Without his 1964 victory over Navy, Dietzel's record at Army would have been 20-19-1, a single game over .500. Players who have been on teams with that kind of winning percentage and no victories against their traditional rival rarely hold banquets for their coach. There is just too much they do not want to have to think about again.

In the case of the 1964 Army team, that sentiment was especially true. Vietnam, where the players had served as junior officers, had left them with more than enough tragic memories to sift through when they thought about their twenties. The clarity surrounding their 1964 win over Navy offered the players a very different perspective on what it meant to come of age in the 1960s. The win provided them with a distinct set of standards for judging themselves and the bonds they had forged with one another. In this context, the players were grateful, not worried, that honoring their old coach turned out to be inseparable from recalling the victory of a lifetime. Their game before the war, as they knew when it happened, had never been just about football.

Army, led by Bill Zadel (76), Barry Nickerson (82), and Sonny Stowers (61), takes the field against Navy. (Courtesy Athletic Communications Office, USMA)

APPENDIX A

Teddy Roosevelt Starts a Tradition

For more than a century, presidents have been coming to the Army–Navy football game. The tradition was begun in 1901 by Theodore Roosevelt, and since then the presidents have followed Roosevelt's example to the letter—spending the first half of the game on one team's side, and then crossing the field at halftime to sit on the other team's side.[1]

But the elevation of the Army–Navy game to a sporting event that the entire nation took an interest in did not follow a smooth course. While the football rivalry between the two service academies generated great excitement from the start, it also produced such rancor that in 1893 West Point's superintendent, Oswald Ernst, declared the Navy game had become "a bad influence," with the excitement surrounding it exceeding "all reasonable limit."[2]

Organized football began at West Point in 1890, well after many colleges in the East had taken up the game. Prior to then, football at West Point was essentially a recreational activity. In his memoirs Civil War general James Longstreet, who graduated from West Point in 1842, wrote of enjoying football, and a decade later, Jerome Napoleon Bonaparte Jr., the grandnephew of Napoleon and an 1852 West Point graduate, noted how, after drill was done, cadets would "all turn out and kick football until parade."[3]

When on November 29, 1890, Army played Navy in the first organized football game in West Point history, the cadets were ill prepared for the challenges they faced from a rival that between 1886 and 1890 had compiled a winning record in twenty-one football games. The cadet behind the first Army football game was Dennis Michie, the son of Lieutenant Colonel Peter Michie, who had served with distinction in the Civil War and who in 1890 was a philosophy professor at West Point. Dennis Michie, who had played football while prepping for college at Lawrenceville, arranged for friends at Navy to issue a formal challenge to West Point; then he persuaded his father to get the approval for the game from Colonel John Wilson, the superintendent of the Academy.[4]

Michie's maneuvering left Army in a vulnerable position. Just two other cadets had ever played football before, and so it fell on him to train, coach, and manage a team that was granted time to practice only on rainy Saturday afternoons when no parades could be held. When the Navy team came out on the field that had been laid out on the southeast corner of the West Point parade grounds, the Army players were surprised to see their opponents warm up with organized calisthenics, and when the game began, the Army players were even more surprised when Navy players used nautical commands—"Helm's a lee," "Reef top sails"—to call out plays they had already practiced.[5]

Navy's 24–0 rout of Army reflected the differences between the two teams. In every phase of the game, Navy was the superior team. As the *New York Times* wrote of the Army team, "It realized before the game was called that it was at a sore disadvantage in its lack of experience, practice, and knowledge of football." But in a losing effort, Michie and his inexperienced teammates had changed the course of sports at West Point.[6]

In his firsthand account of the 1890 Army–Navy game, Michie's classmate, future general John Palmer, recalled that there was so much room on the sidelines that the cadets and officers watching the game could shift with the ball as it moved from one end of the field to the other. The fervor the game aroused was a different story, going far beyond the feelings of the thousand or so spectators who roamed the sidelines. For the press, the game was a front-page story. "Lads who could play football as these cadets did certainly ought to make good soldiers and sailors," the *New York Times* declared. "When bravery was so common and so notable, it would be unfair and unjust to cite one man as braver than the other. Each of these players did all he could to win."[7]

A rematch with Navy became a necessity for Army. As Palmer noted, "Even the most hidebound conservatives conceded that the Army must settle the score with the Navy. Contributions came from every regiment in the Army." Army's anxiousness for a rematch did not, however, preclude sober reflection on what needed to be done in preparation for playing Navy. Army persuaded Harry Williams, a former Yale football star, to coach the team two afternoons a week, and under his tutelage, Army players learned to move as a unit, start on signals, and run prearranged plays. They also set up a fall football schedule designed to test them in a way intramural games could not.[8]

When the second Army–Navy game, this one played on Navy's field at Annapolis, began on November 28, 1891, Army, which had never before sent a team to compete on the home field of another college, was ready. As the *New York Times* observed of the seventeen Army players who were given permission to play, "They remembered the distressing defeat administered by the boys in blue a year ago, and they took measures to prevent its repetition." In a bitterly fought game in which nine players were carried off the field, Army prevailed 32–16, setting off a wild celebration at West Point when the news arrived via telegram. Michie, who in 1898 would be killed during the Battle of Santiago in the Spanish-American War, had gotten his revenge.[9]

The Army–Navy series had begun in the best possible way—with each team winning a game. By the time the third Army–Navy game moved back to West Point in 1892, there was a crowd of three thousand on hand, and the field had to be roped off to make sure people kept their distance from the players. With Michie, who had graduated from West Point in June 1892, now coaching the team, Army lost 12–4, scoring just one touchdown in an era when a touchdown counted four points and a conversion two.[10]

The following year, when the game switched to Annapolis, the anticipation surrounding it had grown exponentially. Special trains from Baltimore and Washington brought large numbers of Army and Navy officers and their wives to Annapolis. When the game began, there was, the *New York Times* estimated, a crowd of eight thousand in attendance. In a defensive battle, Navy eked out a 6–4 victory, but the fiercest battle of all was, it turned out, in the stands.[11]

The Army players had no trouble accepting defeat, but numerous fights broke out among the fans during the game, and the *New York Times* reported that a quarrel between a retired rear admiral and a brigadier general became so heated that it almost ended in a duel. That is when West Point superintendent Oswald Ernst decided the bad feeling generated by the rivalry was too high a price to pay to keep it going. He recommended that Army continue its regular football schedule but drop its game with Navy. Ernst prevailed but only after the Army–Navy game became a White House matter. At an 1894 cabinet meeting at which President Grover Cleveland presided, Daniel Lamont, the secretary of the Army, and Hilary A. Herbert, the secretary of the Navy, made the series between the two schools impossible by forbidding their teams to travel.[12]

It took six years and a change from the Democratic administration of Grover Cleveland to the Republican administration of William McKinley for the Army–Navy game to resume. The new secretary of war, Russell A. Alger, was anxious to restore the game, and when Colonel Albert Mills took over West Point in 1898, Alger had someone who shared his vision. All that had to be settled was when the 1899 game would be played (Army wanted November 25; Navy wanted December 2), and whether Navy players, who at that time had a six-year course of study, should be allowed to play for six years. Dr. William White, a member of the West Point Board of Visitors, was called in to mediate, and both points were settled in Navy's favor. A neutral site, Franklin Field in Philadelphia, was then chosen as the place to hold the game.[13]

For Army, the renewal of the rivalry was a great opportunity to prove to the country that it was an up-and-coming football power. In 1898 *Harper's Weekly* characterized Army as a team that had "won for herself recognition as one of the first class" despite practice times that were essentially limited to one afternoon per week during the football season. Since it last played Navy, Army had achieved a tie with Yale in 1897, a 42–0 victory over Brown in 1897, and a tie with Princeton in 1898.[14]

A crowd of twenty-seven thousand, including the secretary of war and the secretary of the Navy, showed up for the 1899 game, and in exchange for twenty free tickets to the game from Superintendent Mills, the president of the Pennsylvania Railroad gave free transportation to the game to the entire corps of cadets. The trade turned out to be a bargain for West Point. The cadets got to see a powerful Army team sweep to a 17–5 victory and return the Army–Navy game to a headline event. By 1901, following an 11–7 Navy victory in 1900, the rivalry had become more intense than ever and more popular with those the papers called "society people."[15]

The 1901 Army–Navy game, according to the *New York Times*, was seen by "probably the most distinguished gathering that ever witnessed a football game in this country." An estimated thirty thousand people were present, and tickets were in such demand that scalpers sold them for as high as $40 apiece. President Theodore Roosevelt, who sat on the Navy side during the first half and the Army side for the second half, drew the most attention from the press, but Roosevelt and the cabinet members he brought with him were not the only celebrities present. Admiral George Dewey, a hero of the Spanish-American War, spent the entire game sitting on the Navy side.[16]

The result was a thoroughly modern mix of sports, politics, and celebrity that made it clearer than ever to West Point authorities how much they stood to gain from fielding a winning team. Prior to the 1901 season, West Point had accepted as a cadet Harvard football captain Charlie Daly, who had been named to Walter Camp's All-American team three years in a row while at Harvard. Daly, whose appointment to West Point was made by Congressman John "Honey" Fitzgerald, the maternal grandfather of President John Kennedy, picked up at West Point where he left off at Harvard. Older and far more experienced than the Navy players he was up against, Daly made the 1901 game his, scoring all of Army's points as it beat Navy 11–5. Army had its first football superstar, a hero who claimed even President Roosevelt's attention. After the game, Roosevelt shook hands with West Point superintendent Mills. "Extend my congratulations to your boys," he said. "And tell Daly I said this was a great day for the Irish."[17]

A year later, with Daly again leading the team from his quarterback position, Army beat Navy 22–8, concluding a winning season in which they lost only to powerful Harvard. The game was Daly's last for Army. He stopped playing when Navy's complaint that players should not be allowed to compete after three years of college football became a major issue for the two service academies. Daly's retirement did not, however, mean that Army football took a step backward. Army was now a football power.[18]

From 1913 to 1916, with Daly now serving as coach, Army was one of the top teams in the country. In 1914 Army went undefeated, beating, among other teams, Rutgers, Notre Dame, and Navy, and in 1916 Army went undefeated for a second season, prompting Daly to tell the press, "The Army coaches believe that the 1916 Army team could defeat any team in the country. The 1916 team was as effective as the Army team of 1914, and its exceptionally high-grade personnel rate it with the strongest teams in the history of the game." In his halfback, Elmer Oliphant, who starred at West Point in football, basketball, golf, track, and boxing, Daly even had a superstar of his own caliber. On his way to being named to Walter Camp's All-American team, Oliphant showed himself to be a brilliant runner, who also kicked field goals and punted. In Army's 14–0 victory over Navy in 1915, Oliphant scored both Army touchdowns and kicked both extra points.[19]

The public's growing interest in West Point football corresponded to the team's success on the field. By virtue of his presence at the 1901 Army–Navy game, Theodore Roosevelt had cleared a path for other presidents to follow. In 1902 retired president Grover Cleveland attended the Army–Navy game, and in 1913 Woodrow Wilson, along with his entire cabinet, attended the Army–Navy game. The interest in the Army–Navy rivalry was enough for the *New York Times* to declare, "The annual football game between the Army and the Navy holds first rank among amateur sports in this country." To the business community, the money to be made from the game quickly became a lure. In 1914 the Convention Bureau of the Merchants Association of New York City successfully appealed to the secretary of war and the secretary of the Navy to have the game brought to New York City, and in 1915 and 1916 the Army–Navy games drew crowds that jammed the Polo Grounds.[20]

Army's popularity with sports fans in the pre–World War I era meant the West Point football program could withstand setbacks and criticism. In 1909, when Army left tackle Eugene Byrne died from injuries sustained in a rough game with Harvard, Army cancelled the rest of its season, but by 1910, following a series of rule changes that included requiring the offensive team to have seven men on the line of scrimmage at the start of each play, Army was back to football as usual and a rematch with Harvard. Army football now had a life of its own. In 1913 West Point superintendent Colonel C. P. Townley, in his annual report, observed that the injuries from football were so serious that "it is a question whether this form of sport is of sufficient value to the corps to warrant its continuance." But Townley was ignored as the Army football team continued its winning ways.[21]

During this period, even Army's losses brought with them the national spotlight. In 1912, when the Carlisle Indian School, led by Jim Thorpe, trounced Army 27–6, Carlisle was hailed as "among the great elevens of the year." The following season, when Notre Dame, using a passing attack built around quarterback Gus Dorais and end Knute Rockne, upset Army 35–13, Notre Dame was reported by the *New York Times* to have "flashed the most sensational football that has been seen in the East this year." In defeat as well as victory, Army had become a measuring rod for what it meant to be a good team.[22]

With the end of World War I, Army, which had suspended its 1917 and 1918 games with Navy, went back to its regular football schedule. But with the appointment in 1919 of Douglas MacArthur as the Academy's new superintendent, it was anything but business as usual at West Point. The thirty-nine-year-old MacArthur, a highly decorated brigadier general in World War I, had been told by Army Chief of Staff General Payton March that "West Point is forty years behind the times," and on arriving at the Academy, MacArthur found it a shell of its former self, especially because of the classes that had been graduated ahead of time so they could be rushed into battle. "The traditional disciplinary system, so largely built around the prestige and influence of upperclassmen, was impossible in a situation where there were no upperclassmen," MacArthur later wrote in his *Reminiscences*.[23]

For MacArthur, West Point's postwar problems were an opportunity to institute needed change. He immediately took steps to bring hazing (which had led to a suicide in 1919) under control, put the enforcement of the honor code in the hands of the corps of cadets, and made summer military camp meaningful by shifting it to Fort Dix, New Jersey, where the cadets were trained in the use of modern weapons by regular Army sergeants. In sports, MacArthur followed a similar pattern of modernization, making intramural athletics compulsory for the entire corps.[24]

Football was the particular beneficiary of MacArthur's reforms. As superintendent, he went out of his way to make sure that Army remained competitive with its opponents. In an era in which huge football stadiums were being built around the country, he asked Congress to approve a fifty-thousand-seat stadium for West Point. MacArthur also instituted the policy of Army teams playing teams besides Navy away from West Point. The Academy—along with the cadets whom MacArthur now gave permission to attend away games—would be part of a 1920s sports revival in America.[25]

MacArthur did not remain superintendent long enough to see the completion of Michie Stadium (seating capacity sixteen thousand) in 1924, but when he left West Point in 1922, he had set Army football on a new course. However, it was not a new course Army could take advantage of immediately. The speeded-up graduations of cadets during World War I had not only hurt discipline at West Point, they had also hurt athletics. "It will take us four years before we can beat Navy again," Charlie Daly, who resumed his coaching duties after the war, predicted. He proved right. In 1919, 1920, and 1921, Army was shut out by Navy. It did not beat its archrival until 1922, but then it went on a long undefeated streak and did not lose to Navy again until 1934.[26]

From 1926 through 1929, under the coaching of Biff Jones, Army compiled a record of 30-8-2. In its best years, 1926 and 1927, Army lost only one game each season, while running up huge scores against its opponents. Army beat Franklin and Marshall College by fifty-five points in 1926 and shut out Notre Dame 18–0 in 1927. The ability of nonmilitary colleges to now schedule home games with West Point also made Army an increasingly popular team. Throughout the 1920s, good teams wanted to play Army because of the crowds a game with West Point drew. In 1921, in its first game in the Yale Bowl, Army drew seventy-three thousand fans as it lost 14–7. The following year, seventy-six thousand fans showed up to watch Army battle Yale to a 7–7 tie. A similar pattern followed with Notre Dame. The 1927 Army–Notre Dame game drew eighty thousand spectators when it was played in Yankee Stadium. As for West Point's traditional game with Navy, the nationwide interest in it was so great that in 1926, when it was played for its first and only time in Chicago's Soldier Field, over one hundred thousand fans showed up to watch the teams battle to a 21–21 tie.[27]

In Christian Keener "Red" Cagle, Army also produced a 1920s football star comparable to Charlie Daly and Elmer Oliphant in their prime. After breaking football records at Southwestern Louisiana Institute, Cagle came to West Point in 1926. He immediately made headlines. An All-

American halfback who could run, pass, and play defense, Cagle was the dominant player whenever he stepped on the field. In the 1926 Army–Navy game, his long runs allowed Army to gain a tie, and the following year, in Army's shutout victory over Notre Dame, Cagle scored on a run and a pass that were so spectacular they inspired the *New York Times* to observe, "Mercury's time for the 100-yard dash is not known, but he never went any faster than Red Cagle."[28]

The Naval Academy was not happy with Cagle's success, and a week after the Army–Navy game of 1927, which Army won 14–9, Rear Admiral Louis M. Nulton, the superintendent of the Naval Academy, wrote his counterpart at West Point, Major General Edwin B. Winans, a letter that made the old three-year eligibility rule once again an issue for the two schools. Nulton insisted that Navy's continuation of its football series with West Point depended on Army abiding by the rule that limited players to three years of intercollegiate football. The rule, if agreed to, would have made Red Cagle ineligible to play and dealt a severe blow to Army football. Winans countered Nulton's letter with one of his own, arguing that "the authorized enrollment at the Naval Academy is about 50 percent greater than that at the Military Academy."[29]

The dispute became a national political issue with Representative Fred Britten of Illinois, the ranking Republican member of the House Naval Affairs Committee, urging the secretaries of war and the Navy to find a way to get the game played. But a meeting between the two superintendents at the Army and Navy Club in Washington went nowhere, and in early January the 1928 Army–Navy game was officially cancelled. One year later, despite the arrival of new superintendents at both West Point and Annapolis and an appeal by Representative Britten to President Herbert Hoover, nothing changed. In October, the two service academies announced that they would not be playing for a second year in a row. The series that the *New York Times* labeled the "greatest show in football" was for the moment at a dead end.[30]

As for Red Cagle, his glory years at West Point would be followed by public disgrace. Shortly before his graduation from West Point, Cagle announced that he intended to submit his resignation from the Army: "It is with considerable regret that I shall submit my resignation to the War Department after graduation in order to accept two positions in civil life, one as football coach at Mississippi A&M and the other with a large commercial house." His decision was, he declared, dictated by the low

Army pay he would get upon graduating from West Point. "My pay as a Second Lieutenant in the regular army would be $125 a month, plus 60 cents a day ration allowance. That means for many years I would live in the state of genteel poverty," he observed in a formal statement he issued to the press. Cagle then went on to add a caveat: If Congress passed the bill that was before it to increase Army pay, "I would not consider for a moment submitting my resignation."[31]

To anyone who knew Red Cagle, it was hard to imagine him taking such a political stance on his own, and when his statement was followed by Major General William R. Smith, the superintendent of West Point, publicly defending Cagle by pointing out how many West Pointers over the last five years had left the Army for financial reasons, it seemed clear to most observers that Cagle was part of a concerted effort to pressure Congress into raising Army pay. The anger of those who thought Cagle had overstepped his bounds was deep. A few days later, the news was leaked that while on furlough in the summer of 1928, Cagle had secretly married a Louisiana teacher whom he met while both were students at Southwestern Louisiana Institute. The marriage was a violation of West Point rules and Cagle was forced to resign from West Point in disgrace.[32]

With the discovery of his secret marriage, Cagle went from being a football hero to a man branded as a liar. After leaving West Point, Cagle coached for a while at Mississippi A&M and briefly played professional football with the New York Giants, but his life was never the same. At the start of World War II, when he tried to enlist in the Army as an officer, he was turned down by the War Department. West Point, by contrast, came out of the Army–Navy dispute over the three-year-eligibility rule in good shape. Bowing to pressure from Washington, Army and Navy officials agreed to late-season charity games in 1930 and 1931 before finally signing a three-year agreement in 1932 in which they decided that the only pragmatic solution to their differences was to let each service academy set player eligibility standards for itself. The agreement, which gave Army the leeway it had wanted all along, was made still sweeter by its victories over Navy in both charity games, each of which packed Yankee Stadium.[33]

The attendance at the 1930 and 1931 Army–Navy charity games was a good omen for the Army football program. The attendance meant that despite the Great Depression, Army could count on support from a nationwide fan base. Army's games with Notre Dame, even in this post–Knute Rockne era, were almost as popular as those with Navy, and when in 1936 the Army–Navy game moved to Philadelphia's huge Municipal Stadium (which had far more seats than the University of Pennsylvania's Franklin Field, where the service games had been held the previous four years), one hundred thousand fans, including First Lady Eleanor Roosevelt, showed up.[34]

On the football field, the 1930s started out well for Army. In 1933, its best season of the decade, Army came close to a perfect record, shutting out seven of its ten opponents and losing only to Notre Dame 13–12 in a game the Army players dominated until the fourth quarter. The following year, Monk Meyer came into his own as a quarterback, kicker, and runner, and from 1934 to 1936, he made headlines as the star of Army's team. The dark side of Army football in the Great Depression years came in a 1931 game with Yale when Richard Sheridan, a 149-pound end, died from a broken neck as he tried to make a tackle on a kickoff. Army did not cancel the rest of its season, as it had when Eugene Byrne died, but Sheridan's death pointed up the degree to which Army was relying on undersized players to fill key positions on its roster. Monk Meyer weighed at most 145 pounds.[35]

Army was lucky to have skilled, small players like Sheridan and Meyer, but for Army getting bigger as a team was not simply a matter of recruiting bigger players. In 1931, as a result of a directive from the surgeon general, it became much harder for West Point to recruits cadets whose weight topped two hundred pounds. The directive, which would later draw the ire of Red Blaik, was based on the theory that life expectancy was greater for slender men, and it set the ideal weight for cadets much lower than the ideal weight for football players. While Douglas MacArthur, a football enthusiast, was Army chief of staff, it was possible to get waivers to the weight directive without too many problems, but after MacArthur ceased being chief of staff in 1935, waivers became more difficult to obtain. A 1937 directive that said the weight standards for West Point *could* be waived if the excess weight of a candidate for admission was the result of a "robust physique" was generally ignored in practice.[36]

Making matters still tougher for the Army football program were the new rules that in 1938 put an end to the player-eligibility bargain that West Point and Navy had struck in 1932. The new rules, said to have the backing of the White House, limited West Point athletes to three years of varsity play at the college level. Army was now on the same footing as the Naval Academy and other colleges when it came to the football eligibility of its players, but in combination with the size requirements, the new rules left West Point, with its comparatively small student body, struggling to be competitive. Two of Army's prize football recruits at this time—Carl Hinkle, Vanderbilt's All-American center, and Bill Guckeyson, an outstanding running back from the University of Maryland—never played a down of football while they were at West Point.[37]

In 1938 West Point had its last winning football season before the decade ended. The 1939 Army team won only three games, and the 1940 Army team won only its opening game with Williams College, which it beat by a single point. Watching Army lose to the University of Pennsylvania by a lopsided 48–0 score, General Robert Eichelberger, who became West Point's superintendent on November 18, 1940, was shocked. "I was impressed Saturday by the way the cadets cheered our team right to the end," he told the athletic board. "It looks as if we are developing the finest bunch of losers in the world." Eichelberger's sarcasm reflected how far Army's football fortunes had fallen. In 1940 Army marked the fiftieth anniversary of its first game against Navy, but 1940 also demonstrated how in the modern football era Army's success on the playing field would require support that went far beyond the athletic department.[38]

APPENDIX B

The Golden Age of Red Blaik

For Brigadier General Robert Eichelberger, West Point's new superintendent in 1940, the key to bringing Army football out of the doldrums into which it had fallen was one man: Red Blaik. If Blaik, a 1920 West Point graduate and star end, could be persuaded to return as coach, Eichelberger believed that Army football could get back to its winning ways. "So one of the first things I did when I got to West Point," Eichelberger would later say, "was to write to Earl Blaik at Dartmouth and ask him whether or not we could get him back."[1]

In the fall of 1940, with Blaik's seventh season as Dartmouth's head coach at an end, Eichelberger launched his campaign to make Blaik Army's next football coach. "If you have not signed a new contract, don't sign any until you have talked to me first," Eichelberger wrote Blaik in a letter that he typed himself rather than trust it to a secretary, who might leak his intentions. "I understand what you mean. I will see you next week at the Army–Navy game," Blaik replied.[2]

Eichelberger's belief that Blaik was the right coach for Army would pay dividends for the next eighteen football seasons. During its first fifty years, Army's football team had achieved great success playing a schedule that included much bigger schools with better-funded athletic programs. But the two decades in which Blaik coached at West Point were unique. They were the golden age of Army football. Blaik's Army football record was 121-33-10. Under his coaching, Army was twice crowned national champion and produced twenty-nine, first-team All Americans.[3]

When Blaik retired after his undefeated 1958 season, every Army coach who succeeded him was judged by how well he did in comparison. It was an impossible standard to meet, even for those who had played or coached under Blaik, and the comparison was made more difficult because those doing the judging were usually selective in their remembrances of Blaik. They ignored how Blaik benefited from coaching at a time when pro football did not pay huge salaries and Army could recruit top-flight players from across the country. They also minimized the 1951 cheating scandal that occurred on Blaik's watch and resulted in ninety cadets, including thirty-seven members of Army's football team, being expelled from West Point.[4]

In bringing Blaik back to West Point in time for the 1941 football season, Eichelberger was getting a coach who knew exactly what was expected of him. Blaik had entered West Point in 1918, the same year he graduated from Miami University of Ohio, where he played end and was named to the All-Ohio football team. Blaik's reason for applying to West Point had nothing to do with football: He assumed that World War I was going to last many more years. Enrolling in West Point was, he thought, the best way to get commissioned as an officer.[5]

The war did not go as Blaik expected, but his athletic career at West Point was a triumph. Walter Camp named Blaik third-team end on his 1919 All-American team; in addition, Blaik won the West Point Athletic Association Saber, given annually to the best athlete in the Academy. A varsity standout in football, basketball, and baseball, Blaik quickly won the attention of West Point superintendent Douglas MacArthur, who over the years became a staunch Blaik ally and friend.

Blaik graduated from West Point in 1920 as part of an accelerated program put in effect by the Army during World War I, but two years after receiving his commission as a second lieutenant, Blaik resigned from the service. When in 1922 the Army, pushed by Congress to reduce the size of its peace-time force in order to save expenses, offered officers a year's pay to retire, Blaik took the offer. He found his life as a cavalry officer in the West a series of tedious routines. Convinced that promotion through the ranks was likely to come at a snail's pace, Blaik returned to his family's home in Dayton, Ohio, to join his father in the real estate and building business.[6]

It was a smart financial move. By 1923, Blaik had made enough money from building and selling houses to settle down and marry his college sweetheart, Merle McDowell, but he soon found that it was impossible for him to get football out of his system. In 1924 and 1925 he accepted an invitation to travel to nearby Oxford, Ohio, and work with the ends on the Miami University of Ohio football team. Then, in 1926, when his former Miami coach, George Little, asked him to join his coaching staff at the University of Wisconsin, Blaik moved for the fall to Madison.[7]

The move to Wisconsin marked the beginning of the end of Blaik's career in business. In 1927 he accepted an offer from Biff Jones, the head football coach at Army, to join him as an assistant at West Point, and he remained Jones's assistant until the latter's West Point coaching career ended in 1929. But when Jones moved on, Blaik did not. In 1930 he joined the staff of Ralph Sasse, Jones's successor, and stayed with Sasse until Sasse stopped coaching Army football after the 1932 season.[8]

Coaching had now become Blaik's vocation as well as his avocation. The following year, when Garrison Davidson was named Army's head football coach, Blaik signed on once again as an assistant. The decision reflected the loyalty that Blaik felt for West Point, but the decision also forced him to think about what he wanted from a career in coaching. At West Point and in coaching circles around the country, Blaik's reputation as a tactician who inspired those who played under him had grown. At any other college, Blaik would have been the top candidate for the head coaching position after so many years as an assistant. Sasse even endorsed Blaik as his successor, but West Point had an unwritten rule that only a West Point graduate who was an officer on active duty could hold the head football coaching job. In 1933, in the midst of the Great Depression, the Academy was not about to change its unwritten rule for Blaik.[9]

With the end of the 1933 season, Blaik, who had previously turned down head-coaching offers from both Princeton and Ohio State in order to stay with the family building business in Dayton during the off-season, had a big decision to make. Did he want to continue being an assistant coach at West Point indefinitely? Or did he want to strike out on his own? Looking back on that period in his life from the perspective of 1960, Blaik recalled, "I felt that if I was to stay in football, I owed it to myself and my family to accept a head-coach offer. The debt I owed West Point was paid."[10]

It was the uncertainties of a coaching career, not how much he loved football, that worried Blaik. As he later wrote, "At the age of thirty-six, with eight seasons as an assistant coach behind me, I had seen enough of college football to know that a head coach's job is essentially something on which a man cannot plan a solid future." What made Blaik willing to test the coaching waters was his meeting with Ernest Martin Hopkins, the president of Dartmouth College from 1916 to 1945. After sorting through a list of more than a hundred candidates, Hopkins, anxious to improve Dartmouth's football fortunes, made Blaik a coaching offer he could not refuse. At Dartmouth, Blaik would, Hopkins promised him, have complete authority over all matters pertaining to football. There would be no undue bureaucracy to complicate his life. He would report only to Hopkins himself and the Dartmouth Athletic Council.[11]

The Ivy League that Blaik entered in 1934 when he accepted the head coaching job at Dartmouth was still capable of excellent football and fielded teams that achieved national ranking. In compiling a record of 45-15-4 in seven seasons at Dartmouth, Blaik demonstrated that he could be a winning coach at any level.[12]

What defined Blaik's time at Dartmouth and brought him a national reputation as the kind of coach every college football program wanted was the ethos he created. Surrounding himself with a staff of assistants who had worked under such pioneers of college football as Pop Warner and Jock Sutherland, Blaik established a no-nonsense regime in which discipline and sacrifice were the building blocks on which all else depended. "Our major problem at Dartmouth was to replace the spirit of good fellowship, which is antithetical to successful football, with the Spartanism that is indispensable," Blaik later recalled. "Once Dartmouth players understood what we were getting at, I found them little different from the West Point cadets."[13]

Blaik's version of Spartanism meant that he oversaw every detail of the Dartmouth football program. When two Dartmouth athletic officials took several of his players out drinking after a game, Blaik had them relieved of their football duties, and after his first year of coaching, he brought in a trainer, Roland "The Beaver" Bevan, who shared his view that injuries should never be coddled and that a relentless conditioning program was the key to keeping a team healthy. "Bevan could spot a malingering athlete a mile away," Blaik believed.[14]

In the mid-1930s Blaik's Dartmouth team, led by halfback Robert MacLeod, who later played a year for the Chicago Bears, went twenty-two games without a defeat. By the end of the 1940 season, Blaik had established himself as one of the Ivy League's premier coaches, and he had also become a fixture at Dartmouth. It was the kind of coaching relationship that might easily have lasted until Blaik was ready to retire, but when Robert Eichelberger contacted Blaik in 1940 about returning to West Point, Eichelberger struck all the right notes. Blaik was convinced that World War II was coming, and he wanted to be part of it: "I reasoned that if I returned to West Point, I would be in a more advantageous position to return to the service I had left twenty-two years before."[15]

Making Blaik's return to West Point possible were Robert Eichelberger's political skills as much as Blaik's desire to serve his country. Years earlier, when he was adjutant general at West Point, Eichelberger had failed to get the West Point Athletic Board to end its unwritten law that the head football coach at Army must be a graduate officer on active duty. As superintendent, Eichelberger was in a very different position of power, and he did not hesitate to bring the full weight of his office to bear on the athletic board. In short order, the path was cleared for Blaik to take the position he had been denied a decade earlier. West Point ended its policy of hiring coaches who stayed for several years, and then moved to a new military post.[16]

It was a remarkable political achievement that broke with years of tradition, and it professionalized coaching at West Point. But in addition to his demand for a $12,000 annual salary, living quarters, and a five-year contract, Blaik had other conditions that he insisted on before he would agree to coach Army. In a handwritten "Dear General" letter that he sent to Eichelberger on December 16, Blaik spelled out those conditions. He wanted to be able to bring his entire staff of football assistants with him from Dartmouth, and he wanted West Point to abandon the height-weight admissions restrictions of the 1930s that limited those whom West Point could recruit for its football team.[17]

Granting Blaik what he wanted for himself and his staff was no problem for Eichelberger. The challenge was getting permission from Washington to change the height-weight restrictions for admission to West

Point. It was not a matter he could talk over with George Marshall, the Army chief of staff and a Virginia Military Institute graduate, who was focused on rebuilding the Army, but with the help of President Franklin Roosevelt's trusted military aide and appointments secretary, Edwin "Pa" Watson, a 1908 West Point graduate, Eichelberger, as he noted in his World War II memoir *Our Jungle Road to Tokyo*, was able to change the old restrictions. He prevailed upon Watson, who had helped secure the appointment of Rear Admiral Thomas J. Parran Jr. as surgeon general, to persuade Parran to liberalize the most onerous of the 1930s weight requirements for West Point. It did not take long for Parran to see things Watson's way. A new surgeon general directive now said that if a West Point candidate's weight exceeded current standards because the candidate had a robust physique, the standards not only *could* be waived but *should* be waived. In addition, the standards themselves were altered to provide more leeway. Depending on how tall he was, a candidate for admission to West Point could now be twenty-five pounds heavier than in the past. At 6'4" (the Academy height limit at the time) a candidate could weigh up to 226 pounds. "This meant we could get in some candidates who looked like football players as well as officers," a relieved Blaik noted.[18]

At last, Blaik had the freedom he needed to recruit competitively at high schools across the country; still better, as far as he was concerned, he had the mandate he wanted. "My orders," he recalled, "were a 'crash' program to restore West Point football." Although he would not be named athletic director until 1948, Blaik had all the power he needed to build the football team he wanted.[19]

The outlook for Army's 1941 football season was bleak, as the *New York Times* pointed out in a feature story on Blaik. The team Blaik inherited was essentially the same team that the year before had beaten only Williams College. Blaik was, nonetheless, determined to make the most he could of the football talent he had, and his first act was to impose his brand of discipline on the team. This meant, as at Dartmouth, constant scrimmaging on the practice field, little tolerance for minor injuries, and bedtime restrictions even after away games. The change was enough to provide immediate results and, by 1942, to convince the Army that Blaik's most valuable military contribution would be to continue as West Point's coach. In 1941 Army won its first four games, tied a heavily favored Notre Dame, and ended the season with a respectable 5-3-1 record. "At this time, Blaik is looked upon as the nearest approach to a miracle man," the *New York Times* wrote after Army got off to its fast start. In 1942 the team improved to 6–3, and in 1943 it improved to 7-2-1, tying Penn and losing only to strong Notre Dame and Navy squads.[20]

The winning trend at Army was now unmistakable, but over the next three years, the teams that Blaik coached would do more than improve: they approached perfection. Nobody beat them; twice Army was named national champion. Army's success was a tribute to Blaik's coaching and the T-formation that he installed in 1943 and perfected by 1944. But Army's winning ways also reflected the fact that during the World War II years, West Point attracted some of the best players in the country. Along with the Naval Academy, West Point was the perfect place for a young man who wanted to play football and serve his country. The War Department had reduced the time it took to graduate from West Point from four to three years, but during those three years West Point cadets did not have to worry about the draft. They were already in the Army. They could not suddenly be called into service during a manpower shortage, as Notre Dame's star quarterback and Marine reserve Angelo Bertelli was in 1943, and unlike college athletes in the Army Specialized Training Program (ASTP), West Pointers were allowed to play intercollegiate sports.[21]

At eight o'clock on New Year's morning in 1944, Red Blaik gathered his assistants together for their first meeting of the year. Blaik was aware of the imposition he was making on his staff's free time, but he wanted to make it clear to them that 1944 was going to be a special year for Army football. He also wanted to drive home that point to his players. On the first day of fall practice, he told them, "I expect you to be the greatest team in the history of West Point."[22]

West Point now had enough talent to field two equally strong teams for every game. It was no longer vulnerable to opponents with much larger squads who could wear Army down, and in halfback Glenn Davis and fullback Doc Blanchard, Army had two of the best runners and all-around athletes ever to play college football. Davis, a much-heralded school-boy star from California, was fast enough to be a track standout at the 100- and 220-yard dashes. Blanchard, who had already played a year of football at North Carolina, was fast enough to win the 100-yard dash in a track meet against Cornell and strong enough to be Army's best shot putter with very little practice.[23]

In the years they played together, Davis, who became known as "Mr. Outside," and Blanchard, who became known as "Mr. Inside," were an unstoppable combination, and under the supervision of Red Blaik they had no trouble sharing the limelight with each other and their teammates. In 1944 Blanchard and Davis led Army to a 9–0 record that included scoring sixty-nine points against Pittsburgh, seventy-six points against the Coast Guard, eighty-three points against Villanova, and fifty-nine points against Notre Dame.[24]

In their final game of the season against Navy, Blanchard and Davis were the key to Army's 23–7 victory before a crowd of sixty-six thousand in Baltimore. At a time when the war had turned in favor of America and its allies, the game also gave the country a chance to celebrate. Receipts from a sellout crowd added $58,637,000 to the Sixth War Bond Drive. For Blaik, who had been on the losing side during his three previous encounters with Navy, the victory was one that would always stay with him. "I know there must be a moment in every coach's career which surpasses all others for him," he wrote years later. "I believe the number-one moment for me came in that victory of Army's greatest over Navy's greatest in Baltimore." Blaik was not alone in his elation. From Leyte, Robert Eichelberger wrote Blaik, "I cannot tell you how proud we are of you and your fine group of coaches as well as the team that has made the record that will be talked of the next fifty years in the Army." From Douglas MacArthur, then leading the American war effort in the Pacific, came a telegram congratulating Blaik on his "magnificent success."

Everywhere he turned, Blaik, who in 1944 was promoted from lieutenant colonel to full colonel, was honored along with Army's team. In addition to Blanchard and Davis, four other players from the team were named All Americans, and in a souvenir booklet, restricted to the squad and West Point officials, Blaik expressed his own feelings to his players, "Seldom in a lifetime's experience is one permitted the complete satisfaction of being part of a perfect performance," he wrote. "In truth, you were a storybook team."[25]

A year later, Blaik was faced with the challenge of matching his 1944 record. With Blanchard and Davis back for a second year, everyone expected Army to go unbeaten again. A merely good season would be regarded as a failure. In a September 1945 interview with *New York Times* sports columnist Arthur Daley, Blaik tried to play down expectations, pointing to the number of players Army had lost through graduation and insisting his squad did not have the depth of a year ago. But with Arnold Tucker now at quarterback, it turned out that Army had a more versatile attack than it did in 1944. "I would rate that '45 backfield as the best in West Point history," Blaik later conceded. Army topped Michigan 28–7 as Blanchard scored on a sixty-eight-yard run and Davis on a seventy-yard run. It shut out Notre Dame for the second year in a row, this time by a 48–0 score. It overpowered Penn 61–0, and it walloped Navy 32–13, with Blanchard and Davis scoring all five West Point touchdowns.[26]

Army was voted national champion in football for the second year in a row. Blanchard won the Sullivan Award as the outstanding amateur athlete in America, plus the Heisman Trophy as the nation's outstanding college football player. Davis was runner-up for the Heisman Trophy, and he, along with Blanchard and six other Army players, were named to the All-American football team. For Blaik, a second undefeated season in a row was all he could have hoped for, and in the wake of the Navy game, he acknowledged to reporters, "This is the finest team we ever had at West Point, at least in my time."[27]

As 1946 began, the pressure on West Point was even greater than in 1945. For Blaik, "The question was: Could the 1946 team wear the mantle of 1944 and 1945 that had been thrust upon it?" With the war over, other teams were stocked with players who had had their football careers interrupted by their military service, and as a result of graduations, Army was forced to play a line that was outweighed from tackle to tackle by most of its opponents. Even more serious, in the opening game with Villanova Doc Blanchard injured his right knee and was never the same player he had been in 1944 and 1945. Nonetheless, with the exception of its eighth game against Notre Dame, when it was forced to settle for a 0–0 tie, Army won all its games, ending the year with a 21–18 victory over Navy in a game in which a twenty-six-yard touchdown pass from Davis to Blanchard marked the last scoring effort of their careers.[28]

Davis was awarded the Heisman Trophy for 1946. Arnold Tucker received the Sullivan Award, and five Army players, in addition to Blanchard and Davis, were named All Americans. It was a glorious conclusion to the year, but Blaik knew that with the graduation of Blanchard and Davis, the golden era of Army football faced a much tougher future. In the upcoming year, no matter how well it played, Army would not be able to dominate opponents as it had. At the end of the 1946 season, Blaik was voted Coach of the Year, and in his January 3, 1947, speech to the writers who had honored him, he did not hesitate to speak of the previous three years as an era. "I have great pride in the record of the 1944 squad, which was our best squad. I have great pride in the record of the 1945 team, which definitely was our best team," he declared. "But I reserve the warmest affection and the greatest respect for the 1946 team, which, in the face of adversities, playing the best of college opposition, completely and thoroughly demonstrated its right to be classed as great."[29]

With Blanchard and Davis in the backfield together, Army had compiled a 27-0-1 record. The two had scored 537 of the 1,179 points Army had tallied from 1944 through 1946. But Blaik refused to believe that because Blanchard and Davis were gone, Army football was now going to lapse into mediocrity. In 1947 Army's thirty-two-game undefeated streak came to an end when it was upset in midseason 21–20 by a good Columbia University team. The defeat was enough to prompt General Eisenhower to express his regret over Army's loss in a letter to journalist Quentin Reynolds, but the year ended with Army compiling a solid 5-2-2 record that put the team in position to start rebuilding. "I never coached through seasons more exciting and controversial than those of 1948 through 1950," Blaik later wrote.

Army's record in those years reflected Blaik's skill at getting the most from his players. In 1948 Army went undefeated and was ranked sixth nationally. In 1949 Army won all its games and was ranked fourth nationally, and in 1950 Army climbed to number two nationally, losing only in the final game of the season to a powerful Navy team. Blaik had shown that he did not need Blanchard and Davis to make Army a top team. When in a 1950 article for *Collier's* magazine Blaik criticized the "showmanship" and "big fat men" of professional football, he got national attention, and when his son Bob became the starting quarterback for Army, it sparked still more media interest. The two Blaiks were featured in a *Life* pictorial, and in the *Saturday Evening Post* they were heralded as "Football's Greatest Father-and-Son Act."[30]

For Blaik, putting Army in a position to compete nationally in the post–World War II years, when West Point no longer provided a temporary haven from combat, was a difficult task. Army could not, as Blaik was the first to admit, field a powerful football team if it simply chose its players from the cadets who happened to be appointed to West Point: "Such a team could play only at the small-college level." To play nationally ranked opponents, Army needed to go out of its way to recruit good high school football players. The catch was that those high school players often needed help passing West Point's entrance exams, and for many of them that help meant taking a six-week cram course, paid for by civilian West Point alums. Fifteen of the forty-five players on West Point's 1950 team came into the Academy that way, and once in the Academy, a number of players still struggled academically. Al Pollard, a star fullback on the 1950 team, was very open about needing tutoring in math. "If I hadn't received help, I would've flunked out," he admitted.[31]

As a result of this special treatment, the Army football team was able to remain competitive with colleges across the country, but for the players who were getting this special treatment, the downside was that a number came to see themselves as athletes first and cadets second. What followed was the worst scandal in modern West Point history. "West Point Ousts 90 Cadets for Cheating in Classroom; Football Players Involved," the *New York Times* of August 4, 1951, declared in a headline that shocked the nation.[32]

At the root of the scandal was the practice in which cadets passed along the answers to daily written exams to cadets who had not yet taken the same exams. Of the ninety cadets expelled, more than one-third, including the coach's son, were football players, and when West Point officials looked into the origins of the scandal, they traced it back to the fall of 1949. In the words of Major General Frederick Irving, West Point's superintendent, the scandal had mushroomed "due primarily to [its] spread among football players, their roommates, and close associates." They "apparently came to think of themselves as a group apart," Irving declared.[33]

In order to be expelled, a West Point cadet did not need to have benefited from knowing in advance the answers to a test. He simply needed to have known that cheating was going on and done nothing. The West Point honor code says that a cadet will not lie or cheat, or tolerate those who do. The passive act of failing to report cheating was as much grounds for expulsion as actively cheating. At a time when the Alger Hiss perjury trial, Senator Estes Kefuaver's investigation into mob activity, and a college basketball point-shaving scandal were also major news events, the West Point cheating scandal made it seem as if the country had lost its way. To make matters worse, many of the expelled West Point cadets expressed little remorse for their actions.[34]

Soon after the cribbing scandal broke, Al Pollard, one of those expelled from West Point, announced that he had signed a contract to play professional football with the New York Yanks. Harold Loehlein, captain-elect of the football team and president of the senior class, became the poster boy for unrepentant West Point cadets. "Everyone should realize that what we have done takes place in many colleges and universities, though because of the lack of any honor system their offenses hardly cause a national scandal," Loehlein declared in a written statement published in the *New York Times*. "The assistance given by one cadet to another is something that has been going on for years. We did not instigate this by far, but we are the ones to receive the full attack," he argued. "Let it be known that we thoroughly believe in the system, and though we violated one of its principles, we stand behind all the others."[35]

West Point dealt with the scandal by refusing leniency for those guilty of violating its honor code. Knowing what the implications of such mass expulsions would be, the Academy even created a special board, headed by retired justice Learned Hand of the United States Court of Appeals for the Second Circuit, to review its expulsion decisions. Army Chief of Staff General J. Lawton Collins let a group of senators know the scandal was coming before it was announced to the public. For Red Blaik, however, none of these actions could soften the impact of the scandal. He had not known about the cheating system. When a group of his players came to him and confessed the difficulty they were in, he advised them to tell the full truth to West Point officials. "Each one of you should state the facts to the board without equivocation," he told them. The next day, when Blaik learned from his son and his son's roommate that they, too, had known about the cheating, he realized how widespread the scandal was. He immediately offered to resign his coaching position, but what Blaik could not bring himself to accept was the idea that the cadets had committed an offense serious enough to warrant their expulsion from West Point. In *You Have to Pay the Price*, Blaik's chapter on the 1951 cheating scandal is titled "The Ninety Scapegoats," and at its core is a quote from an interview in which General Douglas MacArthur told the sports columnist Bob Considine, "There was no real need for the cribbing scandal that wrecked West Point football. It could have been settled quickly, quietly by a reprimand from the superintendent. That was all that would have been needed except in the case of perhaps two of the boys. And they could have been helped by a kick in the pants."[36]

Blaik was outspoken in defending his players. Less than a week after the cheating scandal broke, he held a two-hour press conference of his own at Leone's Restaurant in New York. Siding with his players and the other cadets who were expelled, Blaik told reporters, "I know them to be men of character. Anything that may have happened has not changed their character." As far as Blaik was concerned, the cheating had started "in an innocuous way several years back and simply pyramided." In Blaik's eyes, the real injustice was the unduly harsh treatment by military authorities of a "tightly knit group."[37]

Blaik's comments backfired. In the past, he had been brilliant at handling the media, but he underestimated the impact of the scandal. His efforts to downplay it made him seem almost tolerant of what had happened, and his defense of his players heightened the criticism of West Point. John Kennedy, then a young congressman from Massachusetts, responded to the cribbing scandal with a *New York Times Magazine* essay, "How Should Cadets be Picked?" Across the country, there were widespread calls for Blaik's resignation. New Jersey Republican congressman James Auchincloss called for Blaik's removal as a way of getting at the source of the cheating scandal. Arkansas's Democratic senator, J. William Fulbright, proposed temporarily suspending football at West Point and Annapolis, and the *New York Times* responded to the scandal with an editorial on the price Army was paying for its overemphasis on football, a column by its Washington correspondent Arthur Krock, and a two-part series by its military affairs editor Hanson Baldwin on the "double standard" West Point football players enjoyed.[38]

The pressure on Blaik was enough for him to reconsider his initial offer to resign as Army's football coach. He was finally persuaded to stay on by, among others, General MacArthur, who told him, "Earl, you must stay on. Don't leave under fire." With MacArthur's backing, plus that of West Point's superintendent, who publicly pronounced Blaik a "forthright gentleman in whom I have the utmost confidence," Blaik finally told the press, "I feel that I can best make people understand these boys and do the proper thing for our fine institution if I remain." But there was no way that Blaik could make people forget the scandal. He had expected that 1951, with his son Bob at quarterback, would be another outstanding year for West Point football. Instead, in August 1951 Blaik began football practice with a varsity squad of just thirty-one players and a tarnished reputation. He was now a coach under the microscope, and his remaining time at West Point would be devoted to showing that he could produce winning teams with players who followed West Point's honor code to the letter.[39]

The challenge was a difficult one. "I had to suit up 'silhouettes,' young men who would have been mainly 'B' squadders, and a yearling group that was the most unpromising since I returned from Dartmouth," Blaik complained. "Badly shaken by what had happened, I could not, try as I would, coach with my normal enthusiasm, drive, and patience."[40]

A year later, as he surveyed his 1952 squad, Blaik was still gloomy. It did not seem like much of an improvement over his 1951 team, and at year's end Blaik was pleased that in a nine-game season, Army finished with four victories and a tie. By 1953, with the talent of his team still thin, Blaik would, however, deliver a turnaround season. Army went 7-1-1 and won the Lambert Trophy as the outstanding team in the East. "I have never coached a team that has given me more satisfaction," Blaik told his players in the locker room, following their 20–7 victory over Navy. "Considering all the conditions since 1951, you have done more for football at West Point than any other team in the history of the Academy."[41]

The 1951 cheating scandal was now sufficiently in the past that Blaik could coach without having to look in the rearview mirror. From 1954 to 1957 Army won more than twice as many games as it lost and achieved a number-seven ranking in 1954. In 1955, in Don Holleder, Army also produced a West Point legend. In 1967, while serving in Vietnam, Holleder was killed after ordering the pilot of the helicopter he was flying in to land and help evacuate a group of wounded soldiers, but it was on the football field that Holleder, for whom West Point's Holleder Center for Sports and Recreation is named, first won fame. An All-American end in 1954, Holleder sacrificed his chance to be an All American two years in a row. At Blaik's request, Holleder switched to quarterback because Army had nobody else to fill that position, and despite having to learn a whole new set of skills, Holleder led West Point's team to a winning season and 14–6 victory over Navy in 1955.[42]

In the comeback he engineered after the cheating scandal, what Blaik had not done, however, was produce a team reminiscent of the great Army teams of the 1940s. All that changed in 1958. "I am certain that this Army team will be interesting," he told reporters as Army began its fall workouts. "It has good team speed, strong runners, and splendid dedication but lacks depth." Blaik was right about team depth, but when Army was healthy, few teams in the country could match it. As running backs, Blaik had returning All-American Bob Anderson and the cadet who in 1958 would win the Heisman Trophy, Pete Dawkins. At quarterback, there was Joe Caldwell, his best passer in years, and at end he had Bill Carpenter, who quickly became known as the "Lonely End" because instead of returning to the team huddle, he lined up fifteen to eighteen yards apart from the nearest interior lineman on every offensive play.[43]

The Lonely End formation was in part a gimmick. As Blaik later disclosed, Carpenter got his signals from the way Army's quarterback positioned his feet. At 6'2" and 225 pounds, Carpenter was a big target who distracted teams even when he was not catching the ball, and with Anderson and Dawkins as Army's featured backs, opponents had their hands full just dealing with Army's running attack. Against Pittsburgh, Army was forced to settle for a 14–14 tie, but against every other team, it was unstoppable in 1958. With its 22–6 victory over Navy, Army ended the season undefeated and ranked third in the nation. Three of its players, Anderson, Dawkins, and guard Bob Novogratz, were named All Americans, and Dawkins added to his football fame by being selected as a Rhodes Scholar.[44]

Blaik could not have wished for more. Seven years earlier, Joe Cahill, the director of sports information at West Point, had predicted that Blaik would never quit while the cheating scandal hung over West Point's football program. "No matter what anyone says, Red Blaik is not going to quit now," Cahill told himself. "He's going to stick it out and rebuild. Then when he finally gets an unbeaten team, when he feels Army football has been vindicated, *then* he'll step out." Cahill was right. On January 13, 1959, Blaik announced that he was retiring from coaching to become a vice president with the AVCO Corporation.[45]

With another undefeated season behind him, there was nothing left for Blaik to prove if he remained at West Point. As the letters of congratulations, including one from President Eisenhower, poured in, he could take pride in going out on top. His personal legacy was complete, and the burden his record would place on his successors was not yet apparent.[46]

INTERVIEWS

Rhesa Barksdale: February 8, 2010
Sam Bartholomew: April 26, 2010
Lucille Braun: June 27, 2013; May 3, 2014
Peter Braun: April 29, 2010; October 29, 2012; June 27, 2013; May 3, 2014; May 27, 2014
Ron Butterfield: May 3, 2010
Russi Champi: April 28, 2014
Sam Champi: February 11, 2010; October 26, 2012; April 28, 2014; June 3, 2014; August 30, 2014
Dan Christman: March 18, 2010
Townsend Clarke: April 8, 2010
Frank Cosentino: April 26, 2010; November 19, 2012
John Cushman: March 25, 2010
Anne Dietzel: May 5, 2014
Paul Dietzel: March 5, 2010
Morris Herbert: April 23, 2010
John Johnson: February 26, 2010; November 24, 2012; May 9, 2014
Mary Johnson: May 9, 2014
Bob Jones: August 13, 2010
Dennis Lewis Jr.: April 30, 2010
Marie Lewis: May 3, 2010
Barry Nickerson: February 12, 2010
Ray Paske: April 26, 2010
David Rivers: February 22, 2010
Thomas Schwartz: March 29, 2010; December 21, 2012

Donna Seymour: April 28, 2014
John Seymour: February 16, 2010; March 12, 2010; November 6, 2012; April 28, 2014
Eric Shinseki: June 15, 2010
Carole Stichweh: May 19, 2014
Rollie Stichweh: April 5, 2010; May 7, 2010; November 12, 2010; May 19, 2014
Charlotte Stowers: May 22, 2014
Sonny Stowers: April 1, 2010; October 12, 2012; May 22, 2014
Ross Wollen: April 1, 2010
Betty Zadel: May 3, 2014
Bill Zadel: February 19, 2010; February 26, 2010

NOTES

PREFACE

1. There is no record of the George Marshall quote anywhere in his papers or in any reliable record. E-mail from Jeffrey Kozak of the George C. Marshall Foundation, June 28, 2010.

2. Interview with Marie Lewis, May 3, 2010; interview with Dennis Lewis Jr., April 30, 2010; interview with Bill Zadel, February 26, 2010; interview with John Johnson, November 24, 2012.

3. Letter from Paul Dietzel to Marie Lewis, October 20, 2009; interview with Paul Dietzel, March 5, 2010.

4. On the awarding of an "A" to Dennis Lewis, e-mail from Rollie Stichweh, June 3, 2010. On the framing of "A," e-mail from Dennis Lewis Jr., June 24, 2010.

5. Interview with Marie Lewis, May 3, 2010; interview with Marie Lewis, May 5, 2014; interview with Dennis Lewis Jr., April 30, 2010; interview with Dennis Lewis Jr., May 5, 2014.

6. Interview with Sonny Stowers, April 1, 2010.

7. James Fallows, "What Did You Do in the Class War, Daddy?" *Washington Monthly*, October 1975, 5–19; Christopher Buckley, "Viet Guilt," *Esquire*, September 1983, 68–72; *The Pentagon Papers* (New York: New York Times, 1971), 542, 567.

INTRODUCTION

1. Earl H. Blaik with Tim Cohane, *You Have to Pay the Price* (New York: Holt, Rinehart and Winston, 1960), 302, 312, 248. For a recent analysis of West Point's victory culture and football, see Dwight S. Mears, "West Point's Fumble," *Washington Post*, February 24, 2014.

2. Video of Army Sports Hall of Fame Ceremony by Army Media Relations.

3. George Vecsey, "Friendships Wrapped in the Army–Navy Rivalry," *New York Times*, September 12, 2012, D18; interview with Rollie Stichweh, November 12, 2012; interview with John Seymour, March 12, 2010.

4. Gene Schoor, *100 Years of Army–Navy Football: A Pictorial History of America's Most Colorful and Competitive Sports Rivalry* (New York: Henry Holt, 1989), 26–27.

5. Hall quoted in William J. Briordy, "Hall Out as Army Coach: Job Open to Non-Alumnus," *New York Times*, December 10, 1961, S1.

6. William C. Rhoden, "Longing for a Return to the Beauty of Imperfection," *New York Times*, September 17, 2012, D2; Richard Sandomir, "Army–Navy Project Ventures Far Beyond Football," *New York Times*, December 14, 2011, http://www.nytimes.com/2011/12/15/sports/ncaafootball/documentary-on-army-navy-rivalry-is-under-way.html; Michael Connelly, *The President's Team: The 1963 Army–Navy Game and the Assassination of JFK* (Minneapolis: MVP Books, 2009), 230.

7. Arthur Daley, "Sports of the Times," *New York Times*, December 8, 1963, 246; Connelly, *The President's Team*, 221–22, 230–32.

8. "Staubach to Get Heisman Trophy," *New York Times*, November 27, 1963, 44.

9. Jesse Abramson, "Navy Beats Army 5th Straight Time," *New York Herald Tribune*, December 8, 1963, section IV, 3; Frank Dolson, "Navy Wins as Clock Stops on Army 2," *Philadelphia Inquirer*, December 8, 1963, S8; Allison Danzig, "Late Drive Fails," *New York Times*, December 8, 1963, 245; George Minot, "Cadets on Navy's Two as Time Runs Out," *Washington Post*, December 8, 1963, C1.

10. Dan Jenkins, "Two Yards and the Clock," *Sports Illustrated*, December 16, 1963, 59; interview with Peter Braun, April 29, 2010.

11. Lincoln A. Werden, "Army Manpower Is at Low Point," *New York Times*, November 24, 1964, 49; interview with Paul Dietzel, March 5, 2010.

12. Allison Danzig, "Streak Ends at 5," *New York Times*, November 29, 1964, S1, S3; interview with Sonny Stowers, April 1, 2010; interview with Tom Schwartz, March 29, 2010.

13. Frank Dolson, "Nickerson's 20-Yd. Kick Sinks Navy," *Philadelphia Inquirer*, November 29, 1964, section 3, 1; Danzig, "Streak Ends at 5," S3.

14. Dolson, "Nickerson's 20-Yd. Kick Sinks Navy," section 3, 1; Danzig, "Streak Ends at 5," S1, S3; interview with Sam Champi, February 11, 2010; "Individual Statistics for Army–Navy Game," *Washington Post*, November 29, 1964, 7; interview with Barry Nickerson, February 12, 2010.

15. Lincoln A. Werden, "Dietzel Confesses: 'Biggest Booboo' Was Made by Him," *New York Times*, December 1, 1964, 56.

16. Frank Litsky, "Long, Gray Wait Ends for Corps," *New York Times*, November 29, 1964, S2; Mervin Hyman, "A Second Fiddle Finishes First," *Sports Illustrated*, December 7, 1964, SI Vault.

17. Carroll Kilpatrick, "LBJ Decries Talk of Wider Viet War," *Washington Post*, November 29, 1964, 1. On deaths for class of 1965, see George Vecsey, "Honoring a Coach and an Upset," *New York Times*, July 20, 2009, D2. On deaths for class of 1966, see Rick Atkinson, *The Long Gray Line: West Point's Class of 1966* (London: Collins, 1990), 3. Figures on Vietnam from Department of Defense Manpower Center, "Vietnam War Allied Troops Levels, 1960–73."

18. Werden, "Army Manpower is at Low Point," 49.

19. William A. Knowlton, "Fellow Graduates and Friends of the Military Academy," *Assembly*, December 1973, 2; Gordon S. White Jr., "Army Plans More 'Realistic' Look at Football Foes," *New York Times*, November 28, 1973, 53.

20. Lewis Sorley, *A Better War: The Unexamined Victories and Final Tragedy of America's Last Years in Vietnam* (New York: Harcourt, 1999), 1–16; Vecsey, "Honoring a Coach and an Upset," D2; *The Pentagon Papers* (New York: New York Times, 1971), 522, 567, 579–80.

21. Interview with Bill Zadel, February 26, 2010. MacArthur's quote is from his West Point farewell speech of May 12, 1962; text is from *Assembly* (Summer 1962): 15.

22. Fallows, "What Did You Do in the Class War, Daddy?" 5–19; draft figures in David Frum, *How We Got Here: The 70s: The Decade That Brought You Modern Life (For Better or Worse)* (New York: Basic Books, 2000), 85; Russell F. Weigley, "360 Pros Reported Exempt from Draft," *New York Times*, April 8, 1967, S23; "Football and America: The Vietnam War Honor Roll," Pro Football Hall of Fame, Canton, Ohio, http://www.profootballhof.com/history/general/war/vietnam/honor_roll.aspx.

1. IKE'S TELEGRAM

1. Telegram with Ike's handwritten changes, November 27, 1964, from Eisenhower's Post-Presidential Paper in Eisenhower Presidential Library (hereafter EPL). See also Ross Wollen, "The 'Ike Telegram,'" *Assembly*, Novem-

ber–December 2004, 51; Paul Dietzel to Dwight D. Eisenhower, December 16, 1964, EPL.

2. Michael Korda, *Ike: An American Hero* (New York: HarperCollins, 2007), 12, 82; Dwight Eisenhower, long-distance telephone call in 1945 to Army team, November 29, 1945, EPL. See also Earl H. Blaik with Tim Cohane, *You Have to Pay the Price* (New York: Holt, Rinehart, and Winston, 1960), 210.

3. Dwight Eisenhower, telegram to Colonel Red Blaik, December 1, 1950, in Pre-Presidential Papers, EPL; Dwight Eisenhower, letter to Colonel Red Blaik, November 8, 1957, EPL. See also James Blackwell, *On Brave Old Army Team: The Cheating Scandal that Rocked the Nation: West Point, 1951* (Novato, CA: Presidio Press, 1996), 287–88; Wollen, "The 'Ike Telegram,'" 50; Stephen E. Ambrose, *Eisenhower: Soldier and President* (New York: Simon and Schuster, 2003), 25, 219.

4. Wollen, "The 'Ike Telegram,'" 50; "Bradley Scores 'Monty' on Gap," *New York Times*, January 3, 1965, 17; Dwight D. Eisenhower to Cadet A. Ross Wollen, November 27, 1964, EPL; Ambrose, *Eisenhower*, 25.

5. Wollen, "The 'Ike Telegram,'" 50, 53. Ike's greeting of Rollie Stichweh in Gene Roberts, "Eisenhower Rejoins His West Point Class of Stars," *New York Times*, June 5, 1965, 1. Rollie Stichweh's record of lunch with Eisenhower in e-mail, December 6, 2011.

6. Eisenhower telegram with Ike's handwritten changes, November 27, 1964, EPL.

7. Dwight D. Eisenhower, *At Ease: Stories I Tell to Friends* (Garden City: Doubleday and Company, 1967), 7; letter from Dwight D. Eisenhower, n.d., in Gene Schoor, *100 Years of Army–Navy Football* (New York: Henry Holt, 1989), 46.

8. Alexander M. "Babe" Weyand, "The Athletic Cadet Eisenhower," *Assembly*, Spring 1968, 11; Eisenhower, *At Ease*, 13.

9. "Good linebacker" quote and *New York Sun* quote in Weyand, "The Athletic Cadet Eisenhower," 12–13, 56; "Army Expects Victory," *New York Times*, November 30, 1912, 11; *Howitzer*, 1915, 80; Carlo D'Este, *Eisenhower: A Soldier's Life* (New York: Henry Holt, 2002), 67–68.

10. Eisenhower, *At Ease*, 14–15; Korda, *Ike*, 93–94.

11. Eisenhower, *At Ease*, 15–16; Korda, *Ike*, 94–95.

12. Eisenhower, *At Ease*, 14–16; John Gunther, *Eisenhower: The Man and the Symbol* (New York: Harper and Brothers, 1952), 34.

13. Weyand, "The Athletic Cadet Eisenhower," 56.

14. Ambrose, *Eisenhower*, 28; Eisenhower, *At Ease*, 16.

15. William C. Westmoreland, *A Soldier Reports* (New York: Da Capo Press, 1989), 32.

16. Eisenhower telegrams cited in Jack Cleary, "A Presidential Tradition," *Army vs. Navy*, Program for 109th Game, December 6, 2008, 20.

17. Paul Dietzel to Dwight D. Eisenhower, December 16, 1964, EPL; Dwight D. Eisenhower to Paul Dietzel, December 30, 1964, EPL.

18. Wollen, "The 'Ike Telegram,'" 52.

2. WESTMORELAND AND HIS COACH

1. William C. Westmoreland, *A Soldier Reports* (New York: Da Capo Press, 1989), 32.

2. "West Point to Get New Chief July 1," *New York Times*, May 14, 1960, 9; "Combat-Ready General," *New York Times*, April 27, 1964, 6; Craig R. Whitney and Eric Pace, "William C. Westmoreland Is Dead at 91," *New York Times*, July 20, 2005, A20; Patricia Sullivan, "General Commanded Troops in Vietnam," *Washington Post*, July 19, 2005; Thomas E. Ricks, *The Generals: American Military Command from World War II to Today* (New York: Penguin Press, 2012), 235.

3. Don Moser, "Westmoreland, the Four-Star Eagle Scout: Starched Courtly Man Gambles to Win the War," *Life*, November 11, 1966, 69; interview with Rollie Stichweh, November 12, 2012.

4. "Combat-Ready General," 6; Westmoreland, *A Soldier Reports*, 18, 32.

5. William Westmoreland, "Plain Talk," *Assembly*, Fall 1960, 1.

6. William Westmoreland, "Plain Talk," *Assembly*, Winter 1961, 1.

7. Lincoln A. Werden, "Army Fans Insist on Cadet Victory," *New York Times*, November 30, 1961, 44; Hall quoted in William J. Briordy, "Hall Out as Army Coach: Job Open to Non-Alumnus," *New York Times*, December 10, 1961, S1.

8. "Hall Candidate to Succeed Blaik," *New York Times*, January 15, 1959, 40; "The New Army Head Coach," *New York Times*, February 1, 1959, S1.

9. Adams quoted in "Hall Out as Army Coach," S1.

10. William Westmoreland, "Plain Talk," *Assembly*, Winter 1962, 1.

11. Briordy, "Hall Out as Army Coach," S1.

12. Westmoreland quote in Ricks, *The Generals*, 232.

13. Paul F. Dietzel, *Call Me Coach: A Life in College Football* (Baton Rouge: Louisiana State University Press, 2008), 30–97; interview with Paul Dietzel, March 5, 2010; Joseph M. Sheehan, "Football Now Fun to L.S.U. Coach," *New York Times*, December 6, 1958, 31; interview with John Seymour, November 6, 2012.

14. Joseph M. Sheehan, "Dietzel Signed to Coach Army for Five Years," *New York Times*, January 7, 1962, 181; Joseph M. Sheehan, "Dietzel Obtains Release

from L.S.U. to Sign as Football Coach at Army," *New York Times*, January 6, 1962, 14; "Dietzel Maps Plans with Aides after Signing as Army's Coach," *New York Times*, January 8, 1962, 30; Dietzel quoted in John Underwood, "Pepsodent Paul at the Point," *Sports Illustrated*, May 28, 1962, SI Vault.

15. Dietzel quoted in Sheehan, "Dietzel Signed to Coach Army for Five Years," 181.

16. Sheehan, "Dietzel Obtains Release from L.S.U. to Sign as Football Coach at Army," 14; "Dietzel Maps Plans with Aides after Signing as Army's Coach," 30; Sheehan, "Dietzel Signed to Coach Army for Five Years," *New York Times*, 181.

17. On formal contact between Westmoreland and Middleton, see Westmoreland, *A Soldier Reports*, 226.

18. On Dietzel's comparison of his leaving West Point to his departure from LSU, see "L.S.U. Acts Today on Dietzel Shift," *New York Times*, January 5, 1962, 21; Paul Dietzel and Mervin Heyman, "I Have Never Broken a Contract," *Sports Illustrated*, September 19, 1966, SI Vault.

19. "Dietzel Weighs West Point Job," *New York Times*, January 2, 1962, 35; "Army Due to Sign Dietzel This Week," 29; "Opposition at L.S.U.," *New York Times*, January 3, 1962, 29.

20. Sheehan, "Dietzel Obtains Release from L.S.U. to Sign as Football Coach at Army," 14; "Bill for More Cadets Is Passed by Senate," *New York Times*, August 10, 1962, 2; Arthur Daley, "Sports of the Times," *New York Times*, January 9, 1962, 26.

21. Dietzel, *Call Me Coach*, 107.

22. Blaik on Dietzel in Underwood, "Pepsodent Paul at the Point." The cartoon is reproduced in Dietzel, *Call Me Coach*, 106.

23. Joseph M. Sheehan, "Army Welcomes Dietzel's Three-Team Football," *New York Times*, May 6, 1962, 225; Joe Cahill, "Down the Field," *Assembly*, Spring 1962, 19.

24. Underwood, "Pepsodent Paul at the Point"; "Cadets Impress as Drills Close," *New York Times*, May 13, 1962, S3.

25. Rex Lardner, "Supercharged Aphorist," *Sports Illustrated*, November 26, 1962; SI Vault; Dietzel, *Call Me Coach*, 110.

26. Lincoln A. Werden, "Army Calls Staubach Key Man," *New York Times*, November 29, 1962, 47; Lincoln A. Werden, "Ace Quarterback Downed in Effigy," *New York Times*, November 30, 1962, 30; Lardner, "Supercharged Aphorist."

27. Dietzel quoted in Robert L. Teague, "Dietzel Says Blocking and Tackling Were Only Differences between Teams," *New York Times*, December 2, 1962, 253.

28. William Westmoreland, "Plain Talk," *Assembly*, Winter 1963, 1.

29. Frank Litsky, "Long Gray Wait Ends for Corps," *New York Times,* November 29, 1964, S2; Lincoln A. Werden, "Dietzel Confesses: 'Biggest Booboo' Was Made by Him," *New York Times*, December 1, 1964, 56.

3. DOUGLAS MACARTHUR'S FAREWELL

1. Interview with John Johnson, November 24, 2012.

2. "Text of General MacArthur's Address to a Joint Meeting of Congress," *New York Times*, April 20, 1951, 4; James Reston, "Profound Division in Capital Caused by General's Speech," *New York Times*, April 20, 1951, 1. In addition, see "President Truman's Statement of Regret in Announcing the Relieving of MacArthur," *New York Times*, April 11, 1951.

3. "Sylvanus Thayer Award Presented to General MacArthur," *Assembly*, Summer 1962, 12–13; Arnold H. Lubasch, "West Point Rites Honor MacArthur," *New York Times*, May 13, 1962, 73.

4. The description of what the players were wearing when they listened to MacArthur is from an interview with John Seymour, November 6, 2012; Paul F. Dietzel, *Call Me Coach: A Life in College Football* (Baton Rouge: Louisiana State University Press, 2008), 128–30; Lubasch, "West Point Rites Honor MacArthur," 73.

5. William Manchester, *American Caesar: Douglas MacArthur, 1880–1964* (Boston: Little, Brown, 1978), 56, 117–27; Geoffrey Perrett, *Old Soldiers Never Die: The Life of Douglas MacArthur* (New York: Random House, 1996), 114–23; Douglas MacArthur, *Reminiscences* (New York: McGraw Hill, 1964), 78–82; Lance Betros, *Carved from Granite: West Point Since 1902* (College Station: Texas A&M Press, 2012), 44–45; Earl H. Blaik with Tim Cohane, *You Have to Pay the Price* (New York: Holt, Rinehart and Winston, 1960), 37; Tim Cohane, *Gridiron Grenadiers: The Story of West Point Football* (New York: G. P. Putnam's and Sons, 1948), 122; "West Point Rally Falls Just Short," *New York Times*, October 23, 1921, 94; "Army Holds Yale to Tie at 7 to 7," *New York Times*, October 29, 1922, 26.

6. Blaik, *You Have to Pay the Price*, 39, 32, 312, 302, 248, 204; Earl "Red" Blaik, "A Cadet Under MacArthur," *Assembly*, Spring 1964, 8–11; Perrett, *Old Soldiers Never Die*, 120–22.

7. "Text of MacArthur's West Point Farewell, May 12, 1962," *Assembly*, Summer 1962, 14–15.

8. William C. Westmoreland, *A Soldier Reports* (New York: Da Capo Press, 1989), 34–35, 39–40.

9. Don Moser, "Starched, Courtly Man Gambles to Win the War," *Life*, November 11, 1966, 68–82.

10. Lewis Sorley, *A Better War: The Unexamined Victories and Final Tragedy of America's Last Years in Vietnam* (New York: Harcourt, 1999), 1–6.

11. Stanley Karnow, *Vietnam: A History* (New York: Penguin Books, 1984), 682–84. Troop figures from Department of Defense Manpower Data Center, http://www.americanwarlibrary.com/vietnam/vwatl.htm.

12. On President Kennedy's decision to begin the gradual withdrawal of American military personnel stationed in Vietnam, see James K. Galbraith, "Exit Strategy," *Boston Review*, October–November 2003; James K. Galbraith, "Kennedy, Vietnam and Iraq," *Salon.com*, November 22, 2003; Robert S. McNamara, *In Retrospect: The Tragedy and Lessons of Vietnam* (New York: Times Books, Random House, 1995), x.

13. Robert Dallek, *An Unfinished Life: John F. Kennedy, 1917–1963* (New York: Little, Brown, 2004), 353–54. The response of President Kennedy and Attorney General Kennedy to MacArthur is from Arthur Schlesinger Jr., *Robert Kennedy and His Times* (Boston: Houghton Mifflin, 1978), 703–4.

14. Earl "Red" Blaik, *The Red Blaik Story* (New Rochelle, NY: Arlington House, 1974), 498; "Cadets Impress as Drills Close," *New York Times*, May 13, 1962, S3.

15. Interview with John Seymour, November 6, 2012. "We'll follow him again" quote is from the 1965 West Point Yearbook, *Howitzer*, 285.

4. SAFETY

1. John Underwood, "Pepsodent Paul at the Point," *Sports Illustrated*, May 28, 1962, SI Vault; Lincoln A. Werden, "Ace Quarterback Downed in Effigy," *New York Times*, November 30, 1962, 38; Rex Lardner, "Supercharged Aphorist," *Sports Illustrated*, November 26, 1962, SI Vault.

2. Mervin Hyman, "A Second Fiddle Finishes First," *Sports Illustrated*, December 7, 1964, SI Vault.

3. Paul Dietzel quoted in Byron Roberts, "Stichweh Full of Praise for Navy's Linebackers," *Washington Post*, November 29, 1964, C7.

4. Staubach quoted in John Dell, "Army Closed in from All Sides," *Philadelphia Inquirer*, November 29, 1964, 7; Jesse Abramson, "98,616 See Staubach's 1-Man Show," *New York Herald Tribune*, December 2, 1962, III, 2; Army Athletic Department, "Final Individual Statistics for 1963 Army–Navy Game," December 7, 1963.

5. Interview with Sonny Stowers, April 1, 2010.

6. Roberts, "Stichweh Full of Praise for Navy's Linebackers," C7; interview with Sonny Stowers, April 1, 2010; Staubach quoted in Dell, "Army Closed in from All Sides," 7.

7. Interview with Sonny Stowers, May 22, 2014; Stowers quoted in Roberts, "Stichweh Full of Praise for Navy's Linebackers," C7; Allison Danzig, "Streak Ends at 5," *New York Times*, November 29, 1964, S1, S3.

8. Interview with John Johnson, November 24, 2012; Allison Danzig, "Army and Navy Battle to 7–7 Tie," *New York Times*, November 28, 1965, S1–S2; Lincoln A. Werden, "Mistakes, Injury Cited by Dietzel," *New York Times*, November 28, 1965, S2; Bus Ham, "Army–Navy Struggle to 7–7 Deadlock," *Washington Post*, December 28, 1965, C1.

9. On Stowers as an outstanding lineman of the game, see Roberts, "Stichweh Full of Praise for Navy's Linebackers," C7; interview with Sonny Stowers, October 12, 2012.

10. Interview with Sonny Stowers, April 1, 2010; interview with Sonny Stowers, October 12, 2012.

11. Interview with Sonny Stowers, October 12, 2010; interview with Sonny Stowers, April 1, 2010.

12. "Gray Eleven Rallies Behind Passing of Johnson to Turn Back Blue, 23–19," *New York Times*, December 26, 1965, S13; interview with Charlotte Stowers, May 22, 2014.

13. Interview with Sonny Stowers, April 1, 2010; interview with Sonny Stowers, October 12, 2012; interview with Sonny Stowers, May 22, 2014.

14. Interview with Sonny Stowers, October 12, 2012; interview with Sonny Stowers, April 1, 2010; interview with Charlotte Stowers, May 22, 2014; interview with Sonny Stowers, May 22, 2014.

15. Interview with Sonny Stowers, April 1, 2010; interview with Charlotte Stowers, May 22, 2014.

16. Interview with Sonny Stowers, October 12, 2012; interview with Sonny Stowers, April 1, 2010; interview with Sonny Stowers, May 22, 2014.

5. THE GANG'S ALL HERE

1. Interview with John Seymour, February 16, 2010; Army Football Game Records, 1964.

2. Frank Dolson, "Nickerson's 20-Yd. Kick Sinks Navy," *Philadelphia Inquirer*, November 29, 1964, section III, 1.

3. Interview with John Seymour, March 12, 2010; interview with John Seymour, April 28, 2014; interview with John Seymour, February 16, 2010.

4. Interview with John Seymour, March 12, 2010; interview with John Seymour, February 16, 2010.

5. Interview with John Seymour, April 28, 2014; interview with John Seymour, February 16, 2010; interview with John Seymour, March 12, 2010; Jim

Ogle, "Army Aims to Put Nix on Sixth Navy Victory," *New York Telegram*, November 28, 1964.

6. Interview with John Seymour, February 16, 2010; interview with John Seymour, March 12, 2010.

7. Earl Blaik with Tim Cohane, *You Have to Pay the Price* (New York: Holt, Reinhart and Winston, 1960), 241; "16 Houston," *Sports Illustrated*, September 11, 1967, SI Vault; interview with John Seymour, November 6, 2012.

8. Interview with John Seymour, November 6, 2012; interview with John Seymour, March 12, 2010; interview with John Seymour, February 16, 2010.

9. Interview with John Seymour, February 16, 2010.

10. Interview with John Seymour, March 12, 2010; interview with John Seymour, April 28, 2014; interview with John Seymour, November 6, 2012.

11. Interview with John Seymour, March 12, 2010; interview with John Seymour, February 16, 2010; Seymour M. Hersh, *My Lai 4: A Report on the Massacre and its Aftermath* (New York: Random House, 1970), 16–43.

12. Interview with John Seymour, November 6, 2012; interview with John Seymour, March 12, 2010; interview with John Seymour, February 16, 2010.

13. Interview with John Seymour, April 28, 2014; interview with John Seymour, November 6, 2012.

14. Interview with John Seymour, February 16, 2012; interview with John Seymour, March 12, 2010.

15. Interview with John Seymour, November 6, 2012; interview with John Seymour, March 12, 2010; interview with John Seymour, February 16, 2010.

16. Interview with John Seymour, March 12, 2010; interview with John Seymour, February 16, 2010; interview with Donna Seymour, April 28, 2014.

17. Interview with John Seymour, March 12, 2010; interview with John Seymour, February 16, 2010; interview with John Seymour, April 28, 2014; e-mail from John Seymour, May 19, 2014.

6. TOUCHDOWN CATCH

1. Interview with Sam Champi, February 11, 2010.

2. Bus Ham, "Nickerson's Kick Turns Tide, 11–8," *Washington Post*, November 29, 1964, C1; interview with Sam Champi, February 11, 2010.

3. Frank Dolson, "Nickerson's 20-Yard Kick Sinks Navy," *Philadelphia Inquirer*, November 29, 1964, section III, 1, 7; interview with Sam Champi, February 11, 2010.

4. Allison Danzig, "Streak Ends at 5," *New York Times*, November 29, 1964, S1; interview with Sam Champi, February 11, 2010; interview with Sam Champi, August 30, 2014.

5. Shirley Povich, "This Morning," *Washington Post*, November 28, 1965, C1; Bus Ham, "Army–Navy Struggle to a 7–7 Deadlock," *Washington Post*, November 28, 1965, C1; interview with Sam Champi, February 11, 2010; interview with Sam Champi, October 26, 2012.

6. Interview with Sam Champi, February 11, 2010.

7. Interview with Sam Champi, October 26, 2012; interview with Sam Champi, February 11, 2010.

8. Interview with Sam Champi, October 26, 2012; interview with Sam Champi, February 11, 2010.

9. Interview with Sam Champi, October 26, 2012.

10. Interview with Sam Champi, February 11, 2010; interview with Sam Champi, April 28, 2014; interview with Sam Champi, October 26, 2012.

11. Interview with Russi Champi, April 28, 2014; interview with Sam Champi, April 28, 2014.

12. Interview with Sam Champi, April 28, 2014.

13. Interview with Sam Champi, February 11, 2010; interview with Sam Champi, June 3, 2014.

14. Interview with Sam Champi, October 26, 2012; interview with Sam Champi, February 11, 2010.

7. ON A HIGH

1. Rollie Stichweh quote in Frank Dolson, "Nickerson's 20-Yd. Kick Sinks Navy," *Philadelphia Inquirer*, November 29, 1964, section III, 8.

2. Ibid., 1, 8.

3. Roger Staubach, *Staubach: First Down, Lifetime to Go* (Waco, TX: Word Books, 1974), 112. See also Roger Staubach quote in John Dell, "Army Closed in from All Sides All Afternoon," *Philadelphia Inquirer*, November 29, 1964, section III, 1, 7.

4. Interview with Peter Braun, April 29, 2010; interview with Peter Braun, October 29, 2012; "Gray Eleven Rallies Behind Passing of Johnson to Turn Back Blue, 23-19," *New York Times*, December 26, 1965, S13; Westfield Athletic Hall of Fame, http://westfieldmj.com/wahf/profiles.htm.

5. Interview with Peter Braun, May 3, 2014; interview with Peter Braun, October 29, 2012; interview with Peter Braun, April 29, 2010.

6. On Al Vanderbush and the 1958 Army team, see Earl H. Blaik with Tim Cohane, *You Have to Pay the Price* (New York: Holt, Rinehart and Winston, 1960), 378; interview with Peter Braun, May 3, 2014; interview with Peter Braun, October 29, 2012; interview with Peter Braun, April 29, 2010; Westfield Athletic Hall of Fame, http://westfieldnj.com/wahf/profiles.htm; "MPH An-

nounces First Inductees into New Athletic Hall of Fame," http://www.mph.net/about/athletic-HOF.

7. Interview with Peter Braun, October 29, 2012; interview with Peter Braun, April 29, 2010.

8. Interview with Peter Braun, October 29, 2012; interview with Peter Braun, June 27, 2013; interview with Peter Braun, April 29, 2010.

9. Interview with Peter Braun, April 29, 2010; interview with Peter Braun, May 3, 2014.

10. Interview with Peter Braun, May 3, 2014; interview with Peter Braun, October 29, 2012; e-mail from Peter Braun, October 29, 2011; Robert Mann, *A Grand Delusion: America's Descent into Vietnam* (New York: Basic Books, 2001), 661.

11. Interview with Peter Braun, April 29, 2010; interview with Peter Braun, October 29, 2012.

12. Interview with Peter Braun, May 3, 2014; interview with Lucille Braun, June 27, 2013; interview with Lucille Braun, May 3, 2014. See also Lewis Sorley, *A Better War: The Unexamined Victories and Final Tragedy of America's Last Years in Vietnam* (New York: Harcourt, 1999), 1–9.

8. IRON MAN

1. Interview with John Johnson, February 26, 2010; interview with John Johnson, November 24, 2012; John Dell, "Army Closed in from All Sides All Afternoon," *Philadelphia Inquirer*, November 29, 1964, S7.

2. Interview with John Johnson, February 26, 2010; interview with John Johnson, November 24, 2012.

3. Allison Danzig, "Cadets Turn Back Boston U. By 30-0," *New York Times*, September 22, 1963, 179; interview with John Johnson, November 24, 2012.

4. Frank Dolson, "Cadets on 2 as Gun Goes Off," *Philadelphia Inquirer*, December 8, 1963, S1; interview with John Johnson, November 24, 2012.

5. Bus Ham, "Nickerson's Kick Turns Tide, 11–8," *Washington Post*, November 29, 1964, C1; interview with John Johnson, November 24, 2012.

6. Interview with John Johnson, November 24, 2012; interview with John Johnson, February 26, 2010.

7. Interview with John Johnson, November 24, 2012.

8. Interview with John Johnson, November 24, 2012; interview with John Johnson, February 26, 2010; interview with John Johnson, May 9, 2014.

9. R. W. Apple Jr., "Bernard Fall Killed in Vietnam by a Mine while with Marines," *New York Times*, February 22, 1967, 1; interview with John Johnson, November 24, 2012; interview with John Johnson, February 26, 2010; Bernard

Weinraub, "Vietnam Protest Blocks Fifth Avenue," *New York Times*, May 16, 1965, 1.

10. Interview with John Johnson, November 24, 2012; interview with John Johnson, February 26, 2010; Bob Brewin and Sydney Shaw, *Vietnam on Trial: Westmoreland vs. CBS* (New York: Atheneum, 1987), 38–46; interview with Mary Johnson, May 9, 2014.

11. Lewis Sorley, *A Better War: The Unexamined Victories and Final Tragedy of America's Last Years in Vietnam* (New York: Harcourt, 1999), 16, 343–46; interview with John Johnson, November 24, 2012; interview with John Johnson, February 26, 2010; interview with John Johnson, May 9, 2014.

12. Interview with John Johnson, February 26, 2010; interview with John Johnson, May 9, 2014; interview with John Johnson, November 24, 2012.

13. *The Pentagon Papers* (New York: New York Times, 1971), 522, 567–68; interview with John Johnson, February 26, 2010; interview with John Johnson, November 24, 2012.

14. Interview with John Johnson, February 26, 2010; interview with John Johnson, May 9, 2014; Robert Mann, *A Grand Delusion: America's Descent into Vietnam* (New York: Basic Books, 2001), 680–81.

9. GAME CHANGER

1. Statistics from the Official Program for the 1964 Army–Navy Game; interview with Rollie Stichweh, November 12, 2012.

2. Interview with Sam Champi, February 11, 2010.

3. Frank Dolson, "Cadets on 2 as Gun Goes Off," *Philadelphia Inquirer*, December 8, 1963, S1; Rip Miller in an interview with Paul Dietzel, March 5, 2010; Mervin Hyman, "A Second Fiddle Finishes First," *Sports Illustrated*, December 7, 1964, SI Vault.

4. Allison Danzig, "Streak Ends at 5," *New York Times*, November 29, 1964, S1.

5. Interview with Rollie Stichweh, April 5, 2010.

6. Interview with Sam Champi, February 11, 2010; e-mail from Rollie Stichweh, August 30, 2014.

7. Interview with Rollie Stichweh, November 12, 2012.

8. Dan Jenkins, "Two Yards and the Clock," *Sports Illustrated*, December 16, 1963, 59–60; interview with Rollie Stichweh, November 12, 2012.

9. Interview with Rollie Stichweh, November 12, 2012.

10. Gerald Eskenazi, "Decisive Ruling Upsets Dietzel," *New York Times*, December 9, 1963, 50; Leonard Koppett, "Dietzel Takes the Blame for Army's Failure to Get Off Last Play," *New York Times*, December 10, 1963, 74.

11. Interview with Rollie Stichweh, November 12, 2012; interview with Rollie Stichweh, April 5, 2010.

12. Interview with Rollie Stichweh, November 12, 2012.

13. George Vecsey, "Friendships Wrapped in Army–Navy Rivalry," *New York Times*, September 27, 2012, B12; interview with Rollie Stichweh, November 12, 2012.

14. E-mail from Rollie Stichweh, December 6, 2011; interview with Rollie Stichweh, May 19, 2014; Eisenhower quote in Gene Roberts, "Eisenhower Rejoins His West Point 'Class of Stars,'" *New York Times*, June 5, 1965, 1.

15. William N. Wallace, "All-America Contest in Buffalo Opens Football Season Tonight," *New York Times*, June 26, 1965, 22; West Point information packet for Rollie Stichweh on his selection to West Point Sports Hall of Fame; Darrell Royal quote in Allison Danzig, "Stichweh Hailed in Army's Gallant But Futile Stand Against Texas Eleven," *New York Times*, October 5, 1964, 48; interview with Rollie Stichweh, May 19, 2014; interview with Rollie Stichweh, April 5, 2010.

16. Interview with Rollie Stichweh, November 12, 2012; interview with Carole Stichweh, May 19, 2014; Vescey, "Friendships Wrapped in Army–Navy Rivalry," B12.

17. Interview with Carole Stichweh, May 19, 2014; interview with Rollie Stichweh, November 12, 2012; George Vecsey, "Honoring a Coach and an Upset," *New York Times*, July 20, 2009, D2.

18. Interview with Rollie Stichweh, November 12, 2012; interview with Rollie Stichweh, April 5, 2010; interview with Rollie Stichweh, May 19, 2014.

19. Interview with Rollie Stichweh, April 5, 2010; interview with Carole Stichweh, May 19, 2014; interview with Rollie Stichweh, November 12, 2012.

20. Interview with Rollie Stichweh, May 19, 2014; West Point information packet for Rollie Stichweh on his selection to West Point Sports Hall of Fame.

21. Interview with Rollie Stichweh, May 19, 2014; interview with Rollie Stichweh, April 5, 2010; Bob Brewin and Sydney Shaw, *Vietnam on Trial: Westmoreland vs. CBS* (New York: Atheneum, 1987), 211, 345–47; Renata Adler, *Reckless Disregard: Westmoreland v. CBS et al.; Sharon v. Time* (New York: Alfred A. Knopf, 1986), 3–5, 10.

22. Interview with Rollie Stichweh, May 19, 2014.

10. THE MARINE

1. Interview with Bill Zadel, February 19, 2010; Bus Ham, "Nickerson's Kick Turns Tide, 11–8," *Washington Post*, November 29, 1964, C1.

2. Interview with Bill Zadel, February 26, 2010; interview with Bill Zadel, February 19, 2010; John Dell, "Army Closed in from All Sides All Afternoon," *Philadelphia Inquirer*, November 29, 1964, section 3, 1, 7.

3. Frank Dolson, "Nickerson's 20-Yd. Kick Sinks Navy," *Philadelphia Inquirer*, November 29, 1964, 1, 8.

4. Interview with Bill Zadel, February 19, 2010; interview with Bill Zadel, February 26, 2010; Dolson, "Nickerson's 20-Yd. Kick Sinks Navy"; Paul Dietzel quote in Army–Navy 1964 Official Program; Bill Zadel, "USMA Class of 1965: Class History Project," January 2011, courtesy of Betty Zadel.

5. Interview with Bill Zadel, February 19, 2010; interview with Bill Zadel, February 26, 2010; Rollie Stichweh, "Eulogy for Bill Zadel," Old Cadet Chapel, October 27, 2011; George Vecsey, "A Love Story Affirmed in Time of War," *New York Times*, October 23, 2011, S6; Zadel, "USMA Class of 1965: Class History Project."

6. Interview with Bill Zadel, February 26, 2010; interview with Bill Zadel, February 19, 2010; Vecsey, "A Love Story Affirmed in Time of War," S6; Zadel, "USMA Class of 1965: Class History Project."

7. Interview with Bill Zadel, February 26, 2010; interview with Bill Zadel, February 19, 2010; Vecsey, "A Love Story Affirmed in a Time of War," S6; West Point Obituary for Mr. C. William Zadel, http://www.west-point.org/users/usma 1965/25571/; Zadel, "USMA Class of 1965: Class History Project"; interview with Betty Zadel, May 2, 2014.

8. Interview with Bill Zadel, February 19, 2010; Vecsey, "A Love Story Affirmed in Time of War," S6; interview with Betty Zadel, May 2, 2014.

9. Interview with Bill Zadel, February 19, 2010; interview with Bill Zadel, February 26, 2010.

10. Interview with Bill Zadel, February 19, 2010; interview with Bill Zadel, February 26, 2010; Milton Viorst, *Fire in the Streets: America in the 1960s* (New York: Simon and Schuster, 1970), 455–62.

11. Interview with Bill Zadel, February 26, 2010; interview with Bill Zadel, February 19, 2010; interview with Betty Zadel, May 2, 2014.

12. Interview with Bill Zadel, February 19, 2010; interview with Bill Zadel, February 26, 2010; interview with Betty Zadel, May 2, 2014; West Point Obituary for Mr. C. William Zadel; Zadel, "USMA Class of 1965: Class History Project."

13. Zadel, "USMA Class of 1965: Class History Project"; interview with Betty Zadel, May 2, 2014.

EPILOGUE

1. Interview with John Johnson, February 26, 2010; interview with Sam Champi, October 26, 2012.

2. Lewis Sorley, *A Better War: The Unexamined Victories and Final Tragedy of America's Last Years in Vietnam* (New York: Harcourt, 1999), 292; Robert Leider, "Why They Leave: Resignations from the USMA Class of 1966" (Washington, DC: Department of the Army, July 1970), 1-1-1; Rick Atkinson, *The Long Gray Line: The American Journey of West Point's Class of 1966* (London: Collins, 1990), 347.

3. Atkinson, *The Long Gray Line*, 347; Leider, "Why They Leave," 1-1-1.

4. Interview with Rollie Stichweh, November 12, 2012.

5. Interview with John Seymour, February 16, 2010; interview with Rollie Stichweh, April 5, 2010.

6. Interview with Bill Zadel, February 26, 2010.

7. Martin Arnold, "Cadets Give Resigning Chief Ovation," *New York Times*, March 18, 1970, 1; David Stout, "Gen. S. W. Koster, 86, Who Was Demoted After My Lai, Dies," *New York Times*, February 11, 2006; Koster quoted in Atkinson, *The Long Gray Line*, 319–20.

8. On "commissions and omissions," see Atkinson, *The Long Gray Line*, 320; Thomas Fleming, "West Point Cadets Now Say, 'Why Sir?'" *New York Times*, July 5, 1970, 126; Seymour M. Hersh, "33 Teachers at West Point Leave Army in 18 Months," *New York Times*, June 25, 1972, 1; Stout, "Gen. S. W. Koster, 86, Who Was Demoted After My Lai, Dies."

9. Interview with Rollie Stichweh, April 5, 2010; "Tom Cahill, 73, Football Coach at Army during the Vietnam War," *New York Times*, October 31, 1992; Gordon S. White Jr., "Law Cripples Army Recruiting," *New York Times*, November 30, 1973, 43; Joseph Ellis and Robert Moore, *School for Soldiers: West Point and the Profession of Arms* (New York: Oxford University Press, 1974), 199–201.

10. Knowlton and Cahill quoted in Gordon S. White Jr., "West Point Dismisses Cahill," *New York Times*, December 14, 1973, 61.

11. William A. Knowlton, "Plain Talk," *Assembly*, December 1973, 2; William A. Knowlton, "Plain Talk," *Assembly*, March 1973, 2; Schuder quoted in Gordon S. White Jr., "Army Plans More 'Realistic' Look at Football Foes," *New York Times*, November 28, 1973, 53.

12. Interview with John Seymour, March 12, 2010.

13. Interview with Peter Braun, October 29, 2012.

14. Richard Halloran, *My Name Is . . . Shinseki . . . and I Am a Soldier* (Honolulu: Hawaii Army Museum Society, 2004), 14.

15. Interview with Eric Shinseki, June 15, 2010; Peter J. Boyer, "A Different War," *New Yorker*, July 1, 2002.

16. Boyer, "A Different War"; Peter J. Boyer, "Downfall: How Donald Rumsfeld Reformed the Army and Lost Iraq," *New Yorker*, November 30, 2006, 56–64.

17. "Bush Looks to Marine to Lead NATO Forces," *New York Times*, April 12, 2002, A22; Eric Shinseki Testimony, "U.S. Senate Armed Services Committee Hearing on FY 2004 Defense Authorization," February 25, 2003, in Michael R. Gordon and General Bernard E. Trainor, *Cobra II: The Inside Story of the Invasion and Occupation of Iraq* (New York: Pantheon, 2006), 522.

18. Gordon and Trainor, *Cobra II*, 102–3; Thomas E. Ricks, *Fiasco: The American Military Adventure in Iraq* (New York: Penguin Press, 2006), 96, 117. Regarding the "on the cheap" charge, see Bernard Weinraub and Thom Shanker, "Rumsfeld Design for War Criticized on the Battlefield," *New York Times*, April 1, 2003, A1.

19. Paul Wolfowitz Testimony, "U.S. House Committee on the Budget Hearing on FY 2004 Department of Defense Budget Priorities," Transcript, February 27, 2003, 8; Rumsfeld quoted in Eric Schmitt, "Pentagon Contradicts General on Iraq Occupation Force's Size," *New York Times*, February 28, 2003, A1.

20. Text of Eric Shinseki Retirement Ceremony Speech, June 11, 2003, http://www.army,mil/features/ShinsekiFarewell/farewellremarks.htm.

21. Interview with Rollie Stichweh, April 5, 2010.

22. Interview with Bill Zadel, February 19, 2010.

23. Interview with Bill Zadel, February 26, 2010; interview with John Seymour, February 16, 2010; interview with John Seymour, November 6, 2012.

24. Interview with John Seymour, November 6, 2012.

25. Evan Thomas and John Barry, "Anatomy of a Revolt," *Newsweek*, April 24, 2006, 26; interview with Eric Shinseki, February 26, 2010.

26. Douglas Robinson, "West Point Class of '66 Eager to Fight," *New York Times*, June 8, 1966, 14; interview with Peter Braun, April 29, 2010; interview with Rhesa Barksdale, February 8, 2010; e-mail from Rhesa Barksdale, January 30, 2010; e-mail from Rhesa Barksdale, August 20, 2014; interview with Anne Dietzel, May 5, 2014.

27. Interview with Rhesa Barksdale, February 8, 2010; Murphy quoted in Lloyd E. Millegan, "Dietzel Signs 10-Year Pact as South Carolina Coach and Athletic Director," *New York Times*, April 7, 1966, 63; Arthur Daley, "Sports of the Times," *New York Times*, April 8, 1966, 16.

28. Paul Dietzel and Mervin Hyman, "I Have Never Broken a Contract," *Sports Illustrated*, September 19, 1966, SI Vault; "Gen. Bennett Takes Over as New Head of West Point," *New York Times*, January 11, 1966, 10; "Athletic

Directors Changed at West Point," *New York Times*, February 27, 1966, S7; interview with Paul Dietzel, March 5, 2010.

29. Interview with Paul Dietzel, March 5, 2010; Paul Dietzel, *Call Me Coach: A Life in College Football* (Baton Rouge: Louisiana State University Press, 2008), 133. Dietzel's report of conversation with General Bennett is from Dietzel and Hyman, "I Have Never Broken a Contract."

30. Interview with John Johnson, February 26, 2010.

31. Interview with Bill Zadel, February 26, 2010.

32. Interview with Paul Dietzel, March 5, 2010; description of Dietzel in Joseph M. Sheehan, "Dietzel Signed to Coach Army for Five Years," *New York Times*, June 7, 1962, 181; interview with John Seymour, March 12, 2010; George Vecsey, "Honoring a Coach and an Upset," *New York Times*, July 20, 2009, D2.

33. Interview with John Johnson, February 26, 2010.

34. Interview with Sonny Stowers, April 1, 2010.

35. Vecsey, "Honoring a Coach and an Upset," D2; interview with Bill Zadel, February 26, 2010.

36. Interview with Bill Zadel, February 26, 2010.

APPENDIX A

1. "Army Football Team Beat the Navy Eleven," *New York Times*, December 1, 1901, 2; "President to Attend Cadet Football Game," *New York Times*, November 29, 1901, 1.

2. "Football by the Cadets," *New York Times*, October 28, 1894, 6; Gene Schoor, *100 Years of Army–Navy Football: A Pictorial History of America's Most Colorful and Competitive Sports Rivalry* (New York: Henry Holt, 1989), 3, 19; Oswald Ernst to Adjutant General, December 12, 1893, in Stephen E. Ambrose, *Duty, Honor, Country: A History of West Point* (Baltimore: Johns Hopkins University Press, 1999), 308–9; Tim Cohane, *Gridiron Grenadiers: The Story of West Point Football* (New York: G. P. Putnam's Sons, 1948), 26–27.

3. Cohane, *Gridiron Grenadiers*, 5–7.

4. Schoor, *100 Years of Army–Navy Football*, 2–3.

5. John McA. Palmer, "How Football Came to West Point," *Assembly*, January 1943, 2–3; Ambrose, *Duty, Honor, Country*, 305.

6. "The Navy Whips the Army," *New York Times*, November 30, 1890, 1.

7. Palmer, "How Football Came to West Point," 2; "It Was a Battle Royal," *New York Times*, December 1, 1890, 3.

8. Palmer, "How Football Came to West Point," 3; Schoor, *100 Years of Army–Navy Football*, 11–12.

9. "Victory for West Point," *New York Times*, November 29, 1891, 2; Palmer, "How Football Came to West Point," 4, 10; Schoor, *100 Years of Army–Navy Football*, 10–14.

10. "Victory for the Middies," *New York Times*, November 27, 1892, 1; Cohane, *Gridiron Grenadiers*, 15, 21.

11. "Middies Again Triumphant," *New York Times*, December 3, 1893, 3.

12. "Less Football Freedom," *New York Times*, March 2, 1894, 6; "Football by the Cadets," 6; Schoor, *100 Years of Army–Navy Football*, 19–20.

13. Schoor, *100 Years of Army–Navy Football*, 20.

14. Harmon S. Graves, "Football at West Point," *Harper's Weekly*, January 1, 1898, 22; James Stewart, *The Black Knights of West Point: A History of Football at the United States Military Academy* (New York: Bradbury, Sayles, O'Neill Co., 1954), 254.

15. "The Navy Succumbs to Army's Prowess," *New York Times*, December 3, 1899, 1; Ambrose, *Duty, Honor, Country*, 310; "Navy Won at Football," *New York Times*, December 2, 1900, 8.

16. "Army Football Team Beat the Navy Eleven," 2; "President to Attend Cadet Football Game," 1; Ambrose, *Duty, Honor, Country*, 310.

17. "C. Daly to Go to West Point," *New York Times*, November 24, 1900; "Army Football Team Beat the Navy Eleven," 2; Schoor, *100 Years of Army–Navy Football*, 24; President Theodore Roosevelt quoted in Cohane, *Gridiron Grenadiers*, 45.

18. "Army Defeated Navy at Football," *New York Times*, November 30, 1902, 1; "Army and Navy Athletics," *New York Times*, December 13, 1902, 11; Cohane, *Gridiron Grenadiers*, 48–49.

19. Daly quoted in "Army Eleven Rated High," *New York Times*, November 28, 1916, 14; Cohane, *Gridiron Grenadiers*, 110–12; Schoor, *100 Years of Army–Navy Football*, 56.

20. "Army Defeated Navy at Football," 2; "Army Smothers Annapolis Team by 22–9 Score," *New York Times*, November 13, 1913, 1; "Merchants Want Army–Navy Game," *New York Times*, March 5, 1914, 7; "40,000 See Army Beat Navy, 14–0," *New York Times*, November 28, 1915, 1; "Army Conquers Navy, 15–7, Amid Cheers of 45,000," *New York Times*, November 26, 1916, S1.

21. "Cadet Byrne Dead; No Army–Navy Game," *New York Times*, November 1, 1909, 1; "Forward Pass Halts Revision of Code of Football Rules," *New York Times*, March 27, 1910, S1; "Wants Football Barred," *New York Times*, November 26, 1913, 12.

22. "Thorpe's Indians Crush West Point," *New York Times*, November 10, 1912, S1; Sally Jenkins, *The Real All Americans* (New York: Anchor Books, 2007), 282–86; "Notre Dame's Open Play Amazes Army," *New York Times*, November 2, 1913, S1.

23. March's quote can be found in William Manchester, *American Caesar: Douglas MacArthur, 1880–1964* (New York: Little, Brown, 1978), 116; Douglas MacArthur, *Reminiscences* (New York: McGraw-Hill, 1964), 80; Geoffrey Perret, *Old Soldiers Never Die: The Life of Douglas MacArthur* (New York: Random House, 1996), 115.

24. Earl "Red" Blaik, "A Cadet Under MacArthur," *Assembly*, Spring 1964, 8–11; Perret, *Old Soldiers Never Die*, 118–24; Manchester, *American Caesar*, 121–24.

25. Manchester, *American Caesar*, 56, 121–23; Perret, *Old Soldiers Never Die*, 119–21; Earl H. Blaik with Tim Cohane, *You Have to Pay the Price* (New York: Holt, Rinehart and Winston, 1960), 37; Cohane, *Gridiron Grenadiers*, 122.

26. Ambrose, *Duty, Honor, Country*, 315; Daly quoted in Cohane, *Gridiron Grenadiers*, 117.

27. Cohane, *Gridiron Grenadiers*, 117, 161; "West Point Rally Falls Just Short," *New York Times*, October 23, 1921, 94; "Army Holds Yale to Tie at 7 to 7," *New York Times*, October 29, 1922, 26; James R. Harrison, "Army's Alert Play Downs Notre Dame, 18–0, Before 80,000," *New York Times*, November 3, 1927, S1; James R. Harrison, "Sports' Greatest Pageant," *New York Times*, November 28, 1926, 1.

28. Schoor, *100 Years of Army–Navy Football*, 70–71, 78–81; Cohane, *Gridiron Grenadiers*, 161–66; Harrison, "Sports' Greatest Pageant," 1; Mercury quote in Harrison, "Army's Alert Play Downs Notre Dame, 18–0, Before 80,000," S1.

29. Winans quote in "Army and Navy End Football Relations on Eligibility Issue," *New York Times*, December 17, 1927, 1.

30. "Break of Army–Navy Aired in Congress," *New York Times*, December 20, 1927, 34; "Officials Cancel Army–Navy Game," *New York Times*, January 8, 1928, 179; "Move to Restore Army–Navy Game," *New York Times*, June 11, 1929, 27; "Army–Navy Break Widens," *New York Times,* October 31, 1929, 1; "greatest show in football" quote in "$500,000 Gate Today as Army Plays Navy," *New York Times*, December 13, 1990, 1.

31. Cagle quotes in "Cagle to Quit Army After Graduation," *New York Times*, May 10, 1930, 21.

32. Cohane, *Gridiron Grenadiers*, 174–76. For defense of Cagle by superintendent of West Point, see the same article, "Cagle to Quit Army After Graduation," 21; "Cagle Wed Secretly, Is Forced to Resign," *New York Times*, May 14, 1930, 22; "Leaving West Point 'Regretted' by Cagle," *New York Times*, May 16, 1930, 17.

33. Schoor, *100 Years of Army–Navy Football*, 82–83; "Army–Navy Football Game Here Lacks Only Agreement on Date," *New York Times*, November 14, 1930, 1; Harry Cross, "Battle Revives Old Pageantry of 2 Services," *New York*

Herald Tribune, December 14, 1930, section III, 1; "Army–Navy Game Plea Favorably Received," *New York Times*, May 29, 1931, 23; Richards Vidmer, "Pomp, Noise, Heroic Play Rock Stadium," *New York Herald Tribune*, December 13, 1931, section III, 1; "Army–Navy Renew Sports Relations," *New York Times*, September 1, 1932, 1.

34. "Notre Dame Upsets Army Eleven, 21–0, as 80,000 Look On," *New York Times*, November 27, 1932, S1; "Army to Play Navy on a New Gridiron," *New York Times*, April 1, 1936, 33; "First Lady a Fan in Throng at Game," *New York Times*, November 29, 1936, S1.

35. "Army Receptive to Rose Bowl Bid," *New York Times*, November 28, 1933, 31; "Cadets Hopes Blasted," *New York Times*, December 3, 1933, S1; Cohane, *Gridiron Grenadiers*, 189–90; "Sheridan, Army End, Breaks Neck in Game," *New York Times*, October 25, 1931, 1; "Sheridan, Army End, Dies of Football Injury," *New York Times*, October 27, 1931, 1; Schoor, *100 Years of Army–Navy Football*, 97. On protests from within West Point on the dangers of football, see "Kingsolving Decries Stress on Football," *New York Times*, January 14, 1932, 7.

36. Blaik with Cohane, *You Have to Pay the Price*, 171–72; Cohane, *Gridiron Grenadiers*, 201–2. For a more detailed analysis of the weight issue and Army politics, see Randy Roberts, *A Team for America: The Army–Navy Game that Rallied a Nation* (Boston: Houghton Mifflin, 2011), 17–19.

37. "Long Controversy Is Ended as Army Adopts 3-Year Sports Eligibility Rule," *New York Times*, December 8, 1937, 34; "Army Rule Affects Athletes on Jan. 1," *New York Times*, December 9, 1937, 34. On the rumors that President Franklin Roosevelt, with his Navy sympathies, was behind the rule change, see Hanson S. Baldwin, "Our 'Sailor President' Charts a Course," *New York Times*, April 3, 1938, 117.

38. Eichelberger quote in Blaik, *You Have to Pay the Price*, 169.

APPENDIX B

1. "Brig. Gen. Eichelberger Takes Up Duties as West Point Head, Succeeding Benedict," *New York Times*, November 19, 1940, 14; Blaik quoted in John Kieran, "Military Intelligence," *New York Times*, March 25, 1941, 29.

2. Exchange of letters in Earl H. Blaik with Tim Cohane, *You Have to Pay the Price* (New York: Holt, Rinehart and Winston, 1960), 169.

3. Blaik's record and All Americans from "Blaik Resigns as Army Football Coach and Athletic Director after 18 Years," *New York Times*, January 14, 1959, 31. The record of wins and losses in the *Times* article is the same as that issued by the Army Athletic Department's "Composite Record of Army Football

Coaches." Blaik's own list of wins and losses includes one loss less than Army officially lists. See Earl "Red" Blaik, *The Red Blaik Story* (New Rochelle: Arlington House, 1960), 559–61.

4. "The Colonel's Stand," *Newsweek*, August 20, 1951, 80; Austin Stevens, "West Point Ousts 90 Cadets," *New York Times*, August 4, 1951, 1. The thirty-seven expelled cadets is the figure Blaik gives in Blaik, *You Have to Pay the Price*, 280.

5. Blaik, *You Have to Pay the Price*, 20–21, 26.

6. "Army to Lose 2,500 Active Officers," *New York Times*, July 19, 1922, 7; Blaik, *You Have to Pay the Price*, 25, 38–39, 57–58, 61–63; Randy Roberts, *A Team for America: The Army–Navy Game that Rallied a Nation* (Boston: Houghton Mifflin, 2011), 29.

7. Blaik, *You Have to Pay the Price*, 18–19, 68–69, 70, 73.

8. Ibid., 77, 95–96, 119.

9. Ibid., 119, 120.

10. Ibid., 119–21.

11. Blaik, *You Have to Pay the Price*, 122–24; Tim Cohane, *Gridiron Grenadiers: The Story of West Point Football* (New York: G. P. Putnam's Sons, 1948); 209–10.

12. Cohane, *Gridiron Grenadiers*, 216; Blaik, *The Red Blaik Story*, 561.

13. Blaik, *You Have to Pay the Price*, 125, 127–28.

14. Ibid., 129–31.

15. Ibid., 150–51, 170.

16. Ibid., 169.

17. Blaik, *You Have to Pay the Price*, 170–72; letter from Earl Blaik to Robert L. Eichelberger, December 16, 1940, Blaik Papers, USMA Archives; Roberts, *A Team for America*, 16.

18. Robert L. Eichelberger, *Our Jungle Road to Tokyo* (New York: Viking Press, 1950), xix–xx; Roberts, *A Team for America*, 17–20; Blaik, *You Have to Pay the Price*, 170–72; Cohane, *Gridiron Grenadiers*, 201–2.

19. Blaik, *The Red Blaik Story*, 406; directors of Intercollegiate Athletics in Lance Betros, *Carved from Granite: West Point Since 1902* (College Station: Texas A&M University Press, 2012), 327.

20. William D. Richardson, "Blaik, New Army Football Coach, Finds Outlook Anything but Rosy," *New York Times*, February 6, 1941, 26; Blaik, *You Have to Pay the Price*, 174–75, 179, 189; Allison Danzig, "Cadets Develop Strong Attack," *New York Times*, October 30, 1941, 30; Army football record in James Stewart, *The Black Knights of West Point: A History of Football at the United States Military Academy for the Period of 1890–1953* (New York: Bradbury, Sayles, O'Neill Co., 1954), 256.

21. Blaik, *You Have to Pay the Price*, 189, 192; Cohane, *Gridiron Grenadiers*, 225; Roberts, *A Team for America*, 64, 86–87, 109. On Army's wartime achievement, see "Blaik Resigns as Army Football Coach," *New York Times*, January 14, 1969, 31; Wilbur D. Jones Jr., *Football! Navy! War! How "Lend Lease" Players Saved the College Game and Helped Win World War II* (Jefferson, NC: McFarland, 2009), 16.

22. Blaik, *You Have to Pay the Price*, 192, 196.

23. Ibid., 187–89, 193.

24. Army scores in Stewart, *The Black Nights of West Point*, 256; Allison Danzig, "Army's Dazzling Speed and Strong Defense Crush Notre Dame," *New York Times*, November 12, 1944, S1.

25. Allison Danzig, "66,639 See Power Army Team Roll Over Navy, 23–7," *New York Times*, December 3, 1944, S1; Roberts, *A Team for America*, 217–18; Blaik, *You Have to Pay the Price*, 202, 204–6; Eichelberger, *Our Jungle Road to Tokyo*, xx.

26. Blaik interview in Arthur Daley, "Sons of Mars and Thunder," *New York Times*, September 13, 1945, 30; Blaik, *You Have to Pay the Price*, 207; Allison Danzig, "Cadet Backs Shine," *New York Times*, October 14, 1945, S1; Allison Danzig, "Davis Tallies Thrice to Set Pace in Cadets' Victory Over Irish," *New York Times*, November 11, 1945, 71; Allison Danzig, "Cadets Start Fast," *New York Times*, December 2, 1945, S1.

27. Blaik, *You Have to Pay the Price*, 211; Blaik quote in "Blaik Calls Cadet Football Team Finest at West Point in His Time," *New York Times*, December 2, 1945, S3.

28. Blaik, *You Have to Pay the Price*, 215–17, 226.

29. Cohane, *Gridiron Grenadiers*, 305; Blaik, *You Have to Pay the Price*, 229–30.

30. "Davis, Blanchard Scored 537 Points," *New York Times*, December 2, 1946, 37; Richard Goldstein, "Doc Blanchard," *New York Times*, April 21, 2009, B11; Dwight Eisenhower, letter to Quentin Reynolds, December 4, 1947, in Louis Galambos, ed., *The Papers of Dwight David Eisenhower: Chief of Staff*, Vol. IX (Baltimore: Johns Hopkins University Press, 1978), 2107; Blaik, *You Have to Pay the Price*, 243, 249, 411–12; Stephen E. Ambrose, *Duty, Honor, Country* (Baltimore: Johns Hopkins University Press, 1966), 317; "Different Game," *Time*, October 30, 1950, 55; Blaik quoted in Stanley Woodward, "The Pro Game Isn't Football," *Collier's*, October 28, 1950, 19, 40–42; Marshall Smith, "Blaik and Son," *Life*, October 9, 1950, 59–66; Stanley Woodward, "Football's Greatest Father-and-Son Act," *Saturday Evening Post*, October 7, 1950, 34, 158–60.

31. Blaik, *You Have to Pay the Price*, 302; Richard Parke, "West Point Tutoring School to Obtain Athletes Disclosed," *New York Times*, August 9, 1951, 1;

Al Pollard quoted in Frank Deford, "Code Breakers," *Sports Illustrated*, November 13, 2000, SI Vault; "Player 'Scouting' in Capital Charged," *New York Times*, August 8, 1951, 12; James Blackwell, *On Brave Old Army Team: The Cheating Scandal that Rocked the Nation: West Point 1951* (Novato, CA: Presidio Press, 1996), 180.

32. "West Point Head Says Cribbing Ring Began in Late 1949," *New York Times*, September 6, 1951, 1; Stevens, "West Point Ousts 90 Cadets," 1.

33. Frederick A. Irving, "The Recent Violations of the Honor Code at West Point," *Assembly*, October 1951, 6–7, 12; Stevens, "West Point Ousts 90 Cadets," 1; Blaik, *You Have to Pay the Price*, 281; Irving quoted in "West Point Head Says Cribbing Ring Began in Late 1949," 1.

34. Anthony Leviero, "Honor Code Binds Cadets for Life," *New York Times*, August 4, 1951, 5; Frederick A. Irving, "The Honor Code at West Point," *Assembly*, October 1951, 6; David Halberstam, *The Fifties* (New York: Fawcett Columbine, 1993), 14–16, 190–91; Ambrose, *Duty, Honor Country*, 318; Joe Goldstein, "Explosion: 1951 Scandals Threaten College Hoops," *ESPN Classic*, November 19, 2003, http://espn.go.com/classic/s/basketball_ scandals_explosion.html.

35. "Pollard, Dismissed Army Fullback, Agrees to Play with Yank 11," *New York Times*, August 31, 1951, 29; "Statement by Cadet," *New York Times*, August 6, 1951, 15.

36. Stevens, "West Point Ousts 90 Cadets," 1; "Hand Calls Decision One of Most Painful," *New York Times*, August 4, 1951, 5; Blaik, *You Have to Pay the Price*, 279, 289–90.

37. Blaik quoted in Joseph M. Sheehan, "Blaik Denies He Will Resign," *New York Times*, August 10, 1951, 1, 8; "The Colonel's Stand," 80–81.

38. John F. Kennedy, "How Should Cadets Be Picked?" *New York Times Magazine*, August 19, 1951, 153; "Blaik's Ouster Urged to Bar New Scandal," *New York Times*, October 9, 1951, 20; "Academies Urged to Ban Football," *New York Times*, August 5, 1951, 1; Arthur Krock, "In the Nation," *New York Times*, August 9, 1951, 20; "Honor at West Point," *New York Times*, August 5, 1951, 118; Hanson Baldwin, "Future of West Point—I," *New York Times*, February 11, 1952, 16; Hanson Baldwin, "Future of West Point—II," *New York Times*, February 12, 1952, 11.

39. Blaik, *You Have to Pay the Price*, 300, 315, 321; "Academy Head Pleased: General Irving Praises Coach," *New York Times*, August 10, 1951, 8; Blaik quoted in Sheehan, "Blaik Denies He Will Resign," 1, 8; "Blaik Musters 31 for Army Varsity," *New York Times*, August 11, 1951, 6.

40. Blaik, *You Have to Pay the Price*, 315–16.

41. Ibid., 321, 323, 335.

42. Blaik, *You Have to Pay the Price*, 346–55; Arthur Daley, "The Old Army Game," *New York Times*, November 25, 1955, 41; Arthur Daley, "Monday Quar-

terback," *New York Times*, November 28, 1955, 36; Robert Cowley and Thomas Ginzberg, eds., *West Point: Two Centuries of Honor and Tradition* (New York: Warner Books, 2002), 249; Blaik, *You Have to Pay the Price*, 336, 346–47.

43. Blaik quoted in "Football Drills Start for Army," *New York Times*, August 26, 1958, 38; Deane McGowen, "West Point Back Honored 2D Time," *New York Times*, December 3, 1958, 50; Joseph M. Sheehan, "Army Eleven Launches Space Man," *New York Times*, October 1, 1958, 47; Blaik, *You Have to Pay the Price*, 373–75.

44. Gene Schoor, *100 Years of Army–Navy Football: A Pictorial History of America's Most Colorful and Competitive Sports Rivalry* (New York: Henry Holt, 1989), 161; Blaik, *You Have to Pay the Price*, 375, 383, 389.

45. Joe Cahill quoted in "Col., U.S.A. (ret.)," *Newsweek*, January 26, 1959, 61; "Blaik Resigns as Army Football Coach," 31; Blaik, *You Have to Pay the Price*, 391.

46. "Army Secretary, Chief of Staff Hail Blaik," *New York Times*, January 14, 1959, 31; "President Adds Tribute," *New York Times*, January 15, 1959, 40; Blaik, *You Have to Pay the Price*, 312, 390, 413; "Industry Beckons Academy Mentor," *New York Times*, January 14, 1959, 31.

BIBLIOGRAPHY

Abramson, Jesse. “98,616 See Staubach's 1-Man Show.” *New York Herald Tribune*, December 2, 1962, III.

———. “Navy Beats Army 5th Straight Time.” *New York Herald Tribune*, December 8, 1963, section IV.

———. “Rollie's Revenge: Army, 11–8.” *New York Herald Tribune*, November 29, 1964.

“Academies Urged to Ban Football.” *New York Times*, August 5, 1951.

“Academy Head Pleased: General Irving Praises Coach.” *New York Times*, August 10, 1951.

Adler, Renata. *Reckless Disregard: Westmoreland v. CBS et al.; Sharon v. Time*. New York: Alfred A. Knopf, 1986.

Ambrose, Stephen E. *Duty, Honor, Country: A History of West Point*. Baltimore: Johns Hopkins University Press, 1966.

———. *Eisenhower: Soldier and President*. New York: Simon and Schuster, 1990.

Apple, R. W., Jr. “Bernard Fall Killed in Vietnam by a Mine while with Marines.” *New York Times*, February 22, 1967.

Army Athletic Department. “Final Individual Statistics for 1963 Army–Navy Game.” December 7, 1963.

“Army Conquers Navy, 15–7, Amid Cheers of 45,000.” *New York Times*, November 26, 1916.

“Army Defeated Navy at Football.” *New York Times*, November 30, 1902.

“Army Due to Sign Dietzel This Week.” *New York Times*, January 3, 1962.

“Army Eleven Rated High.” *New York Times*, November 28, 1916.

“Army Expects Victory.” *New York Times*, November 30, 1912.

“Army Football Team Beat the Navy Eleven.” *New York Times*, December 1, 1901.

“Army Holds Yale to Tie at 7 to 7.” *New York Times*, October 29, 1922.

“Army to Lose 2,500 Active Officers.” *New York Times*, July 19, 1922.

“Army–Navy Break Widens.” *New York Times*, October 31, 1929.

“Army–Navy Football Game Here Lacks Only Agreement on Date.” *New York Times*, November 14, 1930.

“Army–Navy Game Plea Favorably Received.” *New York Times*, May 29, 1931.

“Army–Navy Renew Sports Relations.” *New York Times*, September 1, 1932.

“Army and Navy Athletics.” *New York Times*, December 13, 1902.

“Army and Navy End Football Relations on Eligibility Issue.” *New York Times*, December 17, 1927.

“Army to Play Navy on a New Gridiron.” *New York Times*, April 1, 1936.

“Army Receptive to Rose Bowl Bid.” *New York Times*, November 28, 1933.

“Army Rule Affects Athletes on Jan. 1.” *New York Times*, December 9, 1937.

“Army Secretary, Chief of Staff Hail Blaik.” *New York Times*, January 14, 1959.

"Army Smothers Annapolis Team by 22–9 Score." *New York Times*, November 13, 1913.
Arnold, Martin. "Cadets Give Resigning Chief Ovation." *New York Times*, March 18, 1970.
"Athletic Directors Changed at West Point." *New York Times*, February 27, 1966.
Atkinson, Rick. *The Long Gray Line: The American Journey of West Point's Class of 1966*. London: Collins, 1990.
Bacevich, Andrew J. *Breach of Trust: How Americans Failed Their Soldiers and Their Country*. New York: Metropolitan Books, Henry Holt, 2013.
Baldwin, Hanson. "Future of West Point—I." *New York Times*, February 11, 1952.
———. "Future of West Point—II." *New York Times*, February 12, 1952.
———. "Our 'Sailor President' Charts a Course." *New York Times*, April 3, 1938.
Beech, Mark. *When Saturday Mattered Most: The Last Golden Season of Army Football*. New York: Thomas Dunne Books, St. Martin's Press, 2012.
Betros, Lance. *Carved from Granite: West Point Since 1902*. College Station: Texas A&M University Press, 2012.
———. *West Point: Two Centuries and Beyond*. Abilene, TX: McWhiney Foundation Press, 2002.
"Bill for More Cadets Is Passed by Senate." *New York Times*, August 10, 1962.
Blackwell, James. *On Brave Old Army Team: The Cheating Scandal that Rocked the Nation: West Point, 1951*. Novato, CA: Presidio Press, 1996.
Blaik, Earl "Red." "A Cadet under MacArthur." *Assembly*, Spring 1964.
———. *The Red Blaik Story*. New Rochelle, NY: Arlington House, 1960.
Blaik, Earl H., with Tim Cohane. *You Have to Pay the Price*. New York: Holt, Rinehart and Winston, 1960.
"Blaik Calls Cadet Football Team Finest at West Point in His Time." *New York Times*, December 2, 1945.
"Blaik Musters 31 for Army Varsity." *New York Times*, August 11, 1951.
"Blaik Resigns as Army Football Coach." *New York Times*, January 14, 1959.
"Blaik Resigns as Army Football Coach and Athletic Director After 18 Years." *New York Times*, January 14, 1959.
"Blaik's Ouster Urged to Bar New Scandal." *New York Times*, October 9, 1951.
Boroff, David. "West Point: Ancient Incubator for a New Breed." *Harper's*, December 1962.
Bowen, William G., and Sarah A. Levin. *Reclaiming the Game: College Sports and Educational Values*. Princeton, NJ: Princeton University Press, 2003.
Boyer, Peter J. "A Different War." *New Yorker*, July 1, 2002.
———. "Downfall: How Donald Rumsfeld Reformed the Army and Lost Iraq." *New Yorker*, November 30, 2006.
"Bradley Scores 'Monty' on Gap." *New York Times*, January 3, 1965.
"Break of Army–Navy Aired in Congress." *New York Times*, December 20, 1927.
Brewin, Bob, and Sidney Shaw. *Vietnam on Trial: Westmoreland vs. CBS*. New York: Atheneum, 1987.
"Brig. Gen. Eichelberger Takes Up Duties as West Point Head, Succeeding Benedict." *New York Times*, November 19, 1940.
Briordy, William J. "Hall Out as Army Coach: Job Open to Non-Alumnus." *New York Times*, December 10, 1961.
Buckley, Christopher. "Viet Guilt." *Esquire*, September 1983.
"Bush Looks to Marine to Lead NATO Forces." *New York Times*, April 12, 2002.
"C. Daly to Go to West Point." *New York Times*, November 24, 1900.
"Cadet Byrne Dead; No Army–Navy Game." *New York Times*, November 1, 1909.
"Cadets Hopes Blasted." *New York Times*, December 3, 1933.
"Cadets Impress as Drills Close." *New York Times*, May 13, 1962.
"Cagle to Quit Army After Graduation." *New York Times*, May 10, 1930.
"Cagle Wed Secretly, Is Forced to Resign." *New York Times*, May 14, 1930.
Cahill, Joe. "Down the Field." *Assembly*, Spring 1962.
Cleary, Jack. "A Presidential Tradition." *Army vs. Navy*. Program for 109th Game, December 6, 2008.

Cohane, Tim. *Gridiron Grenadiers: The Story of West Point Football.* New York: G. P. Putnam's Sons, 1948.
"Col., U.S.A. (ret.)." *Newsweek*, January 26, 1959.
"The Colonel's Stand." *Newsweek*, August 20, 1951.
"Combat-Ready General." *New York Times*, April 27, 1964.
Connelly, Michael. *The President's Team: The 1963 Army–Navy Game and the Assassination of JFK.* Minneapolis: MVP Books, 2009.
Cowley, Robert, and Thomas Guinzburg, eds. *West Point: Two Centuries of Honor and Tradition.* New York: Warner Books, 2002.
Crackel, Theodore J. *West Point: A Bicentennial History.* Lawrence: University Press of Kansas, 2002.
Cross, Harry. "Battle Revives Old Pageantry of 2 Services." *New York Herald Tribune*, December 14, 1930.
Daley, Arthur. "Monday Quarterback." *New York Times*, November 28, 1955.
———. "The Old Army Game." *New York Times*, November 25, 1955.
———. "Sons of Mars and Thunder." *New York Times*, September 13, 1945.
———. "Sports of the Times." *New York Times*, December 8, 1963.
———. "Value of Airpower." *New York Times*, December 3, 1962.
Dallek, Robert. *An Unfinished Life: John F. Kennedy, 1917–1963.* New York: Little, Brown, 2004.
Danzig, Allison. "Army–Navy Battle to 7–7 Tie." *New York Times*, November 28, 1965.
———. "Army's Dazzling Speed and Strong Defense Crush Notre Dame." *New York Times*, November 12, 1944.
———. "Cadet Backs Shine." *New York Times*, October 14, 1945.
———. "Cadets Develop Strong Attack." *New York Times*, October 30, 1941.
———. "Cadets Start Fast." *New York Times*, December 2, 1945.
———. "Cadets Turn Back Boston U. by 30–0." *New York Times*, September 22, 1963.
———. "Davis Tallies Thrice to Set Pace in Cadets' Victory Over Irish." *New York Times*, November 11, 1945.
———. "Late Drive Fails." *New York Times*, December 8, 1963.
———. "66,639 See Power Army Team Roll Over Navy, 23–7." *New York Times*, December 3, 1944.
———. "Staubach Excels." *New York Times*, December 2, 1962.
———. "Stichweh Hailed in Army's Gallant but Futile Stand Against Texas Eleven." *New York Times*, October 5, 1964.
———. "Streak Ends at 5." *New York Times*, November 29, 1964.
"Davis, Blanchard Scored 537 Points." *New York Times*, December 2, 1946.
Deford, Frank. "Code Breakers." *Sports Illustrated*, November 13, 2000. SI Vault.
Dell, John. "Army Closed in from All Sides." *Philadelphia Inquirer*, November 29, 1964.
D'Este, Carlo. *Eisenhower: A Soldier's Life.* New York: Henry Holt, 2002.
Dietzel, Paul F. *Call Me Coach: A Life in College Football.* Baton Rouge: Louisiana State University Press, 2008.
Dietzel, Paul, and Mervin Hyman. "I Have Never Broken a Contract." *Sports Illustrated*, September 19, 1966. SI Vault.
"Dietzel Maps Plans with Aides after Signing as Army's Coach." *New York Times*, January 8, 1962.
"Dietzel Weighs West Point Job." *New York Times*, January 2, 1962.
"Different Game." *Time*, October 30, 1951.
Dolson, Frank. "Cadets on 2 as Gun Goes Off." *Philadelphia Inquirer*, December 8, 1963.
———. "Navy Wins as Clock Stops on Army 2." *Philadelphia Inquirer*, December 8, 1963.
———. "Nickerson's 20-Yd. Kick Sinks Navy." *Philadelphia Inquirer*, November 29, 1964.
Drape, Joe. *Soldiers First: Duty, Honor, Country, and Football at West Point.* New York: Times Books, Henry Holt, 2012.
Eichelberger, Robert L. *Our Jungle Road to Tokyo.* New York: Viking Press, 1950.
Eisenhower, Dwight D. *At Ease: Stories I Tell to Friends.* Garden City, NY: Doubleday, 1967.

Ellis, Joseph, and Robert Moore. *School for Soldiers: West Point and the Profession of Arms*. New York: Oxford University Press, 1974.
Ellsberg, Daniel. *Secrets: A Memoir of Vietnam and the Pentagon Papers*. New York: Penguin Books, 2002.
Eskenazi, Gerald. "Decisive Ruling Upsets Dietzel." *New York Times*, December 9, 1963.
Fallows, James. "What Did You Do in the Class War, Daddy?" *Washington Monthly*, October 1975.
Feinstein, John. *A Civil War: Army vs. Navy, A Year Inside College Football's Purest Rivalry*. Boston: Little, Brown, 1996.
"First Lady a Fan in Throng at Game." *New York Times*, November 29, 1936.
Fitzgerald, Frances. *Fire in the Lake: The Vietnamese and the Americans in Vietnam*. Boston: Atlantic Monthly Press, 1972.
"$500,000 Gate Today as Army Plays Navy." *New York Times*, December 13, 1990.
Fleming, Thomas J. "West Point Cadets Now Say, 'Why Sir.'" *New York Times*, July 5, 1970.
———. *West Point: The Men and Times of the United States Military Academy*. New York: Morrow, 1969.
"Football by the Cadets." *New York Times*, October 28, 1894.
"Football Drills Start for Army." *New York Times*, August 26, 1958.
"40,000 See Army Beat Navy, 14–0." *New York Times*, November 28, 1915.
"Forward Pass Halts Revision of Code of Football Rules." *New York Times*, March 27, 1910.
Frum, David. *How We Got Here: The 70s: The Decade That Brought You Modern Life (For Better or Worse)*. New York: Basic Books, 2000.
Galambos, Louis, ed. *The Papers of Dwight D. Eisenhower: Chief of Staff*, Vol. IX. Baltimore: Johns Hopkins University Press, 1978.
Galbraith, James K. "Exit Strategy." *Boston Review*, October–November 1963.
———. "Kennedy, Vietnam and Iraq." *Salon*, November 22, 2003.
Galloway, Bruce K., and Robert Bowie Johnson. *West Point: America's Power Fraternity*. New York: Simon and Schuster, 1973.
"Gen. Bennett Takes Over as New Head of West Point." *New York Times*, January 11, 1966.
Goldstein, Gordon M. *Lessons in Disaster: McGeorge Bundy and the Path to War in Vietnam*. New York: Times Books, Henry Holt, 2008.
Goldstein, Joe. "Explosion: 1951 Scandals Threaten College Hoops." *ESPN Classic*, November 19, 2003. http://espn.go.com/classic/s/basketball_scandals_explosion.html.
Goldstein, Richard. "Doc Blanchard." *New York Times*, April 21, 2009.
Gordon, Michael R., and General Bernard E. Trainor. *Cobra II: The Inside Story of the Invasion and Occupation of Iraq*. New York: Pantheon, 2006.
"Gray Eleven Rallies behind Passing of Johnson to Turn Back Blue, 23–19." *New York Times*, December 26, 1965.
Graves, Harmon S. "Football at West Point." *Harper's Weekly*, January 1, 1898.
Gunther, John. *Eisenhower: The Man and the Symbol*. New York: Harper and Brothers, 1952.
Halberstam, David. *The Fifties*. New York: Fawcett Columbine, 1993.
"Hall Candidate to Succeed Blaik." *New York Times*, January 15, 1959.
Halloran, Richard. *My Name Is . . . Shinseki . . . and I Am a Soldier*. Honolulu: Hawaii Army Museum Society, 2004.
Ham, Bus. "Army Forces Navy to Battle for Bowl Trip." *Washington Post*, December 8, 1963.
———. "Army–Navy Struggle to 7–7 Deadlock." *Washington Post*, November 28, 1965.
———. "Nickerson's Kick Turns Tide, 11–8. *Washington Post*, November 29, 1964.
"Hand Calls Decision One of Most Painful." *New York Times*, August 4, 1951.
Harrison, James R. "Army's Alert Play Downs Notre Dame, 18–0, Before 80,000." *New York Times*, November 3, 1927.
———. "Sports' Greatest Pageant." *New York Times*, November 28, 1926.
Herbert, Morris. "A Dinner for Dietzel." *Assembly*, October–December 2009.
Hersh, Seymour M. "33 Teachers at West Point Leave Army in 18 Months." *New York Times*, June 25, 1972.
———. *My Lai 4: A Report on the Massacre and Its Aftermath*. New York: Random House, 1970.

Herr, Michael. *Dispatches*. New York: Alfred A. Knopf, 1977.
"Honor at West Point." *New York Times*, August 5, 1951.
Hyman, Mervin. "A Second Fiddle Finishes First." *Sports Illustrated*, December 7, 1964. SI Vault.
"Industry Beckons Academy Mentor." *New York Times*, January 14, 1959.
Irving, Frederick A. "The Honor Code at West Point." *Assembly*, October 1951.
———. "The Recent Violations of the Honor Code at West Point." *Assembly*, October 1951.
"It Was a Battle Royal." *New York Times*, December 1, 1890.
Janowitz, Morris. *The Professional Soldier*. New York: Free Press, 1971.
Jenkins, Dan. "Two Yards and the Clock." *Sports Illustrated*, December 16, 1963.
Jenkins, Sally. *The Real All Americans*. New York: Anchor Books, 2007.
Jones, Wilbur D., Jr. *Football! Navy! War! How "Lend Lease" Players Saved the College Game and Helped Win World War II*. Jefferson, NC: McFarland, 2009.
Just, Ward. *Military Men*. New York: Alfred A. Knopf, 1970.
Karnow, Stanley. *Vietnam: A History*. New York: Penguin Books, 1984.
Kennedy, John F. "How Should Cadets Be Picked?" *New York Times Magazine*, August 19, 1951.
Kieran, John. "Military Intelligence." *New York Times*, March 25, 1941.
Kilpatrick, Carroll. "LBJ Decries Talk of Wider Viet War." *Washington Post*, November 29, 1964.
"Kingsolving Decries Stress on Football." *New York Times*, January 14, 1932.
Knowlton, William A. "Fellow Graduates and Friends of the Military Academy." *Assembly*, December 1973.
———. "Plain Talk." *Assembly*, March 1973.
———. "Plain Talk." *Assembly*, December 1973.
Koehler, Herman J. *Koehler's West Point Manual of Disciplinary Physical Training*. New York: E. P. Dutton, 1919.
Koppett, Leonard. "Dietzel Takes the Blame for Army's Failure to Get Off Last Play." *New York Times*, December 10, 1963.
Korda, Michael. *Ike: An American Hero*. New York: HarperCollins, 2007.
Kovic, Ron. *Born on the Fourth of July*. New York: Pocket Books, Simon and Schuster, 1977.
Krock, Arthur. "In the Nation." *New York Times*, August 9, 1951.
Lardner, Rex. "Supercharged Aphorist." *Sports Illustrated*, November 26, 1962. SI Vault.
"Leaving West Point 'Regretted' by Cagle." *New York Times*, May 16, 1930.
Lederer, William J., and Eugene Burdick. *The Ugly American*. Greenwich, CT: Fawcett Cress, 1966.
Leider, Robert. "Why They Leave: Resignations from the USMA Class of 1966." Washington, DC: Department of the Army, July 1970.
"Less Football Freedom." *New York Times*, March 2, 1894.
Leviero, Anthony. "Honor Code Binds Cadets for Life." *New York Times*, August 4, 1951.
Lipsky, David. *Absolutely American: Four Years at West Point*. Boston: Houghton Mifflin, 2003.
Litsky, Frank. "Long, Gray Wait Ends for Corps." *New York Times*, November 29, 1964.
"Long Controversy Is Ended as Army Adopts 3-Year Sports Eligibility Rule." *New York Times*, December 8, 1937.
"L.S.U. Acts Today on Dietzel Shift." *New York Times*, January 5, 1962.
Lubasch, Arnold H. "West Point Rites Honor MacArthur." *New York Times*, May 13, 1962.
MacArthur, Douglas. *Reminiscences*. New York: McGraw-Hill, 1964.
Manchester, William. *American Caesar: Douglas MacArthur, 1880–1964*. Boston: Little, Brown, 1978.
Mann, Robert. *A Grand Delusion: America's Descent into Vietnam*. New York: Basic Books, 2001.
McGowen, Deane. "West Point Back Honored 2D Time." *New York Times*, December 3, 1958.
McNamara, Robert, with Brian VanDeMark. *In Retrospect: The Tragedy and Lessons of Vietnam*. New York: Times Books, Random House, 1995.
Mears, Dwight S. "West Point's Fumble." *Washington Post*, February 24, 2014.

"Merchants Want Army–Navy Game." *New York Times*, March 5, 1914.
"Middies Again Triumphant." *New York Times*, December 3, 1893.
Millegan, Lloyd E. "Dietzel Signs 10-Year Pact as South Carolina Coach and Athletic Director." *New York Times*, April 7, 1966.
Miller, John J. *The Big Scrum: How Teddy Roosevelt Saved Football*. New York: Harper Perennial, 2011.
Minot, George. "Cadets on Navy's Two as Time Runs Out." *Washington Post*, December 8, 1963, C1.
Moore, Harold G., and Joseph L. Galloway. *We Were Soldiers Once . . . and Young: Ia Drang—the Battle That Changed the War in Vietnam*. New York: Ballantine Books, 1992.
Moser, Don. "Westmoreland, the Four-Star Eagle Scout: Starched, Courtly Man Gambles to Win the War." *Life*, November 11, 1966.
"Move to Restore Army–Navy Game." *New York Times*, June 11, 1929.
Moyar, Mark. *Triumph Forsaken: The Vietnam War, 1954–1965*. New York: Cambridge University Press, 2006.
"MPH Announces First Inductees into New Athletic Hall of Fame." http://www.mph.net/about/athletic-HOF.
"The Navy Succumbs to Army's Prowess." *New York Times*, December 3, 1899.
"The Navy Whips the Army." *New York Times*, November 30, 1890.
"Navy Won at Football." *New York Times*, December 2, 1900.
"The New Army Head Coach." *New York Times*, February 1, 1959.
"Notre Dame Upsets Army Eleven, 21–0, as 80,000 Look On." *New York Times*, November 27, 1932.
"Notre Dame's Open Play Amazes Army." *New York Times*, November 2, 1913.
O'Brien, Tim. *If I Die in a Combat Zone, Box Me Up and Ship Me Home*. New York: Laurel, Dell, 1973.
"Officials Cancel Army–Navy Game." *New York Times*, January 8, 1928.
Ogle, Jim. "Army Aims to Put Nix on Sixth Navy Victory." *New York Telegram*, November 28, 1964.
"Opposition at L.S.U." *New York Times*, January 3, 1962.
Packer, George. "Home Fries: How Soldiers Write Their Wars." *New Yorker*, April 7, 2014.
Palmer, John McA. "How Football Came to West Point." *Assembly*, January 1943.
Parke, Richard. "West Point Tutoring School to Obtain Athletes Disclosed." *New York Times*, August 9, 1951.
The Pentagon Papers. New York: New York Times, 1971.
Perret, Geoffrey. *Old Soldiers Never Die: The Life of Douglas MacArthur*. New York: Random House, 1996.
"Player 'Scouting' in Capital Charged." *New York Times*, August 8, 1951.
"Pollard, Dismissed Army Fullback, Agrees to Play with Yank 11." *New York Times*, August 31, 1951.
Povich, Shirley. "Middies Riddle Cadets, 34–14." *Washington Post*, December 2, 1963.
———. "This Morning." *Washington Post*, November 28, 1965.
"President Adds Tribute." *New York Times*, January 15, 1959.
"President to Attend Cadet Football Game." *New York Times*, November 29, 1901.
"President Truman's Statement of Regret in Announcing the Relieving of MacArthur." *New York Times*, April 11, 1951.
Prial, Frank J. "Army Case Recalls That of Mitchell." *New York Times*, March 18, 1970.
Reeder, Red, and Nardi Reeder Campion. *The West Point Story*. New York: Random House, 1956.
Reston, James. "Profound Division in Capital Caused by General's Speech." *New York Times*, April 20, 1951.
Rhoden, William C. "Longing for a Return to the Beauty of Imperfection." *New York Times*, September 17, 2012.
Richardson, William D. "Blaik, New Army Football Coach, Finds Outlook Anything but Rosy." *New York Times*, February 6, 1941.

Ricks, Thomas E. *Fiasco: The American Military Adventure in Iraq*. New York: Penguin Press, 2006.

———. *The Generals: American Military Command from World War II to Today*. New York: Penguin Press, 2012.

Roberts, Byron. "Stichweh Full of Praise for Navy's Linebackers." *Washington Post*, November 29, 1964.

Roberts, Gene. "Eisenhower Rejoins His West Point Class of Stars." *New York Times*, June 5, 1965.

Roberts, Randy. *A Team for America: The Army–Navy Game that Rallied a Nation*. Boston: Houghton Mifflin, 2012.

Robinson, Douglas. "West Point Class of '66 Eager to Fight." *New York Times*, June 8, 1966.

Robinson, Frank. "5th Ave. Sitdown Holds Up Parade of Armed Forces." *New York Times*, May 22, 1962.

Rudenstine, David. *The Day the Presses Stopped: A History of the Pentagon Papers*. Berkeley: University of California Press, 1996.

Rudolph, Frederick. *The American College and University: A History*. New York: Alfred A. Knopf, 1968.

Sandomir, Richard. "Army–Navy Project Ventures Far Beyond Football." *New York Times*, December 14, 2011.

Schlesinger, Arthur M., Jr. *Robert Kennedy and His Times*. Boston: Houghton Mifflin, 1978.

Schmitt, Eric. "Pentagon Contradicts General on Iraq Occupation Force's Size." *New York Times*, February 28, 2003.

Schoor, Gene. *100 Years of Army–Navy Football: A Pictorial History of America's Most Colorful and Competitive Sports Rivalry*. New York: Henry Holt, 1989.

Shanker, Thom. "Retiring Army Chief of Staff Warns Against Arrogance." *New York Times*, June 12, 2003.

Sheehan, Joseph M. "Army Eleven Launches Space Man." *New York Times*, October 1, 1958.

———. "Army Welcomes Dietzel's Three-Team Football." *New York Times*, May 6, 1962.

———. "Blaik Denies He Will Resign." *New York Times*, August 10, 1951.

———. "Dietzel Obtains Release from L.S.U. to Sign as Football Coach at Army." *New York Times*, January 6, 1962.

———. "Dietzel Signed to Coach Army for Five Years." *New York Times*, January 7, 1962.

———. "Football Now Fun to L.S.U. Coach." *New York Times*, December 6, 1958.

"Sheridan, Army End, Breaks Neck in Game." *New York Times*, October 25, 1931.

"Sheridan, Army End, Dies of Football Injury." *New York Times*, October 27, 1931.

"16 Houston." *Sports Illustrated*, September 11, 1967. SI Vault.

Smith, Marshall. "Blaik and Son." *Life*, October 9, 1950.

Sorley, Lewis. *A Better War: The Unexamined Victories and Final Tragedy of America's Last Years in Vietnam*. Orlando, FL: Harvest Book, Harcourt Inc., 1999.

"Statement by Cadet." *New York Times*, August 6, 1951.

Staubach, Roger, with Frank Luksa. *Time Enough to Win*. Waco, TX: Word Books, 1980.

Staubach, Roger. *Staubach: First Down, Lifetime to Go*. Waco, TX: Word Books, 1974.

"Staubach to Get Heisman Trophy." *New York Times*, November 27, 1963.

Sterba, James P. "Scraps of Paper from Vietnam." *New York Times*, October 18, 1970.

Stevens, Austin. "West Point Ousts 90 Cadets." *New York Times*, August 4, 1951.

Stewart, James. *The Black Knights of West Point: A History of Football at the United States Military Academy*. New York: Bradbury, Sayles, O'Neill Co., 1954.

Stichweh, Rollie. "Eulogy for Bill Zadel." Old Cadet Chapel, October 27, 2011.

Stout, David. "Gen. S. W. Koster, 86, Who Was Demoted After My Lai, Dies." *New York Times*, February 11, 2006.

"Study in Military Professionalism." Carlisle, PA: U.S. Army War College, June 1970.

Sullivan, Patricia. "General Commanded Troops in Vietnam." *Washington Post*, July 19, 2005.

"Sylvanus Thayer Award Presented to General MacArthur." *Assembly*, Summer 1962.

Teague, Robert L. "Dietzel Says Blocking and Tackling Were Only Differences between Teams." *New York Times,* December 2, 1962.

"Text of General MacArthur's Address to a Joint Meeting of Congress." *New York Times*, April 20, 1951.

Thomas, Evan. "360 Pros Reported Exempt from Draft." *New York Times*, April 8, 1967.

Thomas, Evan, and John Barry. "Anatomy of a Revolt." *Newsweek*, April 24, 2006.

"Thorpe's Indians Crush West Point." *New York Times*, November 10, 1912.

"Tom Cahill, 73, Football Coach at Army During the Vietnam War." *New York Times*, October 31, 1992.

Truscott, Lucian K. *Dress Gray*. Garden City, NY: Doubleday, 1979.

Turse, Nick. *Kill Anything That Moves: The Real American War in Vietnam*. New York: Metropolitan Books, Henry Holt, 2013.

Underwood, John. "Pepsodent Paul at the Point." *Sports Illustrated*, May 28, 1962. SI Vault.

Vecsey, George. "Friendships Wrapped in the Army–Navy Rivalry." *New York Times*, September 12, 2012.

———. "Honoring a Coach and an Upset." *New York Times*, July 20, 2009.

———. "A Love Story Affirmed in Time of War." *New York Times*, October 22, 2011.

Verna, Tony. *Instant Replay: The Day that Changed Sports Forever*. Beverly Hills: Creative Book Publishers, 2008.

"Victory for the Middies." *New York Times*, November 27, 1892.

"Victory for West Point." *New York Times*, November 29, 1891.

Vidmer, Richards. "Pomp, Noise, Heroic Play Rock Stadium." *New York Herald Tribune*, December 13, 1931.

Viorst, Milton. *Fire in the Streets: America in the 1960s*. New York: Simon and Schuster, 1970.

Wallace, William N. "All-America Contest in Buffalo Opens Football Season Tonight." *New York Times*, June 26, 1965.

Walzer, Judith B. "Literature and the Vietnam War." *Dissent*, Summer 2010.

"Wants Football Barred." *New York Times*, November 26, 1913.

Weigley, Russell F. *History of the United States Army*. Bloomington: Indiana University Press, 1984.

Weinraub, Bernard. "Vietnam Protest Blocks Fifth Avenue." *New York Times*, May 16, 1965.

Weinraub, Bernard, and Thom Shanker. "Rumsfeld Design for War Criticized on the Battlefield." *New York Times*, April 1, 2003.

Werden, Lincoln. "Ace Quarterback Downed in Effigy." *New York Times*, December 30, 1962.

———. "Army Calls Staubach Key Man." *New York Times*, November 29, 1962.

———. "Army Fans Insist on Cadet Victory." *New York Times*, November 30, 1961.

———. "Army Manpower Is at Low Point." *New York Times*, November 24, 1964.

———. "Dietzel Confesses: 'Biggest Booboo' Was Made by Him." *New York Times*, December 1, 1964.

———. "Mistakes, Injury Cited by Dietzel." *New York Times*, November 28, 1965.

Westmoreland, William C. "Plain Talk." *Assembly*, Fall 1960.

———. "Plain Talk." *Assembly*, Winter 1961.

———. "Plain Talk." *Assembly*, Winter 1962.

———. "Plain Talk." *Assembly*, Winter 1963.

———. "A Soldier Looks Back." *New York Times*, June 25, 1972.

———. *A Soldier Reports*. New York: Da Capo Press, 1989.

"West Point to Get New Chief July 1." *New York Times*, May 14, 1960.

"West Point Goes to War." *Newsweek*, July 10, 1967.

"West Point Head Says Cribbing Ring Began in Late 1949." *New York Times*, September 6, 1951.

"West Point Rally Falls Just Short." *New York Times*, October 23, 1921.

Weyand, Alexander M. "The Athletic Cadet: Eisenhower." *Assembly*, Spring 1968.

White, Gordon S., Jr. "Army Plans More 'Realistic" Look at Football Foes." *New York Times*, November 28, 1973.

———. "Dietzel Plan to Pattern Army Along L.S.U.'s Success Lines." *New York Times*, April 8, 1962.

———. "Law Cripples Army Recruiting." *New York Times*, November 30, 1973.

———. "West Point Dismisses Cahill." *New York Times*, December 14, 1973.

Whitney, Craig R., and Eric Pace. "William C. Westmoreland Is Dead at 91." *New York Times*, July 20, 2005.

Wilner, Barry, and Ken Rappoport. *Gridiron Glory: The Story of the Army–Navy Football Rivalry*. Lanham, MD: Taylor Trade, 2005.

Wood, Mark A. "Uncertain Commitment: West Point and the Active Duty Service Obligation, 1950–1964." Digital Library. USMA.edu.

Woodward, Stanley. "Football's Greatest Father-and-Son Act." *Saturday Evening Post*, October 7, 1950.

———. "The Pro Game Isn't Football." *Collier's*, October 28, 1950.

Wollen, Ross. "The 'Ike Telegram.'" *Assembly*, November–December 2004.

ACKNOWLEDGMENTS

An article by George Vecsey in the *New York Times* led me to write about the 1964 Army football team and its experiences in Vietnam and made it clear that the best sports stories never are just about sports.

My greatest debt is to the players from the 1964 Army football team who allowed me to interview them, often multiple times. Their stories lie at the heart of this book. Coach Paul Dietzel and Anne Dietzel went out of their way to speak with me, as did their close friend Rhesa Barksdale, who was assistant manager of the Army football team in 1964 and manager in 1965. General Eric Shinseki took time out from his busy schedule as then–secretary of Veterans Affairs to let me interview him. Marie Lewis and Dennis Lewis Jr. helped me understand in detail why Dennis Lewis was so admired by everyone who knew him. Dan Christman, the former superintendent of West Point (with whom I share the bonds of Western Reserve Academy), gave me perspective on what the 1960s were like at West Point and what has happened to West Point since then. Ross Wollen shared with me his experience of interviewing President Dwight Eisenhower on the day before the 1964 Army–Navy game. West Point Athletic Director Boo Corrigan and Assistant Athletic Director for Athletic Communications Ryan Yanoshak went out of their way to supply me with information and photographs. Suzanne Christoff and Casey Madrick in the division of Special Collections and Archives at the West Point Library were unfailingly generous in helping me find the historic pictures I needed.

Katherine Flynn, my agent at Kneerim, Williams, and Bloom, has been thorough and encouraging in looking out for my welfare as a writer. She is just what an agent should be. At Rowman & Littlefield, Jon Sisk, Ben Verdi, Patricia Stevenson, and Natalie Mandziuk were always helpful, and at the Eisenhower Presidential Library, archivist Mary Burtzloff made my long-distance searches rewarding. Bridget Dooley, a fine photographer in her own right, explained to me how it was possible to make use of old photographs. Warren James Hinckle IV was unrelenting in his close reading of my text. John Seidman was, as he has been in the past, my chief critic and the reader I depended on at every turn.

INDEX